MW00906119

Copyright 2013 by Sharyn Talbert
The author retains sole copyright.

What follows is a true story. As in all creative
non-fiction, some facts and events have been
generalized, condensed, or synthesized to convey
the spirit of the experience while preserving
narrative flow.

To protect privacy, the names of most
characters have been changed.

Sharyntalbert.com

SCHOLAR MINE

An Ohio State Love Story

Contents

1

HISTORY

What I invaded
has invaded me - Denise Levertov

I n September of '85, I gave him the death desk. Maybe it was the tint of his eyes or the way he moved, but what really killed me was the godlike composure, the untouchable cool. He wasn't going to get away with it, so he ended up with the death desk. Despite his innocence.

The History Department had sct aside three rooms for them, bleak, windowless cells where they'd stash their backpacks and coffee cups, where they'd hold office hours and grade piles of papers. When he came to me that September morning, I took one glance and steered him toward the office nearest my own. As we walked, lockstep, a secret took shape: "I'm keeping this one close." He had no inkling, but I felt the surge, like a ripe rumor ready to hit your ear, like the transitory lull of a teakettle just before the boil. Even so, I didn't quite believe. And I couldn't stop to ponder, because History Department business awaited.

I opened the door to 168 Dulles. Other teaching associates milled around, organizing their stuff, chatting. They looked up and I introduced him. Next on my list: his desk assignment. Smack in the center, among the jumble of mismatched desks and chairs, stood the empty death desk. For years, its occupants, one by one, had abandoned their graduate studies, slinking away from the big university, tail between their legs. Even brand new T.A.s knew about the death desk and were glad to have escaped its power. Now, partly to throw him off my scent and partly to get some reaction, I assigned the tainted desk to Joseph Talbert. My joke fell flat. The other T.A.s were silent, and he graciously accepted the seat I'd chosen for him.

Whenever my mind wanders back to the death desk, I can't help but drift a little farther, to March of '85, when his application for graduate school landed in my hands. He would have scoffed at the notion of love at first sight, let alone love *before* first sight. In fact, that turned out to be one of the perks of my new job at Ohio State. And if I hadn't taken just that job, in just that department, in just that university with over fifty thousand students, I wouldn't be telling this story.

* * *

From a young age, I'm aware of the university. My parents call it "State." I don't know what happens there, but when we drive past, I glimpse ingénues in pleated skirts and saddle shoes. They walk in time, their books cradled with easy, feminine confidence. I

2

want to be like them, and by the time I'm eight years old, I feel a pleasant tang when people mention Ohio State.

In the late 1950s, on cold November Saturdays, my dad takes me to a few Ohio State games. Our guys wear red. They are the Buckeyes, and we live in the Buckeye state. Daddy and I sit close in the packed stadium, swaddled in overcoats and scarves. On his head, a fedora with a stiff little feather. The screaming surges, frosty white exhalations. I don't understand the game, and focus on my hot chocolate, sipping carefully from a paper cup decorated with blue-green commas.

Fast forward to fall, 1968. I'm 18, on campus with Kay, my high school friend. We talk about bell bottoms and boys, but we're really assessing our allure. Without warning, an anvil in a tight tee-shirt jogs by. He turns around. Yeah, he says, feet pumping in place, I'm a Buckeye. A half back. And out of all the girls here, I love you the best.

Vin is a different animal. Italian heritage and East Coast accent. He says he can bench press 320 pounds. Thick silver stretch marks across his pecs prove it, violent ribbons of self-embrace. His eyes are drill bits. His roommate, he says, is a douche. "Yeah," Vin shrugs, the small eyes probing. "It's enough to piss off the *Pope*."

After a few weeks, I run away from home to be with him. The Morrill Tower elevator takes me to the topmost women's floor, then I dash up an echoing stairwell into the men's-only section. No job, no money, no college, no promises. I don't worry. We're too busy celebrating. The douchey roommate keeps our secret, and the Beatles' *White Album* helps disguise the reality. But reality intrudes. To keep his football scholarship, Vin has to keep up his grades.

3

Because I can do it, I write his English papers about Hester Prynne and Huck Finn. My writing can't save him. He flunks out. Then we get married. You know what they say. Marry in haste, repent at leisure.

Jump ahead sixteen years. I'm 34. After more than a decade, I'm back in town. My résumé lists the skills I've gained during the ugly marriage and beyond it. Between the lines are the intangibles: I'm quick, organized, a self-starter. That résumé will get me interviews. I'll welcome questions about my strengths and successes, and if they ask about my shortcomings, I'll just say that I'm a perfectionist, too exacting. How could they find fault with that?Along with the spot-on résumé, I know how to dress. And I am one fine listener, head tilted slightly, the precise ratio of intelligence and deference.

Where should I look? A decent environment is almost as important as the paycheck. A big place with room for advancement is the first criterion. State government? One of the hospitals? No. If I have to live here, Ohio State is the best bet. Ohio State has a lot to offer. It will be an even trade, almost like an ideal marriage.

I take the civil service exam, and Ohio State offers me not one but two jobs. I can work in the College of Pharmacy or the Department of History--my choice. Well, it has to be History. I love history, its literary drama, its lessons about politics and art and economics and science and geography and philosophy. I'm no authority, but the idea of history is bracing, and has been from childhood, when I read about the Vikings, the barbarians, the Spanish conquistadors, the little princes in the Tower. History is everything, all rolled up. Besides, in Pharmacy, they experiment on dogs. I try not to think about that.

With my campus ID and parking sticker, it's official. On the first morning, as I brush my hair and smooth my lipstick, I think about Ohio State—a vast expanse of choice and chance. Learning, stability, and the good kind of anonymity, where I can move, unmarked and unchecked. I park in the staff lot. Pulling on my mittens, I plunge into the current, joining hundreds of other walkers streaming in every direction. With a stiff wind at my back, I turn onto 17th Avenue.

To the right is Larkins Hall, the university's gym and natatorium. A constant flow of students moves through its doors, like corpuscles bunching and sliding through a giant venous system. To the left, McCracken Power Plant rumbles, its smokestacks spewing vertical clouds. On the corner, the hot dog vendor, bundled against the morning, is already setting up his quilted steel cart. I pass stately University Hall and glimpse the Oval, the heart of campus, thirty acres of crisscrossing walkways and ancient trees. When I start my job, the deciduous ones are bare.

Tingling with cold and exercise, I wheel into Dulles Hall, a brick bunker of three stories. It isn't corporate America--no walnut paneling or polished brass elevators; only a plain tile floor, grey with darker flecks. Advertisements taped haphazardly on the elevator wall announce math tutors and proofreaders and higher board scores. A lavender flyer urges women to "Take Back the Night!" With a black marker, someone has crossed out "Night" and scrawled "Dykes." From the restrooms, the sound of rushing water crests and fades.

In the reception area, I see editions of *The Chronicle of Higher Education.* Visitors can also look at framed photos of faculty, or they might peer into a tall electrified bookcase displaying new monographs. But I'm no visitor. I work here. So I head for an anonymous space in back, the perch from which I'll oversee the History Department's graduate program. Hanging coat and scarf, I survey the corner desk and Wang computer. A stark, institutional feel. No personality. I'll fix that. Maybe a wall-hanging to soften the sharpness. A radio for my classical music. A desk lamp with a flattering glow to offset the fluorescents above.

As I imagine such things, the Director of Graduate Studies appears, his accent like hot buttered yams. "Well, good mornin', Miss Sharyn. Welcome!"

Motioning with head and hands toward different points in the office, he makes a stab at enumerating my duties. "Okay—we have all the inta-national applicants in heah . . ." He reels open a filing cabinet drawer: zhheeee bock! Peering in, I see manila folders with colored labels, hand marked with a blur of foreign names.

Whirling to another cabinet, he says, ". . .and over heah are the domestic applicants." Many more folders reside in that drawer. "The Admissions Office is the point of contact," he goes on, scrutinizing my comprehension. "—They're at—you might want to write this down—they're at 1800 Cannon Drive, in Lincoln Towah."

He spends all of five minutes before dashing out. I hardly know what to make of my new boss, but what I do grasp is that I'll be in charge. It will be my business to decide how to fulfill my tasks. No faculty supervision to speak of. Hallelujah, I breathe. This place will suit me just fine. As I settle in, I remind myself, Keep your mouth shut and your eyes and ears open. That was my recipe for success in any new job.

In a few days, I master the boring stuff--how to navigate the computer programs and who to call when I have a question. What captivates me is the department's subterranean rhythms. Scouting the hallways in stolen moments, I glance into faculty offices. Some sport oriental rugs and pieces of original art, but most are unadorned: a utilitarian desk and chair, a few crammed bookcases, Venetian blinds, phone, computer. The bare-boned spaces must be good for scholarship--with so little to distract them, the faculty will likely publish rather than perish. I'd heard that little bromide, and like how it sounds.

As winter draws to a close, my sense of belonging deepens. The History Department isn't home. Yet I am at home here. Sipping coffee between tasks, I feel a settling sort of admiration for the accomplished minds around me. The department has a vigor, a rigorous undercurrent of questioning that I'd never experienced in a workplace. Maybe with the right kind of tenacity I can find out what those questions are. And maybe even come up with a few questions myself.

I compare my role in History to other jobs I've held. What a relief to have escaped those cutthroat, can-do settings where an obsession with the bottom line filters from the top guy down through the ranks. Not to mention those deviants in the private sector—the CEO who commanded his employees to vote for Ronald Reagan, the advertising director in the black fedora who tried to shock me with tales of her sexual exploits. I remind myself that there must be some weirdos in History, too. And there's no doubt about its competitive spirit—right away, I notice the good-natured sparring around the coffee pot. But the rivalry in History seems subtle and genial, and unrelated to revenue. In History, the questioning mind is what counts. I immerse myself in the communal soul of the department—rarefied, baffling, and grand.

The salaries at a state university aren't high in 1985, and still aren't. But certain trade-offs in History make up for it. Like my colleagues. Maybe it's dumb to consider the people around you a workplace benefit. But those characters in the History Department. . . .

My boss, Professor Franklin Price, is a Cornell-educated South Carolinian. A medievalist who will teach me the correct pronunciation of schism (*sism*, not *skism*), Professor Price is more courtly and formal than the other faculty, wearing business suits and shiny black brogues. His silver hair is carefully combed. Biding his time as Graduate chair, a two-year rotation that will soon be over, Professor Price can't wait to return to his scholarship.

Professor Douglas Van Curran, a U.S. labor historian, is committed to social justice, and his actions prove it. He drives around campus, three adopted dogs hanging out the pick-up's windows. The Van Currans also have a Black baby born addicted to crack cocaine. I admire the Van Currans, but they're braver than I am. I've already invited a shelter dog into my life but will never have the courage to take in a needy infant with an unfortunate history. A divorced mother of two adolescents, my life is stressful enough.

Winter ends, and on a bright spring day, the staff join the faculty at a luncheon. The department has just received Center of

Excellence status. Professor Lisa Rhys is being honored for something, too. Only a few months older than I, she finished her doctorate at Bryn Mawr at age 26, and is already a full professor, widely published. I'm impressed by her quiet self-possession, her strength to confront the world without cosmetics. I can't imagine that. Now at the Excellence luncheon, Professor Rhys is wearing a sleeveless shell. With her arm casually resting on a chairback, I glance at an unshaven armpit. A lesbian and women's historian, I see that she refuses to be culturally feminized.

Unlike the faculty, History Department staff members are not intellectuals. Well, at least any glimmer of intellectual talent is still untapped. It's true that some of us are educated. Like Elsbeth Wagner, a senior staffer who officially supervises us. But from day one, she leaves me to my own devices. Plenty of other things keep her busy. During the job interview, which turned out to be more about Elsbeth than about me, she says she's working toward her master's in public administration, which requires manipulation of brain-boggling statistical programs. Elsbeth plans to rise in the ranks, and is prepared to swallow the bitter pill.

We become good friends. I try to mimic Elsbeth's self-confident style. Together we take coffee breaks and eat lunch. At our favorite hangout, a Chinese place on High Street, I find out about the History Department, and also about the consequences of war, experienced by one young girl. In her Marlene Dietrich monotone, Elsbeth says she was born in Germany in 1935. As the Allies closed in, "I was a hair's breadth from starvation." She raises her hand, thumb and forefinger meeting. "Yeah. At one point, I gnawed tree bark."

We sit in silence until Elsbeth continues. "My older brother warned me never to eat margarine. We didn't have it anyway, but that was good, because margarine, Siegfried said, was made from Chew bones."

The horror never subsided. Now fifty years old and invested in the American Dream, Elsbeth is buying a house, pursuing advanced education, and shooting for all she can get, career-wise. A certain fondness for Germany lingers, but Elsbeth says the specters of war and privation will always be with her. "Even now," she says casually, "if I mistakenly eat a bite of margarine, I throw up."

I'm speechless, loaded chopsticks in mid-air. Over her teacup, Elsbeth's eyes have a faraway look. Soon enough, she comes around, and with a wave of her hand, she steers the conversation back to our favorite topic, the History Department. "They're basically a good bunch." She doesn't have to tell me she's talking about faculty, not staff. "Smart people, really gifted people. A few bad eppels. But you'll do well here."

I hope so. The History Department is a restless sea. The professors move in a self-propelled hurry, dashing between classes, picking up their mail, dropping off a work order. They toss a pithy comment and catch one in return, never breaking their stride, preoccupied with some secret spinning through their minds. To save time, they prioritize. A few of them even wear the same clothes day after day--getting ready in the morning is quicker if you just put back on what you threw off the night before. The Tudor-Stuart man is wedded to a single pair of pants. Corduroy. Camel-colored. He's the extreme case, but not many are concerned with external trappings. Their real status comes from their scholarship.

This they do in the guarded recesses of office and library and mind. As a pearly shell is slowly dislodged from the ocean floor, the professors pry their insights in patient, focused silence. When they bump against a phantom concept that proves to be not a phantom at all but something rich and muscled, they think, Ahhh, I'm really onto something. As the thing takes on a life of its own, they breathe, This is mine. They become greedy for that feeling. Those who don't get that feeling are shown the door.

The Department's players will shift over time, but at first, that concept doesn't register. Like the child who believes her parents to be immutable, I imagine that History will never change. "As it was in the beginning, is now and ever shall be, world without end, Amen." Not true, of course--with promotions, retirements, dismissals, and new hires, the cast evolves, year by year. Yet the department's hierarchy never changes. It's a familiar recipe in every academic department. At the top is the chair. Then come the other full professors, followed by the tenured associate professors. Below them, the assistant professors, dogpaddling furiously, trying to prove themselves before the seven-year trial is up. Next to last, the lecturers, appointed on a yearly basis. And at the bottom, the on-again, off-again adjuncts, hired at the last minute when student enrollments demand more course sections.

Staff has its own hierarchy, but the creation of knowledge isn't part of it. Confined to our inland sea with smaller waves and fewer fish, the degree of supervision we get depends on our rank, with Elsbeth watching the lowliest of us the most closely. In a scattershot way, the faculty casts a collective eye our way, too, glancing for a sense of our industry. But largely innocent of the rolling tasks at hand, they don't care how we handle the work. Just keep things moving, stay organized, use your head.

We do that, tuning our antennae to the mostly male professors, a habit that ensures both our helpfulness and a detection of their missteps. Some of their foibles amuse us. Professor Bowers pours out the last drop of coffee and waltzes away, thinking about Dred Scott and leaving the pot to burn. Some faculty habits are galling. Professor Auger, a specialist in ancient Greece, glides imperiously past, never making eye contact, never learning our names. We could be dust motes. We don't like it, but we don't tell outsiders. Even when we're resentful, we feel loyalty to the History Department. And to keep our jobs, we have to be discreet.

We also look the other way when one of our own comes in late or stays longer than an hour for lunch. If we don't abuse the freedom, we can keep it. By the early spring of 1985, I'm taking advantage of that deal, stealthily departing the History Department every afternoon. With the fax machine still a few years off, I say I need to deliver some document to the admissions office. Instead I wander around the Oval among the 200-year old sycamore trees, their canopies in green-gold bud. I move past ten thousand tulips, bedded in geometric rows, their pointed blooms like new lipsticks-- shell pink, deep rose, blood red. I explore the buildings, brick and stone, eclectic and imposing. I stroll around Mirror Lake, glassy and dimpled as boiled sugar syrup, watching the mallards and the splashing fountain. Outside the music school, I breathe in floating melodies. Sometimes, Mozart!

And always on Ohio State's campus is the surging tide of students of every shape, size, and nationality. A few older people, but it's mostly youthfulness that surrounds me. I envy the students' new freedom, the honing of their untrained minds, their lives ahead of them.

I'm a student, too. An English major. I'm on the right track now. In the late '70s in California, I studied nursing. When a naked cadaver was rolled out, the other students eagerly prodded the viscera and scrutinized the cells; I tried to avert my gaze, casually holding my nose to deflect the stench of formaldehyde. I wasn't interested in the corpse. I wanted the story. Who had she been? What had he thought? How had she struggled?

Finally, I admit it: I'm too subjective for nursing. It's the humanities I want. It's a craving for the Arts and Letters that leads me to Ohio State in the first place. As a staff member, I can finish my English degree. With Ohio State employment comes free tuition. If I'm working on campus anyway, I can run to class at lunch and after work. I won't have to fight traffic or jockey for a parking spot

Now, everything is falling into place. I've landed a responsible position in the History Department at Ohio State University. Or--*The* Ohio State University, as they're starting to call it. My courses are mapped out. Things are looking up. As my California friends would have said, I am stoked. I see myself in the same boat as the graduate students I work for. Well, we're in similar boats. I'm only an undergrad, but I've paid some serious dues along the way. I'm older than most, and I'm juggling a heavier load--a full time job, two courses every term, and the girls, Tibby and Norah. And I'm managing. I'm brave and spunky. I have nothing to apologize for. Or so I told myself.

***

As far as the work went, some of it was rote and taxing, but I liked poring over the graduate applicant files. Reading through the dossiers was a little like reading the society page. I found out about all sorts of people, where they'd grown up and gone to school, their interests and their prospects. Every transcript was unique and everyone had his own brand of self-disclosure. I tried to picture the applicants, and compared their stories to mine.

Joseph Talbert's application seemed different. As I organized his paperwork and letters of recommendation, something shimmery emerged. His transcript said he'd gotten A's, even in the upper-level courses. I admired that, but good grades are standard for people trying to get into graduate school. Then I saw that he'd written an undergraduate thesis, something about the Paris Peace Conference. He would have needed inventiveness and strong research skills, not to mention discipline.

I looked at the birth date. Unlike other prospective students who were a good ten years my junior, he was the right age, born in January of 1951. Just five months younger. On the current address line, he'd written William Street, Delaware, Ohio. But he'd gone to high school in Greenwich, Connecticut. No chance a hillbilly.

His recommenders were impressed.

"He is both polite and firm in argumentation."

". . . meticulous working habits, a demanding intelligence."

"The brightest undergraduate I have worked with in 20 years."

"He writes with great care, sensitivity, and mature style."

Mysteriously, the recommenders called him José instead of Joseph or Joe. Even odder, his statement of purpose was boldly

14

succinct. Instead of the usual chest-pounding profundity, José hand-wrote one sentence, neatly, on yellow legal paper:

"I wish to pursue an M.A. and Ph.D. in nineteenth and twentieth century central European history to secure a university teaching position."

He tells the unvarnished truth, I thought. He disregards the silly rules. Must be something of a maverick. It dawned on me. This guy has to be the polar opposite of my ex-husband. While Vin had failed miserably in academia, Joseph Talbert was succeeding. While Vin's handwriting was crude and erratic, Joseph Talbert's was fine and controlled. You can always tell something about a person by his penmanship. And then there was that statement of purpose. Even with a gun to his head, Vin could never have explained his goal in one clean, honest sentence. He'd never even had a goal.

Half a year would pass before we'd meet, but I couldn't forget him. My heart would skip at the thought of coming face to face with the phantom. Then I'd scold myself for being romantic and ridiculous—just you watch, I'd tell myself, he'll probably be selfish, boring, and immature, traits that always killed a relationship. Likely homely and clumsy, too. Get a grip, I snapped. But I couldn't help it. Through that spring and summer, Joseph Talbert ruled my dream kingdom.

In September of '85, the new grad students started to come. Their real faces eradicated the mental pictures I'd drawn while handling their paperwork. When they introduced themselves, I said they could come to me whenever they wanted with their questions and concerns. I memorized how each one spoke and dressed, and paid attention to their preferences and temperaments. They were a diverse bunch of young intellectuals, with a few non-traditionals thrown in. José was one of the latter.

His appearance was neither surprising nor disappointing. Six feet tall, lean with long legs, his gait was both cadenced and purposeful. A sensitive mouth, chin with a hint of a cleft. Light brown hair combed straight back from a broad forehead. A wide-set, penetrating gaze. Instead of jeans and tees, he wore trousers and dress shirts. And he did not engage in banal chit-chat as he leaned across my desk to sign my forms.

He'd begin that quarter as a grader for History 111, the first survey course in the European sequence. In his master's program he planned to study Eastern Europe; his Czech language training would be useful in that endeavor. Obviously he was good at languages. Now if he'd only say a few words to me.

From my perch, in between tasks, I watched for him. His natural dignity seemed tempered with keen curiosity and some private amusement. His demeanor set him apart from the clannish younger students who gathered on slatted benches, hooting at an inside joke or whispering earnestly among themselves. Sometimes I'd catch his voice as he strode through the department. Just a word or two, and I'd know. I might be over by the coffee pot or in Elsbeth's office, but when the words drifted to my ear, I could always pick out the voice. It had a certain timbre, almost velvety. At the sound, my heart accelerated.

I tried to engage him, tried to force him to make eye contact. As he collected his mail or made photocopies, I turned on my toe and swished my skirts. I was confident, feminine. And obviously sought after. Other male grad students crowded my office. The military

16

historians were especially ardent: Ray Miller with the Army-short haircut and steel-rimmed glasses, and Kip Richards, tall with dark curls and a perpetual grin. How could José not notice?

One afternoon, he came to me. No flirting. Nothing personal. He asked, "Have you a spare typewriter I could use in 168?" "Let's see . . . ," I said, leading him to a storage room. "—oh, here's an old Royal." He sat down and I stood behind. His hands were beautiful, poised above the keys. Whenever I'd tested a typewriter, I tapped out the standard, "Now is the time for all good men to come to the aid of their country." But as I watched José's fingers, the phrase emerging on the scrap paper said, "The Roman Empire."

The old Royal must have satisfied him. Nodding his thanks, he carried it into 168 Dulles Hall, to its new home upon the death desk.

Apart from that exchange, the fall of '85 ended without any meaningful communication. Afterwards, the long Christmas break. Winter quarter began. On January 28th, 1986, staff and grad students chatted by the reception desk during lunch hour, absently listening to the radio as the space shuttle Challenger lifted off, and with hideous finality, exploded. Six astronauts and a teacher reduced to a spray of molecules. Christa McAuliffe, Ron McNair, Judy Resnick. At home that night, Tibby, Norah, and I watched the footage. For the next few days, everybody in the department moved in somber silence.

The long winter ground on. I still looked for José. Sometimes I'd see him in the stadium lot, emerging from his ancient red Volkswagen as I power-walked to the office. Once, he caught sight of me and wished me a good morning as he hoisted a heavy book bag over the shoulder of his charcoal grey overcoat. I noticed his leather lace-up shoes, not so good on snow and ice. The rising winter sun bathed him in light, gleaming on the place where the hair had receded. Other times, the elevator doors in Dulles Hall slid open, and there he'd be, broad shouldered in a tan trench coat, intense gaze, cigarette between two fingers. He exhaled in a refined way, his upper lip cupped over the lower one, a thin stream of smoke coursing downward toward his chin. He looked like Hitler's Aryan ideal.

But nothing was happening with José, so I finally agreed to go out with Ray and Kip. They always hung together, and for a time, I joined them, a chummy threesome with a History Department connection. We were just friends. They didn't mind that I was a mother in my thirties, and I tried to forget that they'd been toddlers when JFK was shot.

At first, they distracted me with their gregarious intellectualism. Over pitchers of beer, they talked about Thucydides and Sun Tzu and von Ranke. They explained the role of stirrups in warfare. They said that Antietam was the bloodiest day of the Civil War, while Gettysburg, being a three-day engagement, had the highest casualty count.

We liked history, and we liked music. At the Agora, we saw Warren Zevon pound the piano: "Ah-OOO, Werewolves of LONdon. Ah-OOO!"For a minute, I thought it was the '60s again.

After a time, Ray began to invite me to expensive restaurants. We laughed and bantered.I enjoyed drinking wine and eating out. As I savored my meal, I listened to Ray. He held definite opinions, about military history and everything else. He talked about his

18

parents, well-heeled, I gathered. "White is the best color for the exterior of a house," he stated firmly. That was the color of his parents' big place in northern New Jersey. He mentioned his long-haired, liberal brother, whose politics contrasted with his own. But Ray admitted that his brother was just as sharp as he himself was. He glibly discussed his family's religion, Presbyterian, or "Presby," rather than Episcopalian, or "Pisky," as if there were only two choices. He talked about his successes as an undergraduate, and evaluated life in his Columbus apartment.

He rarely cooked for himself, having the money to eat out.But sometimes he did throw a meal together, and when he washed the dishes, he thought it was okay to let the water run full blast. I always tried to save on utility bills, and thought it important to conserve resources. "There's no need to ration water," Ray insisted. "There's no such thing as a water shortage in this country, or an energy shortage of any sort." I wasn't so sure.

After a few weeks, I realized that Ray was becoming possessive. But Ray, Kip, and I kept on eating lunch, and we continued to crack jokes--about the department, visiting faculty, and even the Challenger disaster. Jokes always pop up after terrible events, a release valve. I'd soon learn that in a folklore course.

I thought about Kip and Ray. From day one, deep down, I'd recognized who they were: intelligent, indulged sons of middle-class families, playing life according to well-rehearsed scripts. They were able students, but they balanced their scholarly discipline with a juvenile, presumptuous abandon. Their fantasy lives were shaped by the material they studied--after we'd been going out for a few weeks, Ray asked if I wanted to try a restaurant downtown. I told him I'd never been there. "Well," he said, "I'll just make a re-con."

Ray and Kip had never worked in any serious way. They'd never suffered any serious hardship. They were too young and too smug. Soon enough, their monologues about German fokkers and Hannah Arendt's banality of evil lost my interest. I sighed as they rambled on. I started to pull back.

The bullet heads kept aiming to impress me, but I was thinking about José. Was he gay? Was he involved with someone else? Maybe he just wasn't attracted to me, a notion that stung but which seemed more likely with every passing week. In between the paper shuffling and typing, I watched for him. I tried to stay hopeful, but his books commanded his full attention. I made the effort and sashayed through the Homer Hockett Library, but his eyes were focused, laser-like, on some fusty tome. As I pretended to take care of an errand, I glanced at him. He was perfectly still, but every so often, an involuntary twitch troubled his closed lips, as if objecting to another scholar's argument.

One afternoon in early spring, just before office closing time, I decided to say something. As usual, he was reading in the Hockett Library. "Heavy load for Bamberger's course?"

"A tad bit," he replied. He didn't look up. Yet I thought I detected electricity. He off-handedly remarked that he wished he could read faster. I sat across from him.

"I know what you mean," I said.

We chatted about spring quarter courses. I kept to academic topics. He was most pleasant. I noticed the hazel flecks in the green-blue eyes. Over the next weeks, as I revisited the encounter, a

20

sweetness enveloped me. But the good feeling didn't last, and by May, I'd had enough.

It hadn't been part of my plan to make the first move. Despite my commitment to feminist ideology, I thought it was important for the man to be the pursuer. I'd also lacked the courage to shake things up. Now, I thought, I'll settle this issue.

Soundlessly, I came upon him. "Hi, José," I whispered, in keeping with the studious atmosphere of the library. He was surprised; I'd interrupted his absorption in a journal article about the Eighteenth Brumaire. "Kris and I were going for a drink later this afternoon, but she canceled," I lied. "Would you like to go?"

"—sure," he said. We planned to meet after work. Making a half-assed attempt to finish up my tasks, I trembled with anticipation. When 5:00 rolled around, José and I met in the vestibule of Dulles Hall. We stepped outside, and on that warm spring afternoon, we were actually walking together. Stippled with slanting sunbeams, the campus had never seemed more beckoning. Everything sparkled. The world was pistachio-colored, lit from within. We headed north onto High Street.

From a window of the Library Bar where he was celebrating the weekend with his buddies, Ray Miller spotted José and me as we strolled. On Monday morning, he showed up in my office, close to tears, his features contorted in a jealous fit. But even if I'd been aware of Ray's gaze, I wouldn't have cared. Soon José and I were facing one another at A La Carte, only a clean white tablecloth separating us.

We fingered our drinks. Unanswered questions swirled. He was cordial if not effusive, engaged in a composed, patrician way.

His voice was well-modulated. I noticed how deliberately he articulated his consonants and how carefully he chose his words. Despite his poised demeanor, he was surely wondering why I'd asked for his company. Why were we sitting there at A La Carte? What had been my motive?Holding onto the last vestiges of my feminine mystery, I kept all of that quiet. But I was also dying for information, and wasn't shy about asking for it.

He was born in Houston. No twang, just a flat Midwestern accent. "You don't sound like you're from Texas," I said, sipping my wine.

"When I was a kid, I used to say rahss instead of rice. And y'all."

"Mmm," I nodded briefly. "You trained yourself out of those bad habits."

"I guess I did."

I asked him to go on. He had two older brothers. The first son, John, a good man, was divorced with two young boys. He'd gone to Vanderbilt but hadn't finished his B.A. The second brother was Jim, a yuppie stock broker with a Cornell MBA who lived in New Hampshire with his wife and twin boys. Next on the list was José himself, and five years later, a daughter, Judi. She'd been the wild one.

His parents had lost their firstborn. Baby Carol was three weeks old when she died of a fever, so they tried to replace her with each of the next three children. "Dear old Mom and Pop must have been overjoyed with a third boy," he said, lifting his tumbler of Scotch. Self-disparagement mixed with a reluctance to say much. I studied him. After a few seconds, he lifted his gaze. Green with a turquoise tinge, large irises. As I stared, his eyebrows lifted in shy amusement. The dry sheen of his close-lipped smile said—this is curious, interesting, odd.

At my urging, he continued his story. Because of his father's job, he said, the family moved every four or five years, bouncing from Texas to Chicago to Connecticut to Tulsa. He'd hated Tulsa. In 1969, when he was 18, he enrolled at Ohio Wesleyan, but flunked out at the end of sophomore year. For the rest of the 70s and into the 80s, he held menial jobs, mostly restaurant work. By 1983, he'd had his fill of managing a golf course grill, and with his mother's financial help, finished a history degree at Ohio State.

He didn't say so, but I knew from his dossier that he'd graduated with both honors and distinction. I'd memorized the title of his senior thesis: "Five British Diplomatic Historians: The Paris Peace Conference and the Munich Agreement." I knew that his GRE scores were sky high. And I knew that he'd been inducted into Phi Beta Kappa the year before. Now he was a 35-year old T.A., finishing year one of his master's program.

I listened with rapt attention, consuming a large Chablis on an empty stomach. Suddenly, I remembered the time. "The woman should always decide when the date is over" that was one of my rules. I could have stayed at A La Carte forever, listening to José and gazing at him. But now I steeled myself. I put my napkin on the table and cocked my head to suggest it was time to shove off. I was weak in the knees but somehow exited gracefully through the door he held.

He walked and I floated south on High Street. We angled west through campus toward the stadium lot. His steps were brisk yet dignified. I followed right along, his pace steadying my own. I was hypnotized by his shirt, the waves of light blue and white pinstripe fabric. We reached my Datsun. With a dreamy half-smile, I readied myself for his invitation to go out again. Instead he said thanks for having a drink with me, turned, and made for his car.

It was like being struck. My ears rang with a tinny vibration. Wide-eyed, head spinning, I watched the back of him. He was moving in the wrong direction. I watched as he lowered himself into the red Bug. I watched as he drove away. After all the anticipation and planning, he hadn't asked for a follow-up date. It was too much.

Well, I'm not going to play this ball game by myself, I thought, swaying a little. The nerve. For minutes, I sat dazed behind the steering wheel, reeling with disappointment and the angry buzz. Then, action. In a robotic stupor, I sped towards Delaware. I'd never been to Delaware. I thought it was somewhere north of my house, straight up High Street. As if pulled by a magnet, I flew past car dealerships, a metro park, a Catholic cemetery.

"Delaware," said a big green sign. I turned left from the highway and left again into an old part of town. Frame houses built in the 1910s and '20s stood shoulder to shoulder. I drove along, lightheaded. William Street, I thought. William Street. I turned a corner and somehow, I was on William Street. But I didn't know the house number.

Suddenly, there he was, getting out of his car, parked on a steep driveway. In one arm he carried a small bag of groceries. Lost in thought, he saw my car hurtling forward on the gravel drive. I swerved and sharply braked. He came hastily.

Looking up through the open window, I lifted my chin and tried to appear both helpless and desirable. I kept my eyes half closed. José's surprise turned to alarm when he realized my state of inebriation. He bent into the car, took hold of my shoulder with his free hand, and looked into my eyes.

"Sharyn, can you make it home? Where do you live?"

"Worthington," I said, dimly. I was conscious of acting drunker than I really was.

"Should I take you home?"

"No. --I'm okay. Only, I'm . . . I just don't want to not see you again."

"Oh. Okay." His voice was startled yet softly controlled. He paused and ventured, "Well, what about tomorrow night?"

"Okay, I'm going home now." I'd accomplished my mission, so no need to tarry. I peeled backwards out of the driveway and shifted into drive.

"Okay, Sharyn. Please be careful, Sharyn," he called. He'd said my name twice. In the rearview mirror, he stood motionless, groceries in his arm.

***

As the alcohol buzz wore off, I was both elated and embarrassed. The rest of that evening, I felt that my desire would soon be fulfilled. I was standing at the edge of a sheer drop, terror and euphoria conspiring in my heart.

The next day, Saturday, May 17th, José called. We'd meet that evening at a place near my house called The Fontanelle, a smoky Italian restaurant-bar with a 50's feel: amber panels, pendant lamps with wrought-iron curlicues, heavy dark woodwork. I got there just after 8:00. Old boozers were already hunched at the bar. Waitresses with teased hair and hard eyebrows joked with the regulars. I spotted José at the end of the bar. He rose when I came. I slid onto the stool next to him.

We were quiet at first, vaguely cognizant of the clatter of glassware and the hum of conversation, the occasional burst of laughter. But the people around us didn't matter. That night, the world was just a backdrop. We were the only actors, and time stood still.

I looked at José. He exuded wry humor and a pleasant melancholy. He appeared just as calm as he'd been the afternoon before, but now I could sense a pulse of anticipation. A glance told me that his pupils were dilated, and not from the dusky atmosphere. He was shy but alert and waiting. He didn't know what I had in mind. I sipped my Pinot Noir and gazed unflinchingly. He looked up occasionally from his drink, fixing me with playful glances between fair lashes.

We made the usual pleasantries about the weather, the spring, the weekend. He told me about his courses, and I told him about my upcoming French exam. I said, "I liked hearing about your family at A La Carte yesterday." He had no idea that I was storing the information, keeping careful track. Now I invited him to tell me more. José Talbert wouldn't talk about himself unless urged to do so. I'd known that from the start.

He said he came from German, English, Welsh, and French stock. A Cherokee Indian and a Russian Jew were thrown into the mix, a long time back. But José and I were mostly of northwestern European descent.

"So where did 'José' come from?" I asked. There was nothing Latin about the man.

"It's a nickname from my roommate at Ohio Wesleyan. It just stuck."

He continued. "My dad's name was John Talbert. We kids called him Pop, but his nickname was Red."

A chemical engineer, Red had been a vice president of the Sinclair Oil Company. He was three years dead, gone in his early sixties.

"What did he die of?"

"Lung cancer," José said, eyebrows lifted. His Camels were in his breast pocket.

As he turned back to his drink, I noted his features. The broad forehead. The smooth jawline. The nose--aquiline, sharp at the tip, flared nostrils. The lips at the edge of the Scotch glass. Lightly, with the backs of my fingers, I touched his clean-shaven cheek and held that touch just long enough to feel the warmth of his skin. He wasn't made of marble.

On swiveling bar stools, we sipped our drinks, arm to arm, thigh to thigh. Occasionally, we pivoted, grazing one another's knee or upper arm. We didn't apologize for those luxurious bumps. Forgetting the world and its boiling eddies, we were engulfed in the liquid, hushed fluidity of scuba divers. When the urge hit, we surfaced, speaking comfortably, not in a cocktail-party schmoozing way, but in a disjointed way. The conversation was supposed to be disjointed. Our words were meant to fill in the blanks and shade our understanding of each other.

We talked about our childhoods, sidestepping the embarrassing parts. We gossiped about History. Our connection to the department gave us the freedom, the obligation, really, to discuss the characters we encountered there. José told me of his plans to study abroad in the summer, at Charles University in Czechoslovakia. He'd be doing a Czech language program.

That night at the Fontanelle, we avoided the subject of our living arrangements. Soon enough, José would reveal something I never would have guessed: he was sharing quarters with a woman named Beryl Wentz and her teen-aged son, Tater. They'd met back in 1978 at a restaurant in Delaware, where they both worked. When Beryl's house burned, José offered to shelter her and the boy, a bleakly utilitarian arrangement, the pooling of resources for survival's sake. The setup morphed into a habit. Sometimes it seemed merely awkward to José, a little humiliating. More often, it felt like a soul-deadening lie.

"I don't love Beryl," he said a few weeks after our first date. "I've never loved her. I just feel responsible for her and Tater. And the dogs, too, Sheba and Freeway."

Lacking José's affection, Beryl must have sensed that things were shaky. Superior in the glow of my own desirability, I wondered why any self-respecting woman would settle for a loveless relationship. And why, in his quiet desperation, hadn't José insisted on a change? Wasting five precious years? But José distracted himself from the shipwreck of his life by reading--the denser the material, the better. That was likewise his strategy whenever he visited his widowed mother in her manicured Houston suburb. Reading. For José, always the safe harbor.

28

During those first months, I wondered about José's mismatched life with Beryl. José wasn't much help--he didn't like the subject. Years later, in an envelope holding canceled checks and rent receipts, I found a grainy black-and-white photo of Beryl--heavy jawline and downturned, territorial lips. I saw why José hadn't invited me in when I showed up in the driveway, drunk and frantic.

But at the Fontanelle, we didn't discuss Beryl Wentz or Tater. We didn't consider my girls, Tibby and Norah, or my insolent ex-husband Vin, or my elderly Great Dane, Lady. We were alone in the world. We didn't let anyone else into our small skiff, lest it capsize. It was just the two of us.

I took another swallow of wine.

"Why didn't you ask me out after our drink yesterday?" Any sense of propriety was evaporating. I tipped my head slightly, waiting expectantly. José's eyelashes flickered downwards for a second as he thought about my question. He looked at me. "I thought the date was a failure."

"A failure? You did?"

"I thought you wanted to leave. I thought you asked me out to fill in for Kris. I assumed I was just a cipher."

"Oh, no. You couldn't be more mistaken. I didn't want to leave." He glanced at me. His eyes were ready for me to fill them up with some sign, some knowledge that needed to be expressed.

"Do you like me?" I asked him straight out, level gaze.

"Sharyn, if I didn't like you, I wouldn't be here." His voice had turned raspy. It didn't bother me that I was taking the bolder role, forcing him to express to his feelings.

After finishing our drinks, we left the Fontanelle and drove in my car to the back lot of Colonial Hills School. I shut off the engine and rolled down the windows. The balmy night air entered our space. The dark silence outside matched our moods. The leafed-out trees sheltered us from above. We parked for a while, holding hands. A breeze filtered softly through the open windows. Unconsciously yet reverentially, his left thumb slowly traced and retraced an arc on the thin skin of my hand. My head rested on his tricep. We didn't speak.

After a while, we got out. We murmured and kissed on the grass in the dark, "stuck in a lip lock," he'd later quip. There was no smoky tinge to his breath, only sweetness and heat. I pressed my face against his slightly concave chest. We were stunned into a slow silence. Breathing in the clean scent of his button-down shirt, I felt the world wash away.

***

The following Monday morning, he strolled into my office and dropped a note onto my desk, again in his neat handwriting, on yellow legal paper:

5/19/86

Sharyn,

Did you squeeze me out of your system over the weekend? I thought I was calm until I went to bed Sunday nite and was still staring at the clock at 4:56 Monday morning.

J.,

No, I didn't squeeze you out of my system. Did you accomplish your reading? I thought of you every second.

On Wednesday, he asked if I wanted to join him for a casual dinner after work. We left Dulles Hall and headed to a place he called the fake Italian restaurant. It was nearly empty. We arranged our napkins and sipped water. Sober and proper, we wondered whether Saturday night had really happened. We poked at our chicken Parmigiana and iceberg lettuce. I took small bites, trying not to sully my lipstick.

The conversation was innocuous: we talked politely about academics and the History Department course schedule for autumn. He asked, "Have you any information about Doc Riegert's course load next academic year?"

"Let's see." I had to force myself to think about workplace minutiae. "I think she's doing the Habsburg Monarchy in the winter." His glances had become shy again. He seemed guarded, as if bracing himself for bad news. The brave vulnerability on his face told me that he wasn't concerned about autumn course offerings at all. He was thinking, "I hope it's true that you do like me, but if it turns out to be a mistake, I'm ready."

I played along. I said nothing about how I felt, projecting a manufactured serenity. We are just the same, I was showing him. We're alike in all things. We're a couple now, both of us calm on the outside. But inside, you're buzzing, just like I am. Maybe you think it's scary, but I love it. And I love you.

As we faced one another, slowly eating our fake Italian dinner, I wanted the magic to resume, and could hardly hold myself back as I witnessed the unfolding, the baring of souls, little by tiny little. By the end of the meal, we knew that the spark was burning. We knew it when we held a glance for a few extra seconds. We savored it when our hands collided and lingered a little too long as we reached for the garlic bread.

After dinner, we walked quietly to the stadium lot, our steps keeping a perfect rhythm. This time, as I moved toward my car door, he held me. We didn't have to say a word.

In the office, he began to write notes.

5/27/86

Sharyn,

On Sunday I was talking to Rob about a woman in Middle East Studies (whom we both know), but when I went to say Sandra, it came out Sharyn. Oh well.

6/6/86

Sharyn,

My car is thumbing its nose at me again. I think the problem is wet electrical connections, a common VW ailment. I am going home at 11:00 to dry it/fix it, or destroy it. Je retournerai cette après midi. Can I call directly into your office, and if so, what is your number?

6/7/86

Sharyn,

Sorry I pushed you so hard. May we see each other again— will you still write notes to me? I think I'm crazy about you.

32

As minor members of the History Department, José and I aimed to keep our relationship under wraps. We especially tried to steer clear of my bloviating boss, K. Afton Krebs, who that summer had replaced Frank Price as Grad Studies Director. Krebs laughed loudly and often at his own jokes. He was not one to praise others. During slow times, I used to draw at my desk—caricatures, mostly. Once, Krebs regarded a sketch, hands in pockets, belly extended dangerously close. He pontificated, "Now that camera technology is so advanced, we don't need artists anymore."

Another time, when he was being challenged in some way, I witnessed him thump his chest and bellow, "I *am* the university!" Whenever he jotted a memo, he never signed simply "Afton," but used his three capitalized initials to remind me of his status: "KAK."

After that, José and I never called him Professor Krebs or even Krebs, but only KAK. One afternoon, I absently paged through the dictionary to the those initials. To my surprise, I found the word *Kakistocracy: Government by the worst people in the land.*

A few days later, José commented, "KAK discovered me doing a crossword puzzle in 168 and apologized for interrupting important work before rambling on about the best teachers at Ohio State--does he always think in stream-of-consciousness style?"

It wasn't only KAK who kept us chortling. Anybody in the department could give José and me fodder for speculation and fun. Yet it was important to avoid becoming the topic of conversation ourselves. Romantic entanglements of staffers and graduate students weren't encouraged at Ohio State. After the Ray Miller incident, I thought that José and I should keep things quiet.

By mid-June, José and I were conspiring to meet in Prague later that summer. We put our heads together and sketched our plans over dinner at Delicatessa, an intimate Russian restaurant near campus. He'd leave for his Czech language program at the end of July, and I'd join him there at the end of August. José was ambitious about his education, but there was no denying that Prague would be hard. I'd found out that he was a creature of habit, jarred by change. And in Prague, he'd have to adjust to the food, and would be sharing a room with a stranger, probably a non-English speaker. He'd surely be one of the oldest students.

I selfishly hoped that the most painful thing would be his separation from me, but I knew that the language gap would confound him. He excelled at Czech in the classroom, but being a non-native speaker would bedevil his dignity.

I asked, "Will you take flash cards with you on the plane?"

"The only flash card will be: 'Where the fuck is my luggage?'"

Meanwhile, I was taking computer science and logic courses, which together would fulfill the math requirement for my B.A. I disliked the material. José said encouragingly, "Think binary. Think simple. Day/night. Black/white. Good/bad."

Summer progressed and our love took deep root. "Whether" he would break it off with Beryl Wentz evolved to "when" he would do it. She still had no idea of the coming cataclysm. It was decided that he'd give her the news in late July, just before he left for Prague. But the break meant that he wouldn't have a place to live when he got back to Columbus in September.

My house wouldn't do—I had two impressionable children, and I wanted to set a good example. I also wanted to show José that I *wanted* to set a good example. Yet in mid-June, he hinted that, sooner or later, we would share living quarters.

"When we spoke under the tree yesterday," he said, "you were still not sure that I'll make the move. Brace yourself—I'm liable to land in your lap."

He resolved to lease an apartment for the 1986-87 academic year, but would need shelter at my house for a few days after breaking it off with Beryl. Meanwhile, it was becoming easier to negotiate our travel plans in the office, because KAK had gone on sabbatical.

6/23/86

Sharyn,

According to the "Master-Slave" relationship, where the master depends so much on the slave that the slave becomes the master, you must be . . . Department Kingfish for the summer.

I am going to my bank (my bank?) this afternoon to get a cashier's check to pay for summer school. The check will have to be made out to "Filozoficka fakulta, Univerzity Karlovy. Re: Letne skola slovanskyek studie, ucet (acct.) cis. (cislo-number 19-3923-911." This should be an interesting exercise for the clerk. I will send my passport off to D.C. tomorrow to get the visas.

Miss you, J.

While planning for Europe and sloppily trying to keep our love affair secret, José and I were finding out about each other's habits and quirks. We began to develop our own private system of folklore, as couples will. One item had to do with my Swashbuckler Dress. When José first encountered me the previous September, I'd been wearing a full-skirted shirtwaist of ecru broadcloth with a wide, tight belt. He freely admitted now that he'd noticed me.

"But why didn't you ask me out? Look at all the time we've wasted!"

"I assumed you were married. All pretty women are married," he said.

What a flimsy excuse, and me not wearing a wedding ring. It boiled down to the fact that José was shy, and a big part of the shyness was that he felt unworthy. I'd never understand it—Vin was just the opposite. He had zero to boast about but thought he was God's gift.

Some years later, José would mention being spanked as a child, often and hard. I wondered if that's what had turned him inward. Once, the family traveled from Chicago to Houston in hot summer weather. It was before the Interstate highway system, so they drove on two-lane roads, the windows wide open. Red was behind the wheel. Rachael sat next to him. The three little boys—Johnny, Jimmy, and Joe—were squished together in back.

In the afternoon, Red and Rachael pulled off at a roadside stand. They got a paper bag of ripe peaches and set it on the floor behind the front seat. They took off again.

The three little boys were bored and restless. They squabbled and pinched each other.

"It's my turn."

"I did not!"

"You kids behave!"

Four-year old Joe got a good shove from one of the big brothers, and after that, he was silent. He began to kick the bag. Kick, kick, kick. His parents drove and drove. Kick, kick, kick. He felt relieved as his shoe collided with the bag. Kick. Kick. His mother's talking in the front and the air rushing through the windows masked the sound. When they stopped for dinner a couple of hours later, Red and Rachael discovered that the peaches had been kicked to a slimy mass. Joe got it in the parking lot.

By the time José noticed my white dress with the tight belt, he hadn't been spanked in decades. Now, instead of being punished, he was being kissed and adored. And now that I'd drawn him out, he was revealing his gifts for comedy and word play. He dubbed the ecru dress with the wide belt my "swashbuckler" dress. From then on he always noticed when I wore a skirt with a belt.

"Is that a 'swash-buckle' you're wearing?" he'd ask.

We had no money, so we went on walking dates. Ohio State's campus was a good place to stroll. Closer to home, we'd wander through the Park of Roses or around Antrim Lake. Sometimes we'd just walk languidly through my neighborhood with old Lady along. From his remarks about Sheba and Freeway, I'd found out early that José was a dog person. As we walked, José was gentle with Lady's leash, unhurried when she took her time sniffing. I asked about the dogs he'd had.

His childhood dog was named Monty. "Monty was a shaggy medium-sized stray," he said. "My brother Jim found him and brought him home. Mom wasn't too thrilled." But the Talbert children, which now included Judi, indulged and loved that dog during his long canine life. Whenever Monty made his way into a Talbert family photo, the children aren't looking at the camera, but are instead gazing at Monty.

I told José one of my dog stories. It was a Saturday in October of '57. I was with my father at the empty model home. He sat behind a desk, waiting for people to come and spend money. I was on the sidewalk, eating cookies. A small, friendly dog wandered by. The dog's eyes were dark brown, gentle and merry. His whiskers tickled my hand as he took a piece of cookie. I spent hours with my companion, feeling important when, unbidden, he followed me down the sidewalk and back. He sat patiently by my side.

Twilight descended, and my father said it was time to go. I wanted to take the dog with us. Daddy wouldn't let me. As we pulled away, I looked out the rear window and into the dog's eyes. He was watching me leave. I cried. But Daddy was listening to the radio, something about "Sputnik," which was more important than the dog, whom I'd named Petey.

"Petey! Petey!" I blubbered.

In a few years, my parents got their first Great Dane, and after that, we were never without a dog, purebred, as my mother said. Sometimes we had three or four. As he scouted out houses to buy or sell, my father drove around in his open convertible with the massive, erect dogs in the back seat. The dogs called attention to him. They're good for business, he thought. I'm making a name for myself. In the '70s, he got a vanity plate for his Cadillac, GR8

DANE. Which made sense, because the dogs and my father were Danes, although my mother didn't think *he* was great.

José and I knew that dogs have no delusions about their importance. When you're grouchy, dirty, or sick, they love you anyway. When you make a mistake, they forgive you immediately. When you make a fool of yourself, they join right in. When your parents are impatient and severe, dogs salve the wounds. And maybe being a dog lover gives you insights about human foibles.

José had a knack for bringing human foibles into focus. That summer, as we strolled along or sat on a bench under a leafy tree, his deductions about the human condition reduced me to speechless merriment. The most frequent topics were his own unwitting blunders. In my love-struck state, it was comical enough that this dignified person made any mistakes at all, but the fact that he freely joked about them created an irresistible comic incongruity. The hubris of powerful people was another subject--with his natural ability to pinpoint logical and rhetorical blunders, José could ferret out the tiniest pomposity and eviscerate it. When I laughed, he did, too, feeling appreciated, loved.

It wasn't all moonbeams and martinis. I still had to work, and he still had to study. But the beauty of it was that José and I were employed in the same department. We would collide accidentally-on purpose many times during the day as we headed for the photocopier or the restroom. He'd stop by my desk and ask in mock-courtliness, "Can I coax you into a walk this evening after your class? I enjoyed the one last night."

I nodded with shining eyes.

He bent so that his lips just brushed my hair, and said, low, "Can you stand the excitement of this *faire de coeur*?"

The sense of the permanence of our love grew alongside the ardor. Before we began to date, José had applied to the University of Michigan's graduate program to enhance his academic pedigree. Going to Ann Arbor would also have been a logical way to sever ties with Beryl. Before our first drink at A La Carte, he found out that he'd won a full fellowship to Michigan--tuition and fees waived, and for a year, a monthly stipend for living expenses. No obligation to teach or grade: they would have paid him just to study there. Now, to be with me, he turned down the Michigan fellowship.

In early July, I got my passport. Despite our attempts to keep things quiet, some people in the department knew about our plans to meet in Eastern Europe. Elsbeth and several grad students knew, including Joyce, a woman from the Virgin Islands. With a major field in modern U.S. history, Joyce was born the same year as José— 1951. Joyce and José occupied adjacent desks in 168 Dulles and developed a close friendship, sharing a similar cynicism, wisecracking about the state of the world and the brutalities of being T.A.s. Joyce wore her black hair in a high French twist with a stretchy headband circling her forehead. An off-the-shoulder pink sweater was a favorite item of apparel. With long thin fingers tipped with polished nails, Joyce delicately lifted a glass mug, sipping coffee with cream as she studied alongside José in the Hockett Library. During that summer of 1986, Joyce complained about the French course she was taking for her master's program, and José commiserated, grappling with his own Czech language studies.

Another person who knew our secret was Charles Morley, an emeritus who specialized in imperial Russia. Although retired, he regularly visited the department, collecting his mail and catching up on office gossip. On these occasions, he never failed to swing by my desk. Professor Morley was jolly--white hair on end, stooped shouldered but swivel-hipped, face red as borscht. I told Professor Morley about my plans because he took the time to ask and seemed genuinely interested. Such repartee was one of the best aspects of my job. But José asked suspiciously, "Who put Charles Morley onto me? I've never seen him before. Pleasant gentleman—he became the umpteenth person to assure me that Prague hadn't been bombed in World War Two."

As we planned the trip, friction crept into our budding relationship. Now that I had him, I wanted José to play the dating game, to ask me formally for my company, several days in advance. Then I'd say flirtatiously, "Let me check my social calendar. Umm, yes, I think I should be free next Friday evening." He didn't get it. How could anybody be at the same time so precocious and so naïve? He assumed that because we were in love, we'd be going out steadily, no verbalization needed.

As for me, while a feminist in theory, I was in practice a shameless coquette. I expected things I didn't ask for. When I didn't get them, I pouted. I punished José for not doing something he didn't know he was supposed to do in the first place. I wanted the begging, so sometimes, even though I desperately wanted to see him, I was unavailable. When he showed up at my desk, a look of angelic anticipation on his face, I watched the twinkle disappear.

"I don't remember we were to have gone out tonight," I said.

41

Or, "Maybe you can stop by after my class. I'll let you know how I feel."

But he didn't intrude.

The next day, I told him that I'd waited for his call.

"I didn't want to appear too obsessed with you," he replied.

"I'd much rather deal with your obsession than with your silence," I said honestly.

"Well, I paid for my folly—I bit my knuckle and drank beer all evening."

The game of cat-and-mouse wore us out. I didn't budge, and he didn't beg. But the hunger, the love, were stronger than the game, and even the exhaustion was oddly refreshing. It was like exercise, the pain of the exertion creating denser muscle fiber. Somehow, the vibrating tension didn't harm the ardor, but tied us more tightly.

Despite occasional conflict, we were in sync most of the time. My 36th birthday was coming up, and José formally asked me, a week ahead, to join him for dinner at the Olde Swiss House in German Village. One of the adjuncts recommended it. She said to be sure to get the fresh trout from the trout tank. "You needn't get dressed up tomorrow night," José remarked. "I'm sure haute cuisine will be more honored in the breach than in the observance."

Against the hot humidity, I wore a lightweight dress in a pale blue and white print. The meal wasn't so special, and the trout tank was out of order. But I cared only about the company. José gave me a biography of Thomas More and a collection of H.L. Mencken's writings. He sent a bouquet of red roses which must have broken his budget.

The next day he picked up a battery for his camera so he could shoot me with the long stems, warning, "My pictures will make you brag on your driver's license." Along with love notes and presents, the photos would be one more historical document confirming our union.

For me, dinners out, walks, and also movies were the logical dating venues. But it began to sink in that José despised movies. This both alarmed and fascinated me—I loved cinema, great and merely good, and was almost always in the mood for a movie date. My lifelong habit had been simply to go without caring too much what was playing. On summer weekends in the 1950s and '60s, my father would ask, "Well, should we go to the picture show?" And we always enjoyed it. I saw movie-going as a pleasant diversion. Didn't everybody love movies?

No. José, I soon understood, felt trapped in a movie theatre, unable to escape somebody else's narrative for two long hours. Insulted by hackneyed scripts, affected acting, and implausible storylines, he was skeptical of the very idea of movies. In years to come, he'd go so far as to deny film as a legitimate art form. Yet while we were dating, I learned only by his reactions that he mistrusted movies.

Down and Out in Beverly Hills, which we saw in June, was amusing and harmless in my opinion, but José bemoaned its coarse humor and sight gags. Even serious films tried his patience: after my birthday, we saw James Ivory's *A Room with a View*. José sat sighing and cracking his knuckles. Boy, I thought, not even E.M. Forster can hold his attention. This time, crudeness wasn't the issue. Sentimentality and lengthiness were the culprits.

José's distaste for movies surprised me. But every new revelation about him pulled me more deeply under his spell. Stumbling upon him in the history department of a Midwestern university was like finding the Hope Diamond in a cornfield. I couldn't believe my luck. And so the movie phobia was just another sparkling facet of his singularity: a little peculiar, but it had the bracing effect of teaching the lesson of selectivity. Limit the junk that goes into the mind.

Not that José was a purist. For one thing, he loved the funny paper. But his original wit surpassed the funnies by leagues. His response to even the most mundane question could add another fine brushstroke to my blooming understanding of him.

One night before his departure for Czechoslovakia, over glasses of wine, I observed him as he took a drag on his cigarette.

"Are you healthy?" I asked.

"As far as I know," he said.

Exhaling in his elegant way, he extended his left hand—long fingers, full nail beds with short-cut nails. He wiggled a slightly crooked middle finger.

"I broke it when I was a kid, playing basketball. It didn't knit right."

I sipped my wine. After a minute, I asked, "What's your blood type?"

44

"If you tell me your ring size, I'll tell you my blood type."

I smiled demurely, but was whooping inside.

As July came to a close, the need for José to find an apartment was becoming more pressing. He'd have to store his belongings in my attic while he was abroad--he was more determined than ever to make the break with Beryl. Finally, he said, "I've examined Rob's apartment." Rob was a fellow grad student who would be on fellowship that fall. "It's nice but pretty small. As soon as he gives his notice, I'll get in touch with his landlord."

2

PRAGUE

This little mother has claws.—Franz Kafka

O n the afternoon of July 30, in a Delaware steak house, José ended it with Beryl. She was caught off guard, and as it sank in, she became hysterical. The outburst escalated in the parking lot. Promising financial help, José finally escaped. That evening, José lugged his books and belongings into the hot attic. He'd parked his new car, a second-hand VW Rabbit, on the street. I'd keep an eye on it while he was away. A gift from his mother, the brown Rabbit was a replacement for the red Bug that couldn't be resuscitated.

When he finished lugging boxes, we ate a dinner of salad and pasta. We talked about his departure the next afternoon. In honor of the trip, his friend Joyce had given him two dress shirts, one black with a geometric design, the other, bright blue and green stripes.

They weren't his style, and were too short in the arms, so José refolded them. I'd return them to Joyce so she could exchange them.

For the third time, I checked to make sure I had the right address. My letters had to make it--other than a plane crash, the worst-case scenario would be José cozying up to some pretty Prazan and forgetting all about me. Yes, the address was correct. We talked and drank wine. Our fingers entwined as we listened to Chopin's *Variations on Don Giovanni*. Tibby was spending the night with her best friend. Norah was asleep. José and I finally slept, too—I in my room and José on the couch.

Next day was humid, stifling. To calm our nerves, we drank wine before we headed to the airport. The battle with Beryl had taken its toll. As we drove, he said, "Well, now I'm officially a Displaced Person." Dreading the coming separation, I was silent, too. Anyway, there wasn't much to discuss. Both of us knew the plan: he'd fly to JFK and on to Frankfurt, where he'd change planes again. He'd get to Prague the next day.

Walking through the noisy airport, José projected a poised exterior, but I could feel the nervousness in his clipped, measured responses to the agent. Bags checked and ticket in his hand, we kissed, exchanging hollow words about being careful and missing one another. Then he was gone.

***

José's first and second letters from Prague, mailed to the house, never reached me. As it happened, Vin showed up on my doorstep just hours after José left. We'd been divorced for nearly seven years, but Vin often came, swaggering around in his Tony

Lama boots. He commandeered Norah's bedroom during these periods, dumping his stuff on the yellow carpet.

Norah shared Tibby's bed when her dad was over. But that was the least of the inconveniences. The girls were confused. Vin and I were divorced, but here we were again. We were together, and yet we weren't. There was nothing physical between us. I hated the vibe he gave off, the unspoken, unspeakable readiness for anything I wanted to give him. Feed me! Flatter me! Worship me! Embedded in his every groan, sigh, and comment was a heavy neediness. He was always angling for something.

How awful it was to let him into the house. The girls and I would never recover from his irresponsibility and, yes, cruelty. I didn't love him, didn't like him, and didn't respect him. And yet I braced myself and allowed him to stay with us several times a year, just to relieve a little of the financial distress. He'd give me a few hundred bucks. It was never even remotely worth it.

The marriage to Vin had lasted ten years. The first signs of instability came almost instantly, but I stayed with him for reasons that included my extreme youth and our extreme poverty. I also wanted to prove that commitment and love can help someone become the person he must have wanted to be. Isn't there a syndrome where women fall for misogynist men and stick it out? Maybe there's another syndrome in which gentle, studious men stay with women they don't love? Who knows? But life with Vin was a royal pain.

"Bah, fungool!" he'd yell when things didn't go his way.

"Fuck you and your fucking life!" he shouted as I wept in distress when Tibby was an inconsolable infant, hurling a box of Quaker Oats. It erupted like a pinata.

I hadn't gotten a good deal with Vin, either in marrying him or after the divorce in 1980. When he remembered to send child support, it wasn't enough to pay the utility bills let alone food and clothes for growing children. Never mind trying to save anything. Now it was 1986 and Vin was still surfacing. And I was still compromising my principles for a few bucks.

Vin timed his arrival to coincide with José's departure— typical. Invitation neither needed nor wanted. Knowing too well his jealousy and his penchant for taking things that didn't belong to him—property, privacy, dignity, innocence, and peace--Vin was the reason for José's missing letters. I finally put it together, but by then the first two letters were long gone.

Of the fourteen letters José penned while in Prague, twelve survived, neatly handwritten on yellow legal paper. Lost information survived in a letter to his mother. He told her that his TWA flight had been delayed in New York, causing him to miss his connection to Prague the next day. To pass the time, he spent six hours in the Frankfurt airport reading English newspapers. He got to Prague on Friday evening without further trouble. Much later, I found out that, during the trans-Atlantic flight, José had been subjected to a movie. It was both painful and hilarious to imagine him sitting through *The Mambo Kings*. At 30,000 feet, there was no escape.

Also in the letter to his mother was information about the dorm, typical except that:

. . . they serve beer and mineral water with lunch and dinner. The beer is very good—strong and bitter. For breakfast we usually get cold cuts or frankfurters, either rye or white bread or rolls, a piece of fruit, and heated milk and sweetened tea. Strange fare, but not bad. Lunch is the main meal of the day, and today's was extraordinary: a large slab of wienerschnitzel, mashed potatoes, and cucumbers and onions in vinegar. Less meat at dinner, with boiled potatoes or rice or knedliky (bread dumplings), salad or soup, and a chocolate confection of some kind.

Prague is very beautiful and old. It's also surprisingly hilly—downtown really is down. It's also rough on the shoes--most streets and sidewalks are paved with cobblestones.

The month of August was a time of separation and longing. Before email and reasonably priced transatlantic phone service, we relied on airmail with the inevitable time lapse: José did not receive my first letters until halfway through his five-week stay in Prague. After he got my letters, his mood became more upbeat. But my letters started and ended passionately:

7/31/86

Dearest,

It's been 2.5 hours since your plane left. The wine helped to numb the reality, but emptiness followed me out of the airport and away from your arms. Does school start on Monday? Tell me about the other Americans. How many wild and crazy guys have you seen? I was back in the office for a full 10 minutes before Vin called, asking for overnight refuge. I agreed with the gravest melancholia. Just imagine the neighbors' reactions. We'll have to be resolute. I love you. I miss you so much already.Sharyn

8/1/86

Dearest,

Missing you terribly. Wouldn't it be wonderful to take an Antrim Lake walk again? Are you eating and sleeping well? What is the weather situation? What is the toilet paper situation? Vin is still here, sorry to say. Something startled me in the middle of the night. I thought it was you. In the morning I asked Tibby who had been in my room. Vin overheard and said he'd been looking in my closet for something. Bizarre and chilling. I love you. Sharyn

8/2/86

Dearest,

The shirts have been returned to Joyce. She was incredulous: "He wears a La-a-a-arge?" Well, I told her you're a Handful, but she doesn't believe me. Can't wait to see her next choices. You will boogaloo down Main Street yet.

The sweetheart roses are beautiful. The girls were really touched, especially Norah. For some reason, Norah is quite fond of you.

Can we explore the city together? I'm sure you're dying to see everything now, but please let there be some surprises left for when I get there. Is there a stereo in your dorm? I can see you at the table that last night, listening to the concerto. I am kissing you.Sharyn

Here are José's surviving missives, with my own spliced in:

Monday evening, 8/4/86

Dear Sharyn,

We met the Mayor of Prague today, a greasy bounder with a permanent curl. He appeared to be hung over. This was after we attended the official Summer School opening, which consisted of six dead men on a podium. In between the sessions, I raced all over Old Town and all the way to New Town, looking for a bank, so I could get some crowns and therefore tram tickets and cigarettes. I eventually found one at the south end of Vackowske. Now I have enough money to mail an overseas letter.

My Czech class runs from 9:00-1:20 (about the time you leave for work—I'm still thinking in these terms). Class includes something called "Fonetika" from 12:00-12:30, and sure enough, I managed to get thrown in with the morons. But with 4.5 hours a day, maybe I will finally learn some Czech. Both of my roommates (including the Swede) used the same textbook as I did at Ohio State: Cestiva pro Cizince. So we all have the same gaps and anxieties.

Pani Hana Kornecka teaches the English-speaking morons. She is very pregnant and takes frequent breaks to do whatever pregnant women do. Or maybe she goes out to cry over our Czech. Class is taught in Czech with English provided only upon request. Two Japanese are in the class, and the man seems literate only in Japanese, so I don't think I'll be the caboose. We switched from singular to plural in the prepositional case today—I forgot to bring my Tums.

I just got back from downtown where I sent out some mail. I think the first two letters will beat Vin to the house. I'll mail future letters to the History Department.

We were taken to see an arty Czech film yesterday afternoon—<u>Merry Summer</u>. It was better than <u>Down and Out in Beverly Hills</u>.

I will cross the envelope flap with my pen. One never knows.All my love, J.

8/5/86

Dearest,

I miss you so much, your presence, insights, touch. I'm assuming that your negativity on the last day reflected the turmoil with Beryl only hours before we left for the airport. I want our relationship to start again when we're reunited. I love you, more than I can say. Sharyn

Wednesday Evening, 8/6/86

Dear Sharyn,

A few times during the day, I'm upset that I can't talk to you. I hope Beryl and Vin aren't being problems, to you or themselves. I also hope that my letters to you don't cause raised eyebrows in the History Dept. I frequently gaze at your pictures. I'm not sure this helps the ache. Writing seems to work, though.

Class is too easy. I'll give it til the end of next week and if it doesn't get more rigorous, I'll see if I can transfer to a more exalted section.

Remember to ask the girls what they would like from Prague. Your mother, too. Take care and study hard. Chci skocit vase kosti. Keep these letters so I can find out how things went here when I get back. Love always, J.

8/6/86

Dearest,

In three weeks and two days, we'll be together again. Do you still understand English? I'd write in Czech but suspect you'd get tired of hearing that I love you.

Vin was here again yesterday, on his way to Chicago. He probably spied the framed photo of you next to my bed. He asked Tibby who sent the roses—the poor girl said she thought it was Grandma. Poor kids, stuck in the middle....

Vin's bon mot yesterday was that he and I are "cut from the same cloth." Oh...Help. By the way, Vin's mother knows I'm going to Czechoslovakia. She asked for a replica of "The Infant of Prague." For her sister, who is devoted to it. (him? Him?)

I'm scraping by in class. Can't wait to see how the random choice logic mid-term went.

The department is quiet. Many of the faculty and grad students are vacationing. Several grad students are throwing a good-bye party for Shirley on Saturday evening. I'm going, to be out of the house while Vin is there (he's returning for his "once monthly" visit this weekend). I expect there will be a good-sized group. Rob is bringing Shirley late, after everyone's assembled. Love you, Sharyn

Friday evening, 8/8/86

Dear Sharyn,

Sorry if my letter of Wednesday seemed a little morose. I'm just worried about what may be going on while I'm incommunicado. By this I do not mean that I think you're fooling around. I'd just like to get a word in edgewise before you come to any drastic conclusions about the future of us.

My phone number here is 34-73-518, Ext 441. The calls are much cheaper in Czecho than out of it (about $1 a minute, according to my American roommate), but don't call unless you need to. A dollar a minute is still pretty expensive.

My roommates and I, plus the American's Czech wife, went to a wine bar in the Old Town last night. We had two platters of hors d'oeuvres and three liters of wine for under $25. Good wine, too. The American "knows just enough Czech to make himself misunderstood," as his wife puts it. Their 3½-year-old bilingual daughter forgets vocab from one language when speaking for a while in the other. The Czech wife spent the evening telling us Czech Chernobyl jokes. She says there are hundreds of them. These people really hate the Russians—and the Slovaks. When I asked her if there was a chance that the next president would be a Czech, she said, "No, just another dumb Slovak." Czechoslovakia has a great future.

Class is going all right. I'm beginning to understand the instructor (a little) when she flies off on a tangent. This is a minor miracle.

On Sunday, we're taking a field trip to the camp at Terezin. But when you come, we'll hire a boat, lay in a lunch, and punt off into the Vltava. I'm told this is the best way to introduce a lady to

Prague—and oneself to the lady. When you come, bring a corkscrew and a bottle opener—two things I forgot. We can make use of a "Czech refrigerator": tap water in a basin. The water here is unbelievably cold.

I wish I could be with you tonight. All my love, J.

8/9/86

Dearest,

I was speaking with Dr. Cline today—recently back from a trip to Soviet Union and eastern Europe. I asked about Prague and was surprised to find out that "one needs at least 2.5 hours in the airport before departing Czechoslovakia." Cline said that the lines are interminable, foreign dignitaries constantly breaking through, bags searched in an impossibly slow manner. Passports are double- and triple-checked. (Do you think they have a problem with "trust"? Do you think you'll ever get this letter?) But in Dr. Cline's view, Prague has remained the most beautiful city in all of Europe, surpassing much of what is Italian, surpassing Paris.

I love you very much and miss you every second. Sharyn

Sunday Evening, 8/19/86

Dear Sharyn,

The tour of Terezin started with the cell of Gavrilo Princip— remember this guy? He died in Terezin during the first World war. My Swedish roommate is angry. He thought Terezin was filled with propaganda. This is probably true. The "Arbeit Macht Frei" over the entrance looked too freshly painted, and with Jews and Roma pushed into the background, Terezin is a memorial to the brave Communist struggle against fascism.

After Terezin we went to Litomerice. I figured out why. It wasn't for the baroque chapel (very beautiful) but to see occupied Czechoslovakia. A Russian regiment is garrisoned here, with silly slogans on red banners. Prague has no such blatant military presence.

I've passed page 300 in the Dreyfus book [The Affair by Jean Denis Bredin]. Thanks for such a long book—it might last another week. At night, I lie here and identify with Dreyfus, socked away on Devil's Island. The truth is, I have more important things to do this summer than to study Czech. If you decide not to come, Sharyn, let me know. I will not stay in Prague without you. I don't want to stay anywhere without you.

I'll write again tomorrow, and I'll send a note to Joyce, too. Give my best to Tibby and Norah. I will love you always. J.

The next day, José did write a letter to Joyce, thanking her for the too-small shirts:

Dear Joyce,

Sorry about "le debacle des chemises." You should have caught me in a movie theatre and taken my measurements while I slept. You also should not have bought me TWO shirts. But they are much appreciated.

I've gotten fat and complacent this summer. Four and a half hours of Czech per day is exhausting. Courting, of course, has been arduous (and ardorous) enough to keep me in some sort of tone. And my legs should be especially magnificent when I return: Prague is uphill in every direction.

I've tried to educate my Swedish roommate about American politics. He takes Reagan's speeches seriously: for instance, the one he made at the D-Day ceremonies in 1984, when the U.S.S. Eisenhower cruised past his shoulder just in time for the morning "news" programs. I've told him only a Swede would be so idealistic.

Take care of yourself. I will bring you a copy of Rude Pravo: it'll make you long for The Columbus Dispatch. I've also discovered some tidbits about Czech racial foibles. Miss you. A toute a l'heure, José

Monday Evening, 8/11/86
Dear Sharyn,

I wrote this down as my Czech instructor said it. "The most of Czech verbs is in pairs." For an hour this morning, we all had a "conversation." The instructor speaks rapidly, and most of it whizzes by my ears. The subject: eating out in restaurants, a topic which has its uses. But I'm not sure how I'm going to work it into my thesis.

The headaches of the first week must have been a result of caffeine withdrawal: I've been drinking only one cup of coffee a day. I've reached page 345 in Dreyfus: the general staff conspiracy has come undone but the revision of Dreyfus' conviction is still stymied.

I hope my letters aren't proving an embarrassment in the office. Now that I think of it, you will probably go through the mail delivery yourself. I guess I ought to study perfective-imperfective differences in Czech verbs now. I'll probably fall asleep reading Dreyfus. Scratch Lady's chest for me. I love you. J.

8/12/86

Dearest,

Got your first letter yesterday! It made great time—six days! But, I suspect it came out of sequence. Had you written before the 6th? You mentioned Beryl and Vin: Vin has been here since late Saturday night. He's playing it to the hilt. As for Beryl, it will be easier for her in the long run if she realizes that she must proceed without you.

Will St. Vitus Cathedral be open in early September? Joyce returned the shirts and got two replacements (same patterns, size large). She wants me to bring them to Prague. Do I have to?

Be careful, study hard. I'll write again tomorrow. Love, Sharyn

Thursday afternoon, 8/14/86

Dear Sharyn,

Have I ever told you the story about my hitting the Trifecta at the Delaware County fairgrounds on the last race of Little Brown Jug day in September of '81? My combination was 8-1-6. Horses 8 and 1 were by far the best in the race—the only question was, which horse would show? I picked Hanley Hanover, a six-year old mare who appeared to have seen some hard use. Oddly, I can remember the 6 horse's name but not the names for the 8 or 1. Sure enough, 8 and 1 far outdistanced the other horses, and managed to finish in the proper order. With only a furlong to run, Hanley Hanover exploded

60

out of the pack, went three-wide, and blew the rest of them off the track. She closed so fast she almost caught the 1 horse. I was standing at the finish line in ankle-deep mud, almost in tears. Hitting a trifecta is so improbable it seems to transcend mere luck—it's more like being kissed by an angel.

All of this is a preface to what happened yesterday afternoon. I got back to the dorm at 1:45 and checked the ledge where they lay out the mail. I thought that if I didn't hear from you that day, I probably wouldn't for another week. I hadn't made a big deal about you writing to me, but I was definitely acquiring a Dreyfus complex. When I got to the mail ledge, I realized I had mail. This was understatement. In front of me were your letters of 31 July, August 1, 2, 5, and 6. And on my way up to the cafeteria for lunch, I thought of the trifecta and the angel's kiss. You made my day—my week. I stopped in the commissary and fell into two bottles of beer while I read.

I'm sorry Vin has been such a pain. Maybe he will retire from the field with some dignity. Maybe?

About Norah: I have to admit something. Every time you assume your "Himmler" stance, I give her a behind-your-back smile. For this alone, she cannot dislike me. Actually, I think you handle your kids with great affection, especially when you are coercing them into doing something. Tell me, is Norah more organized in August than she was in June?

I can hunker down and live without music for a month, but god I miss reading a real newspaper—especially one with comics. We vulgarians read those first. We have no stereo, the only towel is the one I brought, and it smells sour by now, even after washing, But frankly, I'm glad we have hot water.

As for Prague, I've walked a lot and have just barely begun to see it. Ninety percent of what we see together, I will probably be seeing for the first time.

Thanks for the The New York Times op-ed. Women wear pants, men wear trousers; women wear stockings, men wear socks; women wear panties, men wear shorts (well, some little boys never grow up). Isn't this common knowledge? Am I really the only person you know who carries a hankie? We traditional guys not only carry hankies, we use them.

I will not return to Beryl. I have been out of control of my half of our relationship since June. The negativity on my part which you mention was halfway attributable to the turmoil of leaving. I think it was the most screwed up week of my entire life. Being with you on the last night was all that saved it.

The other half of my negativity was trepidation. In late July, you mentioned that we would be too "busy" in September to spend as much time together; your tone bordered on a reproach. That remark still disturbs me. I don't know if it was something I did, or if you were having an attack of cold feet. After all, September and October are the two finest walking months in Columbus. In my humble view, if two people are in love, they find the time to requite one another's love.

The ache, the feeling of emptiness, was persistent on the night before I got your letters. I read Dreyfus from 7:00-9:00 (I'm up to page 550), and studied Czech rigorously until midnight. At 3:30, I was still wide awake. Now that your letters have started to come, I don't think I'll have another episode like that. Thank you. Keep writing.

Give Tibby a pat on the back for me: it's admirable to lie when the occasion warrants it. She has my appreciation. I would like to have a group photo of you three. (Vin unnecessary.)

I've never heard of the "Infant of Prague." But there are sellers of trinkets on Charles Bridge every evening and on weekends. If they have not heard of him (Him), maybe they can create him (Him).

When you get to Prague (which you'll notice looks like Port Columbus circa 1969, but a little shabbier), after the two passport checks, walk straight ahead into the baggage room. After you get your bag, they will check it at the customs booth and send you into the main lobby, where I will jump all over you. If you miss your connection in Frankfurt, please have Lufthansa page me in Prague so I will not go crazy.

It's 10 p.m. here; you are just about to get off work. I still have to do my Czech homework. I'll write in the morning. I'll love you always. I never get tired of hearing you say you love me. J.

8/14/86

Dearest,

Your fourth letter came first, next your third letter. The first two, sent to the house, haven't shown yet. When I read your passage, ". . . so I think the first two letters will beat Vin," I shuddered, because he was there at that moment. Vin has a history of intercepting my mail.

I laughed at the image of your mad quest for cigarettes. Language school sounds hard, interesting, and a comedy-show. Wish I had the first two letters so I could put together a more solid picture of your classmates and roommates.

Everyone at home is fine. Including the Great Dane. Tibby and Norah start school in two weeks. Mom would really enjoy getting a card. Must run to politics class. Love you, dearest. Sharyn

Friday, 8/15/86
Dear Sharyn,

I have all of your pictures here with me in Prague, but I've hauled them out only three times. They're a sterile reminder of what I left behind. I did show the "bunny" pic to my American roommate. He said, "She's cute." He didn't fool me—I saw his knees wobble. While I'm on the subject, I haven't yet seen a woman in Prague who can hold a candle to you.

Czech dorms don't have bathtubs, but elevated shower stalls (about 15 inches)—perhaps to promote bathroom accidents. I have avoided these, so far.

My Swedish roommate has the flu and refuses my offers of aspirin. Bull-headed type. Of course, his flu seems to abate each evening when he goes out to chase a particular Italian girl. The dreaded illness rears its head again each morning just before class.

I want to sleep with your body against mine and wake with it still there. And not just in my dreams. And yes, we will go to Antrim Park the first chance when we get home.

Have you scratched your dog's chest today?

When you come, bring cash, not travelers checks. Cash is more versatile. Also, tipping in hard cash is much appreciated. Not to mention that finding a bank in Czechoslovakia requires cunning and determination. Bring your sneakers, probably the best footwear for Prague.

At the end of class yesterday, we were told to go to another room in the philosophy faculty where a woman would teach us Czech songs. Gee whiz. I went straight back to the dorm to eat lunch and write my magnum opus to you. So the first thing this morning, the instructor asked us to sing the songs we learned. You can imagine my beatific look as my classmates/nerds broke into merry song. Perhaps I can work a Czech song into my thesis defense. Maybe a capella. *This might cut short the defense. Maybe the examiners would throw in a Ph.D. if I agreed to shut up. Class isn't always this trivial and cute, but it is often enough.*

I think of you all the time. I love you alone. J.

Sunday evening, 8/17/86

Dear Sharyn,

A few questions for you, Madame. Are you worried about Vin giving the girls the third degree while you're in Prague? How have you explained my car? Have you driven it? Better yet, have you taken Tibby out in it? If you don't teach her, I shall feel duty-bound to do so myself—Tibby willing.

A couple of students have mistaken me for a Slav. Is this true? And if so, what should be my response? Several times, I've been approached on the street by people looking for directions. They were disappointed. The other day, I helped a mother unload her

65

pram off the tram. I knew what to do, and so didn't pay much attention to her staccato Czech. She must have thought I was retarded.

I walked around Old Town yesterday, avoiding the Square because of the tourists, but we still have to stop there at least once to watch the Town Hall clock do its schtick. Last night, Ola and I went to Mala Strana for a beer and stopped in a tourist trap, U Svate Tomase. They serve dark beer (very good) which is brewed in Prague. The place was crawling with Germans. Even our waiter attempted to speak German. Ola said, "That was some kind of very bad German language, I tell you, Josef." On our way back we got off the tram at Hradcany Square and walked down Nerudova Street almost to the river. Ola thinks it might be the most beautiful walk anywhere. Steep and cobbled and haunting. We'll walk Nerudova, and continue to Charles Bridge, gazing at the right bank of the Vltava, which is completely lit from the House of Artists to the National Theatre. It is remarkable.

Since May I've been granted the chance to make my life over. Shy people understand that opportunity knocks rarely, and never more than once. Only you have the power to veto our relationship. Since the first evening at the Fontanelle and Colonial Hills School (I can't tell you how beautiful you were that evening—I was staggered), my life has been too good to be true. Only several months before, I'd concluded that I'd either have to spend my life with a woman I did not love, or else alone.

Now I have a chance for a lasting relationship with the woman I love. I've tiptoed around Dulles Hall, passing notes to you like a bashful school boy, as if I needed someone's permission to

66

court you, to fall in love with you. I think and hope that we will be more solidly one when we leave Prague. So much so that any objections will seem Lilliputian; the interferences, grossly Brobdingnagian. The department will simply have to get used to us. Be resolute and unafraid. We will out.

8/18/86

Dear Sharyn,

Since Wednesday of last week, I've heard nothing from you. I am selfish. You must keep writing to me. And I do miss the catharsis of music. Particularly at your house. I have felt both out of place and very comfortable in your house, especially when talking to you at the den table late in the evening, the only time we were together without undergoing a public inspection, except by an occasional daughter.

Sometimes I have the frightening thought that my letters aren't getting through. Remember I told you I'd buy a journal here? My letters to you are it. But the post office clerk just cancels them and flings them into what looks like a laundry basket. "This little mother has claws." She also inspires paranoia. If my mail does not get through, I will be a long time forgiving the little mother.

This morning, my American roommate and I went to East Prague to get our visas extended. He'd been to the place before and claimed to know exactly where it was. We took the metro to Sokolovska Street and walked east three miles, clear off my map, past a tractor factory. When we came upon a cornfield, we gave up and took the tram back. We were about a mile north of the proper street. I'll go myself tomorrow morning and to downtown Prague to see about hotel reservations for us. One recommended place is just across the river from Old Town, with easy access by tram. Or we might end up in a place on Vaclavski Namisti. The hotels on Wenceslas Square are more elegant, but I think they're also clip joints, and we'd be financially freer outside Old Town. Wherever, I'll lay in a supply of provisions.

I'm going to bed now. I am pushing back your hair, and kissing you. Love you always, J.

8/19/86

Dear Sharyn,

I just received your letter of August 8. Eleven days seems excessive. My errands today were to get my visa extended and make hotel reservations for us. This time I went to the right boulevard, stood in line for an hour, underwent a 3-minute interview followed by the fastest rubber-stamping this side of Lincoln Tower. I'm legal again until September 8.

The other part of my mission was more frustrating. It seems the good local hotels get their bookings from the Czech agency Cedok on the first of the month. So I'll go to Cedok tomorrow and have them find us a room. We'll take what Cedok gives us, but you will have shelter, my sweet. Maybe even hot water. When I see you at the airport at customs check, I'll probably fall down with palpitations. J.

8/21/86

Dear Sharyn,

Prague has definitely cooled off. On the uphill jaunt to the tram stop this morning, I could see my breath—the coolest weather I've ever experienced in August. You'd best bring a sweater, and maybe your flannel nightgown.

I'll be in the dorm until the 31st, and then the Hotel Savoy. You can reach me there by telegram if you have to. If the hotel proves to be too modest, we can look for something else after September 1. Tourist season ends at the end of August—everyone breathes a sigh of relief when the Germans depart.

I doubt you'll get this letter before leaving for Prague. Hurry here. Love, J.

8/24/86

Dear Sharyn,

I realize that this note has virtually no chance of reaching you, but I wanted to write anyway. You and I will have plenty to see and do, but I hope our weather is better: today is 55 degrees and drizzling. A great morning to have washed my clothes.

On Tuesday, we take one last field trip. This time, to Lidice, the town razed by Nazis after the assassination of Heydrich. It will be interesting to see how they handle the commentary, and probably aggravating, too.

I will see you a week from tomorrow, with bells on. Miss you and love you.

As the month of August drew short, I was in a flutter. I'd shelled out $862.26 for airfare, and charged a red Geiger jacket of boiled wool. Oh, yes, and a silky bathrobe. I also got a pair of cowgirl boots. These were anomalous. Western wear had never been my thing. Maybe the boots symbolized a break with all that had gone before. A "step" in a new direction. Erect and shining, the boots almost sang, "Let's get goin', you hot, unbridled girl!"

To acclimate myself to the coming time change, for days and days, I got into bed before dark and rose at 4:00 next morning, drinking coffee and applying my makeup in the dark as I listened to Mozart's *Prague Symphony*. When José and I were together again, I didn't want to waste one second on jet lag. Going about my chores at home and work, I thought of nothing but José. I was starving for him.

Saturday, August 30th came. Mom drove me to the airport. In a khaki jumpsuit and the cowgirl boots, I was ready. On the flight from Columbus to JFK, it hit. I looked at my cleanly manicured nails and felt my smoothly washed hair. No job or kids to think about. "Wow," I thought. "How crazy is this? I'm on my way to eastern Europe to meet the man of my dreams in a romantic tryst."

Faced with a two-hour delay at JFK, I clomped around, releasing nervous energy, passing one gate after another. I headed outside, sun penetrating my clothes, noise and movement everywhere. I strode with business-like purpose even though I didn't have one, observing New Yorkers and international travelers jump into cabs and town cars. But the cowgirl boots weren't broken in, and a deep, bleeding blister on my heel put an end to the hike.

On the transatlantic flight, I sat next to a married couple, the man, a retired Columbia University professor. As they dozed, I took in their comfortable compatibility, the grey heads nodding toward each other. "Yes," I thought, "--a metaphor for my own future. Mine and José's." Like the old couple, I settled down and closed my eyes. But I was still wide awake when the plane landed in Frankfurt next morning.

After disembarking, I decided to redo my makeup. I'd look perfect when José and I embraced. He'd take in every contour of my face. I'd see the hungry devotion in his eyes. It would be a moment to remember. The public restroom was just ahead.

With airport soap and wet paper towels, I removed the stale makeup. I rinsed well with warm and then cool water. After patting dry, the usual products in the usual steps: foundation, blush, powder. Next, the eyes: a touch of eyebrow pencil blended well, silvery tan shadow, eyeliner carefully drawn and smudged with ring finger for a natural look, and mascara, cleanly stroked to avoid clumps. Despite two days without sleep, my eyes were not a bit bloodshot. Finally, fresh lipstick. I gave my long hair a comb and a toss. The image in the mirror pleased me. I took up my bag and made for the gate.

"Oh, sorry, Miss," said the German ticket woman in lightly accented English. "You have missed your connection to Prague." Disbelief followed by panic. But nobody could help. So for hours I wandered glumly around the Frankfurt airport, lugging my suitcase, limping with my blister, dodging mashers who surely appreciated my flawless grooming. To kill time, I ate an overpriced salad. In one of his letters, José said to have Lufthansa page him in Prague if

71

I missed my connection. I was too upset to remember that. Finally, I was allowed to board a Czechoslovak "OK" aircraft. After a seriously bumpy ride, the plane landed in Prague at 3:50. I stood in the customs line until 4:55.

Meanwhile, José had been waiting at the airport for eight hours, chain smoking. When he spotted me, he sucked in sharply, teeth almost clenching, eyes bulging. Exhaling, his features relaxed. He rushed forward. We collided with delirious joy.

In the back of the taxi, we snapped together like magnets, an endless, devouring kiss as the driver made his way to the Hotel Savoy. The cinematic flavor of the moment wasn't lost on me. It was exactly like one of those 1940s war films, a scene of thwarted and regained love.

We got to the hotel. We climbed a flight of stairs. Carrying my bag, José opened the door. A clean and functional room, table and chairs positioned near the sink. There I saw José's toothbrush and shaving kit. His suitcase was in a corner. His clothes hung on a metal bar. A green armchair cozied up to a tall window. Twin beds neatly made with down comforters.

Setting my suitcase next to José's, I went down the hall to shower. The un-private bathroom echoed as I moved around inside, a bluish, cobwebby place with a high, horizontal window. I hurried to dry off, and applied the lightest touch of cosmetics. Cinching the belt of the silky pink robe, I fluffed out my wet bangs.

José was pouring wine. We sat and took a deep swallow. His free hand caressed mine. He put his glass down. Taking my hands in his, he closed his fingers gently around. Looking into my eyes, he asked in soft, cadenced words, "Sharyn, will you marry me?"

72

My heart flipped. But I was cagey enough to hesitate. Without speaking, I got up, deliberately slow and graceful. I slid onto his lap, my arms softly embracing his neck. And as we kissed, I murmured, Yes, Yes, Yes.

Next morning, we ate breakfast in the Savoy's restaurant. With my blister tightly bandaged and wearing white sneakers, we walked from Nerudova Street to Charles Bridge, to Old Town Square and the Prague Synagogue. We drifted slowly through the Old Jewish Cemetery, where seven centuries of Prague's Jews had been buried and reburied, stacked three or four deep, coffins crammed into every last inch of ground. Ancient trees devoured the mossy tombstones, some almost entirely consumed, just a decrepit edge and greenish Hebrew letter visible in the trunk's curving cleft. Souls triply swallowed.

Dinner that night at the Hotel Savoy again—we ate spicy chicken breasts and drank a good deal of wine. Next day, the second of September, we set out for Hradcany Castle, gazing for hours at the relics and jeweled monstrances. We strolled to Franz Kafka's house on Golden Lane, and headed back to Old Town. Tea at Malostranska hit the spot. I found an etching of Charles Bridge for Tibby. We also picked up some post cards, including one featuring The Infant of Prague.

On to Old Town Square for hot dogs. Biting into mine, I also bit into a bee hiding in the bun. Stung, I threw my lunch onto the cobbles near the massive bronze statue of Jan Hus, burned as a heretic in 1415. For days after, I was self-conscious of my ballooning lip, but José didn't notice.

That night, more wine and conversation at a Malostranska café. "We'll definitely go to France together in the next five years," José said between sips of his cabernet. It was understood that, as a someday professor of European history, such a trip would involve scholarship and research. We felt not only the electrical charge of our love but serene confidence in the health of our future. In that holy state, we were shielded from everything hateful and unjust. But riding back to the hotel, the bliss was interrupted by German youths, hurling expletives and gyrating obnoxiously. I ignored them, touching my swollen lip and gazing at the city from the window of the cold tram, the darkness punctuated by glowing lamplight. "You sickos are not allowed into our private bubble," I thought firmly, eyes fixed on the magic outside. If not for the modern tram, I would have sworn it was the 19th century.

The days of joy melted together. Quiet breakfasts, sipping coffee and eating all we could of rolls, apricot jam, butter, sliced ham, succulent cheeses, tanking up for the day ahead. We took a tram up Petrin for a view of the city and held hands along cobbled paths. Perfection surrounded us. One day, I bought a tee-shirt for Norah, and one evening, we walked in the rain to U Labuti Bar, where a rosy housewife in an apron was just trotting out with two brimming pitchers. It was a scene from long ago but happening right now. Noting my surprise, José said, "Yes, that's how beer is bought here, for family use. Six-packs don't exist in Prague."

Next day, we took photos at the Bridge Tower and ate goulash and knedliky on Old Town Square. We went to a bakery, a cheese shop, and a vintner, returning to the hotel in late afternoon with our delicacies. But first, a rest.

José lay down. I relaxed in the green armchair. It was very quiet. I looked around. The walls were light ivory, some sort of thick, European paint with a low sheen. The ceilings were lofty. The high casement windows with wide transoms were spread open. Unlike American windows, there were no screens, and the windows cranked into the room instead of out. Sheer curtains above the transom slowly fluttered.

José was sleeping now. Lying on his back, hands folded on his chest, his profile contrasted against the sun-filtered curtains. His lips were closed. His skin looked waxen. He was utterly still. In that instant, I understood that one day I would see him dead. I blinked, once, twice. His motionless form strobed, from orange to blue to violet, like the after-effect of a flash bulb. It wasn't José but a phantom--exquisite, ephemeral.

Things shifted back. We were in the Hotel Savoy again. It was sunny, an Indian summer afternoon. José's breathing was steady and rhythmic. I watched his chest rise and fall. From outside came a peal of laughter. A bicycle whirred past. I kept gazing. It's just a nap, I told myself. It's just a flight of fancy.

True to form, this one soundlessly retreated to some dusky recess in my mind.

On Friday the 5th, we ate breakfast again at the Savoy. José automatically gravitated there. I wondered why we weren't sampling other venues. I knew that José was reassured by routine. But I liked to jazz things up a bit--since we were in Prague, we should be experiencing all sorts of breakfasts. I didn't mention this minor irritation. The relationship was still too new. I resolved to keep the small disappointment to myself.

On Charles Bridge, I bought a pair of earrings for Joyce and an etching for Elsbeth. José took my picture as I cuddled a basset hound puppy who came along at that moment. After wine and tea across from the National Theatre, we strolled down Vaclavske Street and drank three more glasses of wine at an outdoor café, The Green Frog. Dinner that night was again at the Savoy, many glasses of beer for José, and light, delicious wienerschnitzel. We stayed until the restaurant closed. The waitress spoke to us in German instead of Czech. We didn't know why.

By the 6th of September, our week was coming to an end. It was that morning that I first heard José mention "morning ablutions," a term he'd use countless times in the coming years. I'd thought the phrase meant only the toileting part of getting ready in the morning. Now I understood that it included the whole spectrum of washing, shaving, dressing, grooming, and in my case, the application of my beloved makeup. For José, the best part of his morning ablutions was reading *The New York Times* whenever he could get his hands on a copy. But any print publication would be an improvement over *Rude Pravo*.

After another day alternating between sightseeing and eating, we took a taxi to the Alcron Hotel. Here we celebrated our final night in Prague. The atmosphere brought to mind a scene in the film, *Doctor Zhivago*, the red velvet restaurant in Moscow where Lara and Victor Komarovsky dine on French cuisine and whirl under the chandeliers. We were in love, and the rightness of that love was confirmed by the succulent, slightly exotic food, the wine, the warm glitter of lights, the sweet pulsation of a Strauss waltz.

Next morning, we boarded a flight to Germany. The leg back to the U.S. was especially comfortable—deep seats and brown travel socks. I listened to Mozart's *Haffner Serenade* over and over. José and I held hands, and I didn't have the slightest impulse to disengage myself. Before, whenever a man held my hand, a confining dampness took over and I pulled away. José's touch was warm and comforting.

In Columbus we took a taxi to the University Parke Hotel. Early next morning, I left for a mandatory staff meeting in the History Department, a ridiculous intrusion to my way of thinking. Afterwards, I rushed back to José's embrace. At noon, we headed for my house. It was silent, early autumn sunlight streaming through. Vin had just left and the girls were at school. Dear old Lady wagged passionately.

The following weekend, after a romantic meal at The Spot in German Village, José sat on the edge of my bed and dialed his mother in Houston. I was tipsy, and not only with alcohol. Arranging myself next to him, I listened to the one-sided conversation. "Well, Mom," he said, "it looks like wedding bells are in my future.

3

THREE OF A KIND

The imperfect is our paradise – Wallace Stevens

I hadn't planned to wear white, but it was hanging on the wrong rack, in the bridesmaid section. It fit perfectly, with three-quarter sleeves and a scalloped neckline. A short train floated behind. What the heck, I considered, admiring my confection-reflection. This is the real thing. I'm going to do it right this time. With a long hesitation, the manager admitted that I shouldn't have to pay for the store's mistake. He let me have the dotted Swiss gown for $40.00 instead of the true price, $440.00.

While we were in Prague, José and I talked about getting married in winter. But February is a nasty month, and why should José pay rent when we could live together, happily married? They say that two can live just as cheaply as one. Well, in our case, four. So José reneged on the apartment and moved in with an old friend,

René. It would amount to only a few weeks of inconvenience for José and René. Our wedding day was approaching.

It was my favorite time of year--early autumn, the leaves showing the barest tinge of red gold, like gilt on book pages. To me, autumn never seemed melancholy. It's a time of honest, cozy industry that the other seasons lack. Spring is a time of stirring; fall is a time of ripening. In the still perfection of Indian summer, the warm, dry air itself is rich with promise.

On the morning of October 5, 1986, I kept glancing at the sky. The weather had to cooperate, because the ceremony was going to be outside, on Ohio State's campus, near Mirror Lake. Our church would be a place called the Browning Amphitheater. Our guests would sit on stone steps encircling a flagstone stage. Luck was with us: overcast at first, the weather turned soft and clear by mid-morning. By 11:30, only a few transparent clouds drifted across a robin's egg dome.

For $15 each, I'd hired four grad students from the Music School to play Pachelbel's *Canon* and Handel's *Arrival of the Queen of Sheba.* Asher Levine would speak the words. A rabbi as well as a historian of modern Judaism, he was enthusiastic about presiding over us. José's mother, a staunch Southern Baptist, might have been scandalized, but the unconventionality charged me. Professor Levine's words would proclaim my rejection of Catholicism. It would show my appreciation for the poetry of an even more ancient mythology. Professor Levine chose the most exquisite passages from Song of Solomon. I am my beloved, and my beloved is me.

Thirteen-year old Norah was the bridesmaid. Dressed in a turquoise shirtwaist belted around her little waist, she seemed to need the honor more than her sister did. José's best man was René, his temporary roommate. A free spirit who owned a self-serve car wash, René taught English as a second language. Witty and handsome in a spare sort of way, he showed up in a dark suit and running shoes. After the ceremony, René went off to Indonesia and disappeared. We never heard from him again. Even his mother had no idea what had become of him. On that perfect October day, nobody could have predicted such a strange turn of events.

We wanted an intimate celebration, mostly immediate family. The guests sat close on the semi-circular steps. In a holding pattern twenty yards away, I waited, unseen behind tall boxwoods and a corner of ivy-covered Pomerene Hall. As I listened for the musicians' cue, my knees bent and locked, bent and locked, in rhythmic tension, like a diver about to negotiate the end of the high board. Looking at the seated guests steadied me. Everyone was conversing, quietly, politely. His mother Rachael was conventional and proper, in royal blue silk and a mink stole, her short hair cleanly cut and brushed. My mother Betty's silver brown hair flowed loose, a barrette at her right temple. She wore a cream-colored skirt and leather boots; a brown suede vest concealed her crooked spine.

José's brother Jim couldn't make it, but his other siblings, John and Judi, were there along with his Aunt Sadye from Texas, and my friend Elsbeth from the History Department. Sixteen-year old Tibby, tall and graceful with layered blond curls and pearl earrings, wore a wraparound dress in tones of turquoise and lavender. Meanwhile, on the amphitheater stage, José, René, and the rabbi stood in solemn silence, hands folded.

The musicians drew their bows. Something Baroque, but I couldn't tell what. Norah was walking next to me, but that didn't register. I was blasting into space. Foregoing the traditional cadenced pace, I walked too briskly. None of that "one-and, two-and" routine. In my flowing bridal gown of dotted Swiss, I almost trotted.

And so we were married. That night, after everybody was gone, the remnants of the food put away, and the house straightened, José and I retired to the bedroom, our room now. A few minutes later, Tibby knocked timidly on the door. "Mom? Are you in there?"

I was, and so was José. I called out yet another goodnight from behind the closed door of the wedding chamber. Tibby, Norah, and I would never again be a trio. But I saw no problem. Now we were a foursome. And the new member was somebody we could all look up to, literally and figuratively.

Nineteen-eighty-seven. Newly married. Saturday mornings. José baking biscuits.

"Good morning, sweetheart," he'd say as I came into the kitchen in my robe. I poured a cup of coffee, glanced at the day's headlines, and watched him from my perch on a bar stool. Neatly dressed and stirring biscuit batter, he bent occasionally to follow a recipe in *A World of Breads*, opened flat on the counter. The page was pocked with splatters of egg and batter. It was worth the trouble: his biscuits were hot, light, delectable. Butter. Red napkin in the basket.

And six months after our wedding, I was pregnant. The baby was due just before Christmas. I was in Dulles Hall that April morning when I found out. Pregnant again, after fourteen years. With thrumming heart, I hunted him down and told him in a first-floor alcove.

"Oh?" he asked doubtfully, with sober eyes. "What do you want to do?"

Of course, of course, I wanted our child. But José's response showed that he would respect my decision. He was attuned to feminist ideals, that women have the right to decide their reproductive paths. He knew that women give their bodies, their lives, to bring children. Practically speaking, I already had two teenagers, we were struggling financially, and I was the primary breadwinner. José knew the challenges we'd face. But for me there was no question.

As we adjusted to the news, and in between his course work and grading, José was preparing for a presentation. He'd be one of the contributors in a symposium called "The Historian in Society." He spent one long night writing his commentary. The next morning, I was battling morning sickness but managed to pick up Mom and drive her to the Mershon Center. We settled in plush red seats. As we took in José's poised delivery, I was sure that his performance would warrant an affirmation. But sometimes Mom threw a curve ball.

My Mom. Betty. She considered herself a highly astute judge of people, but her perceptions were densely pixelated by prejudice. When she evaluated someone, she spoke in hyperbole. Sometimes she gave high praise--"What a stupendous performance!" More often, she was critical. People generally disappointed her, causing her to become "flabbergasted," "crushed," "outraged." Not so José. When I introduced them ten months earlier, her features expanded and relaxed. I could tell she was seeing what he was, and what he wasn't. It was his essence she zeroed in on. To those who paid attention, José gave off a subtle aura: I can be trusted. If you tell me your secrets, I'll keep them. I am gentle. But I'm honest, too.

"What a difference," Mom whispered admiringly when José was out of earshot. She didn't have to say that she was comparing him to Vin. Now, at the Historian in Society conference, I realized that she was spellbound by the assurance of his words as they filled the auditorium. The place was silent, taking him in.

José's topic was the civil war among professional historians. Marxist historians and neoconservative historians, he said, should quit beating up on one another, because the real enemy is the natural sciences. Scientists, he said, crunch bigger and better numbers. Historians' use of quantitative analysis must therefore. . . *become more sophisticated, and our use of them more sparing and harshly governed. For if we do not protect our freedom to interpret, with the*

84

coming generations of super computers, one day the scientists will
show up at our door with the unassailable numbers, and they will
present those numbers to us as if they were our heads.

At the end of the talk, Mom clapped energetically, with a low, rapturous, "Bravo, Joseph! Oh, that was just outstanding!"

A few days later, José wrote my mother a note of appreciation.

4/30/87

Dear Betty,

Hope the Symposium didn't wear you out too much. Next
year I think they'll reduce it to two sessions, and this should help a
little. I would like academics more if they had eraser fights, as we
are grasping children by nature. I might schedule celebrity chair
races in Dulles Hall to coincide with the next symposium.

Hope you've recovered from the shock of Sharyn's
pregnancy. I've been thinking about names. How about something
with a Latin touch—Accidentalus. Or maybe classical English—
Happenstance.

Take care,

José

Four months pregnant, I underwent amniocentesis. At 37, I wanted assurance that the baby was healthy. My Ohio State benefits would pay for it—people always feel a little freer if the money doesn't come directly out of their pocket. I considered my low paycheck to be partly offset by Ohio State's excellent health benefits. The procedure would pose a small risk to the pregnancy; I tried not to think about that. Nor did I consider what we'd do if we found out that something was wrong. Mainly, I wanted to remove one element of worry from my mind. Everything went smoothly--"totally text book," said Dr. O'Shaughnessy. It was painless and quick. In a few weeks, we found out that, yes, the baby was healthy. And it was a boy. For his mother's sake, José was hoping for a girl. Rachael had four grandsons and wanted a granddaughter to sew frilly things for. But I already had two girls, and a boy had been my dearest hope. The fact that I was carrying José's son proved not only the soundness of our marriage, but its magic.

Before dawn one morning soon after, as he was driving to Dulles Hall to do some grading, José was broadsided. The nurse who slammed into him had just come off a 12-hour shift and failed to stop at a red light. José was unhurt, but the brown Rabbit was demolished. There were no witnesses, and we found out that the insurance company wouldn't pay for a replacement car. José exploded in frustration, punching a hole in the laundry room wall before storming into the garage and lighting up. I'd never seen him show despair and rage.

Well, we can both use my Datsun, I said to soothe him. If one of us needs to get somewhere earlier, that person can take the COTA bus. It wasn't a big deal, I said, looking into his eyes. But he was elsewhere. He seemed stressed and careworn.

Later that summer, José's brother Jim in New Hampshire called to say that his wife's father was selling a car, another VW Rabbit. This one was yellow, carefully maintained with low mileage. So José flew to Boston and drove to Jim and Cathie's. He kicked the wheels of the yellow Rabbit, bought it, and drove it home.

86

While he was away, I found out that I'd won the 1987 Melton Prize for the best seminar paper in Jewish history. The previous fall, I'd written "Anti-Judaic Policies of the Church and the Church Fathers: from Constantine to Agobard of Lyons." José, Mom, and Elsbeth took me to the ceremony in late August; the historian Martin Gilbert handed me the prize. I walked up, visibly pregnant and flushed with enjoyment. José seemed proud.

Meanwhile, the T.A.s in 168 Dulles were razzing José about impending fatherhood. Three of them put their twenty-something heads together to come up with a name for José's offspring. Something from the Old Testament! How hilarious. When they had the name, they drew a cartoon of a baby with a cunningly-drawn face that looked like José's. The baby's receding hairline was crowned with a single vertical curlicue. A cigarette dangled from his lips. That was "Baby Boaz Talbert." Copies of the flyer circulated through the T.A. offices. José only smiled at the affectionate antics. His reserved dignity made his fellow T.A.s howl.

In October of '87, José and I celebrated our first anniversary. I made reservations at a place called the 94th Aero Squadron. I thought how surprised José would be. After all, he was a historian of modern Europe, and he loved planes. It would be perfect. The restaurant resembled a bomb shelter, heavy beams criss-crossing the ceiling and artifacts from the First World War strategically placed— vintage posters, German helmets on splintery wooden shelves, biplane wings suspended in the corners, waitresses dressed as Red Cross nurses. Through the windows, diners could watch aircraft land and take off at nearby Port Columbus.

"Isn't this cute, dear?" I asked as we walked in.

He looked distinctly professorial that night, a sweater vest under his dark brown herringbone sport coat. His hair had grown. As usual, it was combed straight back, but two or three curls touched his shirt collar. At my question, José tilted his head slightly with a look of noncommittal amusement. Maybe he thought the restaurant was a sanitized representation of a terrible period, crassly commercial. But he didn't say so. We had fun. I was seven months pregnant, but we still felt the charge that came from being near one another. It would be the last time we'd go out before the baby was born. For the anniversary, José gave me a box of stationery with my new initials, "ST," engraved in silver. His note said, *Remember, the first is paper. Love, José.*

In late November, the History Department staff, faculty, and graduate students threw us a baby shower. Although gracious, José was out of his element, looking abashed and peaked. He'd been grading papers, and was trying to finish his master's thesis, due in the Graduate School by the end of December. His title, decided at the last minute: "The Czech Creation of Czechoslovakia."

My husband's progress was always a big deal, but for several months, I'd been in pregnancy land, navigating morning sickness and wondering how the baby would alter family dynamics. I'd also been worried about the birth—because I was 37, the doctor had deemed me high risk. And now, the shower. In a borrowed maternity dress, I was central to the celebration, a fifty-person love fest. From the department came a stroller, car seat, and mechanical swing, and we got a windfall of individual gifts, too: baby clothes, hand crocheted blankets, toys. Thanks to the shower, we didn't have to buy much. Cards were signed by over seventy-five members of the department. Even haughty Dr. Auger wrote a (self) congratulatory note: *Start him on Latin and Greek as soon as possible -- Great Uncle Jack.*

On December 10th, José defended his master's thesis. After the defense, Professor Hugo Bamberger, one of José's committee members, came to my desk. With a trim build and neat salt-and-pepper beard, Bamberger was friendly with many people in the department; he seemed especially eager to engage in chit-chat with me. That day, his topic was serious: he wanted to report his assessment of José's performance.

"Well, he did a good job," he said. "The thesis needs some fleshing out, and one of the key arguments is a little flimsy."

Bamberger's tone struck me as patronizing, his words indiscreet. There is such a thing as academic confidentiality, and there I was, the candidate's wife. I was due in about two weeks and could no longer fit behind my desk.

"Thanks for letting me know. Actually, I see the M.A. thesis as just one milestone along the road." I looked him in the eye and said nothing more. Impervious to my slight irritation, he smiled broadly and gabbed a little longer. After wishing me a good weekend and good holiday, he left my office.

***

In the early hours of Sunday, December 13, 1987, José climbed into bed after finishing three seminar papers for his own courses and grading undergraduate exams. The deadline for turning in grades was Monday, and the deadline for submitting his thesis to the Graduate School was in a couple of weeks. His document still needed work. He was beat.

Meanwhile, although I didn't recognize it, I'd spent the day nesting. I washed, dried, and folded the laundry. I baked Christmas cookies and cleaned up the kitchen. Popping a cookie into my mouth for sustenance, I lugged in the Christmas tree, set it up, and decorated it. After that, I clambered up and down the steep attic steps, retrieving heavy pieces of the baby crib, on loan to us. My bulk made it tricky. On the way down, I gripped the iron rail with my free hand and placed my feet deliberately on every step. When all the pieces were laid out on the bedroom carpet, I set about putting the crib together. "Oh, shit on it!" I muttered, trying to align screws and metal bars. With only one set of hands, it took a while.

After assembling the crib and pushing it to my side of the bed, I pulled on the fitted mattress pad and sheet. I smoothed the blankets, sighing with satisfaction. Pretty soon our bedroom would accommodate three instead of two. In only ten days, give or take.

Next I fed Lady, and when she finished, I bathed her in the tub. She'd needed a good bath for weeks. I dried her and cleaned her ears with Q-tips. When I released her, she ran around the den on stiff legs, shaking the remaining drops, wheeling dangerously close to the Christmas tree and charging back towards me. Her eyes were both reproachful and frisky.

My work finished, I ate a yogurt, curling on the couch to watch an old movie. José was still grading on campus. The girls were out. I got up and took a shower, and as I dried off, glanced at my distended belly. Geez Louise. I went to bed. In a little while, the girls came in. I heard them make snacks and turn on the TV. After a long time their bedroom doors closed. I fell asleep.

At about 1:00, something woke me from a vivid dream. I listened, but the house was soundless. Then I felt the cramping. In the bathroom, I realized that my water had broken. No, not yet. The face in the mirror looked strangely normal. But I'm not ready. It's too soon. The icy jewel in my throat contrasted with the hot radiating pressure below. After a few minutes, I went back to bed. I pulled the blankets around my chin and lay motionless. Maybe if I don't move, if I'm absolutely still . . . .

Finally, José came home from Dulles Hall. He moved around, a soft padding of feet, a whispered swish of fabric. He pulled off his socks and lowered himself between the sheets. In a minute his breathing slowed. He was drifting off. But the contractions were intensifying. When another wrenching twist gripped me, I gently rubbed his arm.

"Dear? How many more papers do you have to grade?"

He replied groggily, suspiciously: "Why do you ask?"

At five o'clock, we left for Ohio State University hospital. As we sped along in the darkness, José joked to cheer me, but I was in no mood. It had been almost fifteen years since I'd given birth, and the baby took his time. It wasn't over until eleven. I didn't take any sort of painkiller. I also refused the internal fetal monitor that tethers laboring mothers to a hospital bed; I wanted to be mobile for as long as possible, to speed things up.

Ethan's birth was all the things women say about the process. It hurt like nothing else, it took too long, I was scared. When it was over and everything was okay, I was overcome with relief and joy, my legs a-tremble. José never left my side, rubbing my back, calmly telling me that he loved me. He didn't say much, but his shadowed eyes were intensely focused and soft with emotion. He breathed sharply several times.

After the baby was born, Dr. O'Shaughnessy directed José in the cutting of the umbilical cord. The baby was seven pounds, six ounces, and scored a perfect 10 on the Apgar scale. When he was clean and swaddled, a nurse put a knit cap on his head. I held him, and saw that he'd have a wide smile. After the trauma of being born, Ethan was content to lie in my arms and peer at the world with just opened dark blue eyes. I scoffed at having been categorized as high risk. I felt fine, and even put on my rose-pink lipstick.

Mom set out from Reynoldsburg as soon as she got José's call. She took the long way, on surface streets, because she was afraid of freeways. When the Interstate Highway System came on the scene, Mom was only in her thirties, but she'd always refused to drive on freeways. Just too complicated, not to be trusted. When she got to the hospital, she climbed several flights of stairs because she was scared of elevators. This was something of an ordeal for a person with arthritis and a bent-up spine. Eventually, she found us. Wearing a paper hospital gown over her street clothes, she leaned in to get a look at her new grandson. Saint Joseph's child, she breathed, smiling.

An hour after giving birth, I insisted on taking a shower. So much for my invincibility: as I lathered myself, I nearly collapsed in the stall. I unsteadily turned off the water and made my way back to bed.

The girls came that evening. "Awww!" Tibby was close to tears. "Mom, he's so cute!"

Norah cooed to Ethan, "Hi, sweetie! Hi, sweetie! It's me, Norah, your big sister!" She couldn't wait to get her hands on him.

We had the hospital's "V.I.P. Suite." It was just dumb luck. When we took a tour a few weeks earlier, they'd said, "you'll get the V.I.P. Suite if nobody else is using it." On top of that, thanks to my Ohio State benefits, we didn't have to pay one nickel for the pre-natal care or the hospital delivery. It wasn't yet a co-pay world.

In two days, I was ready to go home. José gathered the diapers and other hospital promotions, and we dressed Ethan in his "planes, trains, and automobiles" pajamas. As we rode down the hospital elevator, a maintenance man chuckled at our new infant.

"You just watch out, now," he said in a deep, musical voice, wagging his long, creased finger. "By next Christmas, she'll be into everything!"

We didn't correct him, but only smiled at our little bundle.

When we got home, José carried Ethan and I brought in my overnight bag. I walked into the kitchen. On what had been a smooth gold-brown countertop, an ugly mark shouted out. My eyes fixed on it. "What--? Oh no! What happened!?"

"Norah was making spaghetti, dear," José said in a conciliatory tone.

"Oh, no! Just *look* at that." I fingered the black circle, 12 inches across. On one side, a smaller, darker sphere bubbled up. It was obvious: Norah had set a red-hot pot on the unprotected counter. Always fussy about my surroundings, the needless damage turned my mood from joyful to bitter.

Norah wasn't careful at home, and she wasn't following the rules at school. In mid-January, the middle-school principal called.

Norah wasn't manageable. She was wreaking havoc and failing all of her courses. He stated loudly: "The onus is on you, now!"

When the call came, I'd been bathing month-old Ethan in the kitchen sink. Now I held the wet baby in a towel, trying to think of something both honest and reassuring to tell the principal. I had no idea what to do with Norah. Nothing had motivated her to achieve in school or to act responsibly at home. The phone call ended without a resolution.

I sighed in frustration and disappointment. But for once, I didn't rant or implore. I'd held onto the possibility that maturation would lead to Norah's self-regulation. But as the bite of the principal's words subsided, it dawned that Norah would never be ruled by anybody but herself. I quietly absorbed the reality.

With Norah, the best I could hope for was a few islands of calm in a sea of trouble. We'd had some good times. Norah and I liked to go to the pool, sunning ourselves and taking a dip when we got too hot. We liked to go out for lunch. Every so often, we'd become absorbed in a TV show, sitting comfortably in each other's presence. And movies. When we watched a good movie, Norah and I were suspended. The knots of anger unraveled and love and peace returned, if only for a few hours.

Shortly after the phone call, I took Norah to see *Moonstruck*. It was a deathly cold Saturday night. Sandwiched between the other movie-goers, I held five-week old Ethan. He slept the entire two hours. As Norah and I sat in the packed theater, the unspoken thought was that we were the responsible ones, jointly overseeing our precious charge. As the movie got underway, the synchrony deepened: we both recognized the skillfully drawn Italian family, a

94

mirror of Vin's relatives. Ours wasn't the only seriously screwed-up family. And no matter how deep the rifts, the love was stronger. I hoped.

***

On the morning of May 24th, I woke to find Lady in convulsions, heaving and gasping. I called the vet but she died before we could get her there. Seven years earlier, I'd sprung Lady from a shelter in California. A man in Arroyo Grande had bred her and subsequently dumped her at the shelter. When I looked at her behind the bars, I loved her beautiful face and saw that she had a gentle disposition. Rail thin with distended nipples, I knew she'd fill out. She deserved a chance. I took the plunge and brought Lady home to the girls.

A week later, she gave birth on my bedroom carpet to nine black puppies with white splotches on their chests. Lady had been so emaciated that I hadn't known she was pregnant. It was clear that she wasn't robust enough to nurse her pups, so I set aside two of them, a male and female with the least amount of white, and took seven back to the shelter to be euthanized. As I drove, tiny cries came from the back seat. "It's okay, baby dogs," I said, heartsick. "It's . . . okay."

Lady managed to nourish the two remaining puppies. I called them Hansel and Gretel. Their father was a mystery, but the two pups turned out to be real Great Danes, conforming to all of the standards of the breed. In a few months, we found Gretel a home, and in 1983, when the girls and I came back to Ohio, Mom adopted two-year old Hansel.

When Lady died in the spring of 1988, she was more than ten years old. She had been my California friend, and all of us loved her. José was devoted to her. After Ethan was born, when I became preoccupied, Norah noticed and gave Lady some of the love and attention she deserved.

On June 7th, Tibby graduated from high school. In her dark blue cap and gown, she seemed impossibly statuesque. As I changed Ethan's diapers that night, I wondered how Tibby could have grown up so fast. For the graduation, Vin and his mother came from New Jersey. When I was the young wife of her son, she worked the night shift at a plastic factory, leaving the house around dinnertime, getting back after midnight, and sleeping until noon the next day. Cooking for family was her thing--she woke up thinking about what to fix for dinner. The pasta, the red gravy with its thin sheen of grease. The beef stew with unscraped carrots. I thought of her thick fingers, scrambling over Sicilian pizza dough. In the evenings, she enjoyed a piece of homemade cake and a good cup of cawfee.

To save money on everyday meals, she never used cloth napkins, or even paper ones. Instead, she and her children wiped their fingers on "the family towel," passed from one person to the next. Connie ordinarily scrimped and saved like a champion, but then I thought of Thanksgiving at her place—the antipasto and manicotti with meatballs first, then turkey and all the sides, and afterwards, a truckload of homemade desserts.

Now she was in José's and my house. Surveying our place with small, shrewd eyes, she said, "Verry nice, Shaaa-ryn." After saying hello to José, she stepped into the backyard and pulled dry laundry from the line. José watched from the window as Connie folded our towels and underpants. Meantime, Vin made himself comfortable on the couch, looking expectantly for refreshments. Did he or his mother comment on the beauty of my baby? No. They only said, "He's so big! He's so fat!"

Truth be told, Ethan was a healthy 21 pounds at six months. He'd been sitting since four and a half, bobbling unsteadily in his crib. Now he was straining to pull himself up. He willingly opened his mouth as we spooned in oatmeal, soft barley, egg yolk, a tender carrot, pulverized peas. He was still nursing. I'd been able to stay at home with Ethan for the first three months, but in March of '88, I had to go back to the History Department. For the next eight months, José took care of Ethan during the day. The first weeks were rough. Ethan refused the bottles of breast milk I'd left, and by late afternoon he was frantic with hunger. Both father and son were worn out when I got home at 5:30. "I don't have mammary glands, dear," José said, handing me our tear-stained infant before heading to the garage for a smoke.

We soon established a routine. Every day at noon, José put Ethan in the car seat and drove to campus. In the stadium lot, José set up the stroller and pushed it east on 17th Avenue, striding in his dignified fashion, his button-down shirt tucked into belted trousers. By the spring, the weather had turned warm, and it would stay hot all summer. During those months, Ethan was lightly dressed in a white tee-shirt and diaper. When José handed me our son, I used the History Department master key to let myself into a rarely-used faculty office. There I nursed Ethan in a professor's cushy Barcalounger. After half a day without him, I cuddled my baby and stroked his satin cheeks and arms. I cupped my hand over his head, breathing deeply.

At home, both girls doted on their half-brother. Norah especially had always wanted a younger sibling, and at age 15, she finally had one. She played with Ethan, held him and kissed him. But she was still causing problems. Her friends, her social status, were paramount. Norah lived for the society of her peers. When she wasn't with them physically, she was on the phone. To make sure she didn't miss anyone, she ordered "Call Waiting" from AT&T. We found out when the hefty phone bill came.

Norah had never been a biddable child, and Vin encouraged her unruliness. "That kid is something else," he said proudly. "She won't take anybody's guff!" Making things worse, our lives were marked by divorce, poverty, and continual moves. While the stresses made me determined to whip life into a pleasing shape, and while Tibby turned inward, Norah became more belligerent. And then, the big accident.

It happened in May of '83, a few years after the divorce from Vin, when the girls and I lived in central California. Ten-year old Norah was spending the night with a friend named Claire. The girls were horsing around. Michael Jackson's *Thriller* blasted on the stereo. At midnight, instead of tucking them into bed, Claire's parents let the girls fry cookies in an electric pot filled with boiling oil. Somebody stumbled into the cord, and the contents spilled on Norah's leg and foot. She was wearing knee socks, which held in the heat. The squad came. Emergency room doctors said that Norah had third-degree burns. A few days later she got a skin graft from flesh taken from her upper hip. She was hospitalized for two weeks and had to wear a tight burn stocking for a year.

Norah's burn was the most upsetting thing but not the only upsetting thing that happened in central California. At first I enjoyed our two-bedroom house, the quiet privacy, the herd of deer on the hill behind the shed in the morning, the soft hooting of owls at night. It had taken some serious finagling to convince the mortgage company that I'd be a decent risk, but I'd done it. Unasked, my dad had sent $5,000 for the down payment. The mortgage carried a 17% interest rate, and in five years a big balloon payment would come due. But I wasn't worried. The bungalow was what mattered. I was sure we'd achieved permanence. The kids and I are set, I thought, kissing the live oak tree in the front yard.

As the months passed, I began to feel the isolation, 16 miles from my job at Cal Poly State University. One summer day, a tarantula sedately crossing the patio sent me into a tizzy. Soon after, I woke to the sight of neighbors slaughtering chickens, the couple bent over a chopping block, headless birds hanging by their feet on a low clothesline. After that, the septic tank backed up and next the roof had to be replaced. One hot, dusty afternoon as they rode their bikes, the girls spied a coiled rattlesnake at the edge of our property. Norah's picture-perfect orange kitten went missing, and a few weeks later, his flattened body turned up on our gravel driveway. And soon after Norah's accident, a brush fire swept the hills behind the house. The volunteer firemen put out the furious blaze just short of the backyard.

Things weren't any better at work. I quickly became dissatisfied with my boring duties, and resented the bossy woman who spewed cigarette smoke my way. Finding another job in San Luis Obispo was out of the question. In such a small town, there were few openings. A lot of people were unemployed during the recession of the early '80s, and people with jobs held onto them. I'd been lucky to land the Cal Poly job in the first place, but I wasn't being challenged. And the pay was too low.

Maybe it had been reckless to move to central California, a single woman, relatively penniless and unskilled, and with two young girls along for the ride. As the weight of the little and big traumas piled up, I had to admit it: the seven-year experiment had gone bad. Oddly, when I faced that fact, the edifice fell without much dust.

In November of '83, I sold the bungalow, so lovingly cleaned and painted. The rosebushes I'd planted in the stone beds looked their last at us. We were moving to Ohio, the place I'd grown up. Two adolescents, two Great Danes, and a single mother. As we drove east through desert and mountains and plains, the knowledge that I was leaving behind the California Dream crouched in a corner of my heart, but another idea took its place: if we couldn't have the California Dream, we'd grab the Ohio Dream. We'd keep the California memories.

That's how it always was with me. When I wanted a chocolate pecan turtle but had only a strawberry Twizzler, I was good at convincing myself of the merits of the Twizzler. So as we made our way back east, I saw it not as the end of anything, but as another beginning. I was 33. I had all the time in the world.

I decided we'd roost with my mother until we had our own place. They say you can't go home again, but with my mother's temperament and idiosyncrasies? It would have been tough with just myself in the equation. Throw in two girls and two dogs--hello, chaos. So I bought the first house I qualified for in Worthington. Everybody raved about the schools. Mid-America, conventional, safe, stable. Playgrounds and a shelter house for voting and community meetings. And sidewalks. Our place in central California had been too rural for sidewalks.

When the realtor opened the door to the vacant ranch, it just felt right. Each of the three bedrooms had a built-in bookcase, a sign that the girls would soon be reading with a purpose! Norah would get the room with the yellow and white wallpaper and yellow carpet. Tibby would love the larger room with pale blue carpet and two windows.

The living room with a wood-burning fireplace seemed dark and cold. But the galley kitchen would be easy to keep clean. Next to it, a laundry room with storage cabinets, and next to that, a one-car garage. Snug and cozy. Built in 1941, the house had solid brass door knobs and, the realtor assured me, solid oak floors under the carpets. Tall maples softened the angularity of the front and back yards.

The selling point was the airy family room with a deck outside: nine tall windows, a skylight, and a sliding door. In the coming years, we'd spend all our time in that room with its warm southern exposure. It was big enough for a dining table at one end and a couch and TV at the other. We'd call the room, the den.

The girls, Lady, and I moved in on January 9, 1984, mountains of snow piled up. Through the arctic whiteness, I drove a U-Haul truck away from Mom's, loaded with boxes that I'd mailed in stages from California. After ten long weeks with Mom, I felt both battered and euphoric, like an escapee from the gulag. "Ahh, privacy and freedom. Not a minute too soon." But for Norah, the move represented one more new school. Again she'd be the outsider, struggling to establish herself in the friendship hierarchy, but with the added dimension of full-throttle hormones.

Four years later, when José and I were newly married, Norah was still trying to find her niche on the high school totem pole. Studying? It still wasn't happening. José's and my happiness? Forget it. I picked up the umpteenth wet bath towel from her bedroom carpet. She was on the phone. "Dawn! What is your problem? You act like we're gonna have a huge rumble!"

I sprinkled Comet in the bathroom sink and rubbed it. I rinsed and polished the faucet.

". . . Well, my Mom didn't bring *me* up to be some loud crass bitch!"

I Windexed the bathroom mirror and swiped the door of the vanity and the toilet lid.

"I'm not going to listen to you say you're gonna—*quote*— knock me on my ass! I didn't do jack to you!"

I went into the kitchen, filled the watering can, and began hydrating the plants. Philodendron, African violet, peace lily.

"I can fight my own battles, thanks!"

Wiping a spill under a pot and dusting the table, I tossed the rag into the washer. Now, my studies. I arranged the books and binder. I had to get in a little brain work before starting dinner. Norah's harangue interrupted that.

"Don't you call me a little freshman! I should be a sophomore, and you're no older than me and *definitely* not more mature!"

Norah fought with her friends and she fought with Tibby over the petty things sisters tangle over. They fought with me, too, and I snapped back. Their needs were complex and usually at odds with mine. I couldn't gauge what they required--my yardstick was my own messed-up experience as a teenager.

José didn't interfere. His arms swung almost comically as he maneuvered the domestic battleground. His face took on a genial, noncommittal expression, but with a hint of sadness. Steering clear of the girls seemed the wisest course, yet he greeted them politely, offering gentle witticisms in passing. José understood that he was the usurper, that the girls and I would never again be the three amigos—a phrase of Tibby's from the California experiment. Ah, the three amigos. The girls and me against the world, surviving on movies, caramel corn, and, yes, plenty of Twizzlers. Maybe it was his own bleak history with Beryl that made José sensitive to the girls' and my back story. Whatever it was, he didn't tangle with the girls. He didn't criticize them. And he never complained to me about them.

We didn't fight about the girls, but like all newly-married couples, José and I fought sometimes. The discord centered on three issues. The first problem was José's academic inertia. As the 1980s drew to a close, he seemed stuck, dead in the water. He was still taking courses, but wasn't participating in discussion. And he was ignoring his advisor, Professor Riegert. After months of reaching out without a satisfactory response, she let him know that she wasn't willing to work with him anymore.

So José abruptly changed direction, leaving Eastern Europe behind and focusing instead on France. I didn't question his decision, but I wasn't reassured by it. José arranged to collaborate with a historian of modern France, Professor Charles Thorndyke. Thorndyke kept to himself, rarely speaking to a staff member, and not too chummy with his colleagues, either. A Harvard Ph.D., Thorndyke was respected in his field. From the grad students, I knew that he demanded a lot in his seminars. Ok, I thought, José must know what he's doing. He must need the intellectual challenge.

But his new historical field and new advisor didn't inject vitality. His anxiety and depression only deepened. I remembered that, twenty years before, he'd flunked out of Ohio Wesleyan. I'd thought it was just male immaturity, but now I feared that a chronic debility was surfacing. Where it came from, I couldn't tell, and he wouldn't explain. I was sorry for José's unhappiness, but feeling vaguely betrayed, I thought, don't we all have to face the injustices?

I was also becoming resentful of the time he was spending on his doctorate. We were closing in on our fortieth birthdays, and secretly, I wanted progress. I kept quiet, not wanting to injure his masculine pride, but I didn't have to say anything. We both worked in academe, and we both knew that tenure-track jobs are few and far between, especially for white males in the humanities, and especially for 40-year olds. And he hadn't even passed his general examination yet. José must have sensed my growing frustration, which hard-spurred his melancholy.

The second issue was our lack of income. Everybody knows that when you marry a grad student, you're marrying poverty. I expected to be poor early on. Yet some financial security, some savings, and a movie or dinner out once in a while would have been good.

The third problem was José's smoking. It started decades earlier. His father was his model, and José was a keen observer. A pack-and-a-half man, Pop put a cigarette to his lips and flicked a shiny metal lighter. His sucking breath turned the end of the cylinder a glowing red-orange. Taking it from his mouth, it went lifeless, but when Pop kissed it again, it glittered anew, the hatchwork of tiny flakes igniting in rolling bursts, a secret hiss, a shriveling of paper. When it was almost gone, Pop squashed it in an ashtray. For a while, he was less likely to find fault with his youngest son. Magic.

At the age of ten, José started sneaking cigarettes from his father's dresser. His allowance and money from odd jobs fed the habit. By the time we met, José smoked more than a pack a day. From the start, I worried about his smoking, half-heartedly trying to bargain with him, saying that I wouldn't take the plunge until he quit. He regarded me silently with raised eyebrows.

The habit disturbed me. It was a vicious cycle: the stress of academia led to more smoking, and more smoking led to more friction between us. At home, he'd get up from his work and stroll into the garage to smoke. He'd do the same at Dulles Hall, stepping outside in every kind of weather to take breaks from grading, paper-writing, lecture preparation, general exam prep. Every morning he drove to the Duper for his *New York Times* and a few groceries, but also for the all-important cigs.

While I was pregnant, the pediatrician warned us about José's smoking. We'd had to fill out a questionnaire about parental health, so she knew that José was a smoker. Smoking hadn't been on my mind; I asked the doctor about postponing the pertussis inoculation. "There are pros and cons for waiting," the pediatrician said. "Really, your son should be fine either way. But his father's smoking—now that's another matter."

My worries about the smoking, my frustration over José's slow progress, and the angst that came with our poverty swirled together. Another problem plagued us, too. José was seriously put off by the light-hearted chit-chat I engaged in with men in the department. He'd always been quietly jealous of male grad students and faculty who paid me too much attention. He witnessed such encounters frequently. I'd flit around Dulles Hall, enjoying the positive feedback. José would amble into my office and accidentally squelch the banter of some male student or professor.

When he encountered the flirtations, José became silent and grim. But I'd take my small enjoyments wherever they popped up. I sat at my desk as if at court, relishing the compliments and beaming at the intellectual repartee. And I enjoyed using my power to make my reticent husband react.

The worst offender was Professor Hugo Bamberger. Supremely self-confident, he joked and laughed as he swooped through the department in his sport coat, brown eyes crinkling. With Svengali-like magnetism, Bamberger commanded a fawning group of graduate students in modern German history. Whereas José was humble and mild, Bamberger was dynamic and loquacious. While José worked silently and thanklessly at his scholarship, seeing it as an end in itself, Bamberger was a brilliant schmoozer.

Bamberger's persona was an affront to all José idealistically believed about academia and personal conduct. But a bigger problem was that, despite being married, Bamberger was consistently attentive to me. He often stopped at my desk, making small talk and enlightening me about fractals and "Chaos Theory." José silently swallowed the ire as I basked in the reflection of my own charm.

In early 1989, Bamberger announced with great fanfare his upcoming Holocaust Symposium. Always interested in my husband's professional progress and eager for him to embellish his résumé, I urged him to submit a paper. He didn't respond. I became irritated by his lassitude: why wasn't he more assertive about his standing in the department, about his career? My future and Ethan's were on the line, too. After a week of my harping, he blew up. I wrote a petulant demand for an apology and slammed it onto the kitchen counter. José slept in the den that night. He wrote a note in reply.

S.,

I'm out of options for courses next quarter. The classes I <u>*should*</u> *take are taught by people I can no longer stomach. I never imagined that personal animus would leave my education dead in the water, but such is the case. The lectures I'm sitting through are given by someone who knows as little about the 19th and 20th centuries as I do about the 11th and 12th.*

HB is proving to be a roadblock in my schoolwork, and on top of that, he spends his time buzzing around my wife. And I couldn't even escape him at home last night. Now suddenly I must either agree to participate in the Hugo Bamberger Holocaust Extravaganza, or give a cogent reason why I should not. And you are right—I saw red. Maybe I haven't been jealous enough. But jealousy is a sign of weakness.

On the one hand I must be polite when men flirt with my wife. I think I've been reasonably tolerant, but when someone flirts w/ you 3 or 4 times a week, sometimes for hours at a stretch, and you even skips a class so it can continue, I begin to wonder what would happen if the shoe were on the other foot.

I've had a belly full of HB's megalomania and I certainly do not want to see him in a panel discussion promoting himself and his cockamamie schemes at the expense of dead Jews.

The real question is: Am I greater than the sum of my vices and habits? Does a smoker deserve to have his feelings taken into consideration just as would be those of a non-smoker, or does the smoker have to pay an emotional penalty?

I'm sorry if I've hurt you. I might seem uncaring, but I only feel threatened. I love you.– J.

We made up. I'd been a brazen flirt and had baited my sensitive husband into self-defense. Once more, José's wisdom prevailed. I resolved not to be so conceited or callous.

The tensions didn't end, though. Our poverty persisted, and José kept right on smoking. He was also spending too much time in 168 Dulles Hall. His T.A. funding had been approved for another year, so he was in the office from early morning until evening, alternately shackled to his grading and his reading for the upcoming general exam. I'd have preferred to perform those tasks at home, but José chose institutional Dulles Hall. That was the place where he felt legitimate, official.

He was now the most senior member of the T.A. office, in both age and longevity. Sitting at the death desk in front of the manual typewriter, one leg slung over the other, foot dangling, he was the glue that held together a group of students who shot the bull, read *The New York Times,* and got José's take on things. A patient, good natured listener, he nodded with first-hand understanding when fellow students complained, often about Hugo Bamberger.

He was a hard nut to crack, but once you got to know him, José's sense of humor was addictive. There was his physical style, too, a style all his own. In chilly or rainy weather, he'd wear the tan trench coat over his sport jacket. At the end of the day, he'd pull on the trench coat with a little hop and quick jerk of the shoulders to knock it over the top of the jacket underneath. The motion contrasted with his cool demeanor, giving a comic effect. It was one of his signature moves. After observing him for a few months, the younger T.A.s would mimic this mannerism in unison, as if they were part of a gang.

Baby Ethan was admitted to Ohio State's Daycare program in December of 1988, when I was closing in on my B.A. We were captivated by Ethan. His face was irresistibly chubby and we admired the shape and size of his skull; sometimes José called him "U-Haul Head." Ethan gave us the levity we needed as José read the last of 129 books on his generals list.

In the spring of 1989, as the Communist Bloc crumbled in a death spiral, José passed his generals. With three fields--modern European history, African history, and the history of science, he finished the written portions in early May, and on the 9th of that month, passed the two-hour oral with high praise. Progress! Passing generals was the penultimate hurdle on the road to the Ph.D. The final step--the dissertation.

Later that spring, José was nominated a second time for a University Teaching Associate Award, which carried a $1500 cash prize. He didn't win. "Always a bridesmaid, never the bride," he said lightly. The absence of envy always surprised me.

In June, I graduated. I'd already been admitted to the English M.A. program and would begin that fall. It wasn't all smooth sailing, though. Norah was still making friends abroad and trouble at home. Her bedroom was still littered with dirty dishes and towels. Despite threats and pleas, she kept on using José's razor. He never complained when he found it lying on the edge of the tub, wet and untidy, but I was furious at Norah's lack of respect. I set a curfew, which she ignored, instead coming home in a state of rowdy drunkenness, waking the household. So in late summer of 1989, I dragged her mattress to the curb. I'm practicing Tough Love, I told myself. Norah didn't see it that way. José remained silent.

After 16-year-old Norah went to New Jersey to live with her Italian grandmother, I wondered if I'd been premature. Maybe she would have come around. Well, it was too late now. Would the failure be visible on my face, coarse and calcified? I wondered if I'd take on the sun-blinded expression of a myopic person groping for her glasses. But after all the strife, it boiled down to Norah's willfulness versus the well-being of the rest of us.In utilitarian terms, I'd done what was best for the greatest number.

Life rolled along. I went to campus early. José came in later, after feeding Ethan and dropping him at child care. On his way into Dulles, he usually stopped at a campus food place called The Cellar, buying some refreshment for both of us. If I was out of the office when he came, he left a note on my desk.

S, Juice in fridge.
Love, J

Or,

S, Ethan was pretty good. This greasy sinker was all the Cellar had left.
Love, J

He was supposed to be writing his dissertation, but the money came from his History Department T.A. job, and grading papers and exams for classes of 45 undergraduates was a constant chore, taking much longer than the expected 20 hours a week. "Dead time." That's what José called grading. When faced with a confusing passage in a student's paper, he'd occasionally write one word in the margin: "Huh?" But when students challenged him, he went above and beyond.

One student was irate over a C grade on a paper about Martin Luther. José typed his single-spaced explanation on the black Royal.

Mr. Wapshott,

Your thesis is clear—that Luther rebelled against the Church because of a psychological compulsion to glorify himself. Then the problems begin.

Paragraph 4—You write that Luther rejected the Catholic faith in a "political manner," but don't explain what that means. You go on to say that Luther wanted to " . . . add to his ego by being the head of this new institution." You provide no evidence that Luther, in Dec. 1520, intended to erect a new Church. There is no doubt that Luther made himself the star of the reform movement in Germany, but he was never the head of the "Lutheran Church"; the secular princes in the Germanies oversaw these churches, and Luther deferred to their authority. You also need evidence that Luther's faith—not just the reform movement—centered on himself.

Paragraph 5—When you mention Luther's advocacy of the right of the priesthood to marry, you must take note of Luther's concept of the "priesthood of all believers" and not simply claim that Luther wanted to eat his cake and have it, too. You cannot ignore good evidence—you must attempt to explain it away. You also present no evidence that Luther desired to be worshipped. This is bizarre; Luther had a high opinion of himself, but not that high.

Paragraph 6—I will admit that Luther enjoyed his preeminence within the reform movement, and he did have many followers, but you provide no evidence (say, from Luther's letters) that Luther merely used these people to glorify himself.

Paragraph 7—You write that Luther ". . . interpreted scripture to fit his own personal belief and led people down the path." Yet there's a difference between a mere personal belief and a scrupulous scholar's interpretation of Scripture. In class, I mentioned the TV evangelists because of their fast and loose interpretation of Scripture. Luther's writings amount to 100 thick volumes—and his translation of the Bible is still in use in some German-speaking congregations.

Paragraph 8—No one ever thought that Luther was the original Christian martyr. You must cite a specific source for this assertion.

The best way to go about a paper like this is to quote Luther to his own detriment—he was an intemperate man and said many foolish things—and therefore use Luther's own words against the usual historical interpretations. But you cannot merely ignore the evidence and arrive at contrary conclusions by assertion. This is why you got a C. Considering the fact that you put some thought into it, I gave you a C+.

José Talbert

Another grumpy student was Mr. Sullivan. After he threw a tantrum in the T.A. office, angered by a poor grade he'd gotten on a paper about Leonardo da Vinci, José wrote:

Mr. Sullivan,

My general objections to your paper is that it does not say much. You bring up a number of possibilities for discussion, but don't follow up.

Paragraph 1—The only sentence which advances an argument is the last: "His work was not always respected yet he left his impression on many and his ideas were carried on by his contemporaries." The rest of the paragraph is fluff. Everyone is entitled to one empty sentence per paper. After that you must get down to cases. Why was such a brilliant man "not always respected"? Which of his ideas were "carried on" by which contemporaries?

Paragraph 2—You need a real definition for "naturalism." I know what this means, and to whom it refers, in American literature (Frank Norris, Theodore Dreiser, etc.), but all you write about Leonardo is that, " . . . he held nature with great respect," and that, "his painting centered on what his eye captured in reality." Is this not true of all painters? Was it not true of Monet and Van Gogh? Yet no one ever called them naturalists. Worse, you state that, "The Mona Lisa's mysterious gaze fills the observer's mind with conclusions about the statement being made." What conclusions? What does it fill your mind with? As for the pressure to satisfy a patron, why did Leonardo have more trouble than other painters, who also relied upon patrons for support?

Paragraph 3—Did Leonardo's portrayals of women " . . . influence the male population to observe women in a more positive aspect . . ."? How? And what is the, " . . . beauty that only a woman can possess"?

Paragraph 4—"His contributions to the world of science could have played a dramatic role in his society had someone believed in him." The Duke of Milan apparently believed in him. What else stymied Leonardo's technological revolution?

Paragraph 6—In which ways would the Renaissance have been reduced without Leonardo's contribution? You talk around several things, but never attempt to explore them in even brief detail. If you were a student in a technical field, and never put a pen to paper except to draw figures or calculations, I wouldn't be surprised. But you are a junior in the social sciences and I expect better work than this.

José Talbert

***

By March of 1990, José and I walked the neighborhood with two-year old Ethan holding our hands. Lots was going on. We saw neighbors taking out the trash, washing cars, sweeping sidewalks. We'd say hi, and Ethan would say hi. We saw big kids playing basketball and people walking their dogs. We always asked if it was okay before Ethan could pat one. That spring, a fellow T.A. from the History Department bought a Cape Cod in the neighborhood. One evening, José and I chatted with him.

"I got a pretty good deal on the interest rate," Fred said. "But, wow, there's a lot of yard to take care of!" We nodded, well acquainted with the suburban lawn routine. Fred sighed with satisfaction. We couldn't help notice that his new house was painted a vivid salmon pink. As we walked on, I could tell by his staring eyes that José was thinking about the color. When we were far enough away, José breathed, "Golly Ned, Fred!"

José had gotten into the habit of buying Ethan a little metal truck or car from the Duper every weekend, and Ethan had come to expect it. "Here you go, Scoots," his dad would say.

By the spring, Ethan had more than 20 small vehicles. Ethan was transfixed by fire engines, garbage trucks, and tractors. He did not share his father's fondness for aircraft. "Large, plebian land vehicles are more to his taste," his father pointed out. Partly because of José's weekly presents, Ethan was familiar with a variety of vehicles on the road. At age two-and-a-half, he said from his car seat, "That's a bucket truck!" "That's a crane." "A steam shovel!" There has never been an absence of construction on Ohio State's campus.

On Sundays, Ethan and I walked to the "forest," a wooded ravine with a brook behind Colonial Hills School. We held hands as we maneuvered the steep trails. Throwing rocks and sticks into the water, our feet got muddy. In the spring, we saw snow trillium and naturalized daffodils. Here, Ethan was utterly preoccupied. Once he fell down and landed hard on his stomach, but no whimper came out, only a gasp before scrambling back to his exploration. For a few weekends, final exams and chilly weather curtailed our visits to the forest. One Sunday, he asked solemnly, "Is it wahm enough?" That meant he wanted to be outside.

But I'd been busy inside. During the month of May, I repapered and recarpeted Ethan's bedroom, which had been Tibby's room. That spring, twenty-year old Tibby moved out. Now both girls were gone. Ethan had outgrown his crib, and was big enough to sleep in a twin bed in his new room. At first, he'd wake up and come to us during the night. I'd return him and he'd go back to sleep.

José was the only T.A. in the History Department with a young child. The other T.A.s turned to their dignified older colleague for advice about academics and other things, and they were curious about how marriage and fatherhood could mesh with the demands of graduate school. Thus, the conversation in 168 Dulles sometimes centered on child rearing.

One master's student, Rick Sands, explained his method for teaching children. Childless himself, Rick's advice to parents was to avoid nagging, and to avoid supervision, for that matter. "Just let the kid touch the hot stove. He'll never do *that* again!" Rick said with conviction.

José took a dim view of Rick Sands's technique, and let me know it on occasion when, during my watch, I was slow to respond when our toddler flirted with danger. "I see you subscribe to the Rick Sands School of Childcare," he'd say.

One Saturday, to make $25, I enlisted two-year old Ethan as a human subject in an experiment conducted by Ohio State speech and hearing faculty. The NIH aimed to develop a device that would loudly warn parents if a child approached a hot oven or electrical outlets--in other words, the "non-Rick Sands School of Child Care." The researchers promised that the noise wouldn't harm Ethan's hearing. First, Ethan's cognitive development was evaluated. Ahead of the game. Next, the audiologist tested his hearing. Fine. As Ethan the young guinea pig played, I sat nearby, watching. Every corner of the toy-filled room was equipped with a speaker, and two cameras were poised, ready to videotape us. I was told not to interact with Ethan, but to comfort him if he experienced distress.

The experiment began. At two-minute intervals came siren blasts, each lasting six seconds. At the first sharp blast, Ethan came to me. I reassured him. He went back to playing. More blasts sounded. At one point, Ethan attributed the noise to a fire engine he was holding. After repeated blasts, Ethan said, "I'm sick of that sound. Please stop it." Only a few more blasts, and we left. It was then that Ethan cried, but not because of the noise. He wanted to keep on playing.

That spring, José was teaching European history survey courses at both Ohio State and Ohio Wesleyan. He also got stuck with jury duty, spending two weeks waiting at the courthouse. In the end, he wasn't picked. "They were looking for people who are fairly easily persuaded," he told me. The defense tried to put together a jury for a case in which, as José told it, "a hillbilly who managed a pornographic bookstore on the south side was charged with shooting in the back and killing an ex-con high on cocaine who'd just robbed the store." The robber had been shot at a distance of 20 yards.

The defense attorney asked potential jurors whether they thought it was okay to keep a weapon.

"Yes," "Yes," "Yes."

Then he got to José, who said, "As long as it's used to protect life and not property."

At this, the defense lawyer shouted, "Get him OUT!"

José enjoyed the experience, but I was glad that jury duty was over. The camaraderie in the T.A. office was better, and even his T.A. job was more lucrative than jury duty, which paid $7.50 per day. Just to park downtown cost $4.00. We couldn't afford jury duty. Especially when, after only a couple of years, the yellow

118

Rabbit died in our driveway. The malady was fatal, yet José refused to get rid of it. So I got behind the wheel and he pushed the deceased vehicle into the garage, neighbors watching. José insisted that he'd learn to repair the Rabbit himself. When he found the time.

That summer, while he was mowing the lawn, José spotted something. He killed the mower. A fledgling had fallen from the silver maple. It lay on the grass, moving feebly but apparently unhurt. José looked up and spotted the nest. He hauled out the extension ladder and set it against the tree trunk. Placing the bird delicately into a cupped hand, he climbed.

At that second, I glanced out. There was my husband: left leg on the second to the top rung, left hand gripping the trunk, right hand holding the bird, right leg extended along a thick branch. He slowly lowered his torso. Stretching his fingers, he placed the fledgling into the nest. We never knew if the little creature survived. But I couldn't forget the sight of my husband poised at the top of the ladder, risking life and limb to save a baby bird.

Nature continued to call to us. At the end of June, we planned an outing. We bought supplies for a cookout and drove up to Highbanks Metro Park off North High Street on the way to Delaware, across the highway from the Catholic cemetery. We spread a blanket and José fired up a grill. Afterwards, we three took a walk through the Really Big Forest.

We were alone. A breeze swept the leaves of the huge deciduous trees. We listened to birdsong and heard small animals scampering in the undergrowth. After dinner, we played on the playground. José tirelessly pushed Ethan and me as we soared on the swings. José and Ethan climbed the big slide, hurtling down as an interlocking unit, José echoing Ethan's thrilled laughter with a high-pitched shriek of terror and delight.

4

LEARNING

I am not young enough to know everything –J.M. Barrie

In late July of 1990, I got a call from Norah. It had been almost a year.

"Hi, Mom." She sounded both embarrassed and remorseful.

"Hi, Norah. How are you getting along?"

"Clifton's okay, Grandma's pretty nice. But I have to sleep in a little room in the basement, which I hate. Plus it's hard to adjust."

"Well, I'm sorry to hear that."

"Plus, I don't have good friends here."

"Well, your friends are the most important thing, so starting over must be tough."

"Mom, can't I come back home?"

"Norah, it's not just about the last outbursts. It's because you've been out of control for a long time"

"Mom--"

"--and I'm out of patience."

"Mom, I will try hard in school from now on. You have my word."

"The grades weren't all of it, Norah. You could have stayed at home indefinitely if you'd been responsible and respectful."

"Mom, please consider me and my happiness, and I'll consider yours!"

"Well, that comes a little late."

"But what have you got to lose, Mom? What have you got to lose, if I come back home?"

"Well, let's see. For one thing, maybe my peace of mind? Freedom from ugly outbursts, screaming on the telephone for hours on end?"

"I promise I wouldn't . . . "

"I'd lose my clean house. I'd lose my happy family, my unbroken sleep at night--"

"Mom—"

"--and I'd certainly lose my self-respect."

"Mom, I know you have José and Ethan now, but don't you love me even a little?"

"It's not because I don't love you. I certainly do love you. But I won't sacrifice my life, and my husband's and my baby's, to your behavior, Norah."

Silence on the other end now.

"Norah, you are so talented and you have such a sense of humor. You're a wonderful person. But you're dangerously obsessed with your friends--"

"Don't bring my friends into this, Mom--"

"--to the point where you're willing to destroy all the important relationships in your life, the people who can determine your future—"

"Such as?"

"Well, your mother. Your teachers."

"Yeah, like my mother and teachers ever did me any good."

"Listen, Norah, if it weren't for your grandmother, you'd be on the streets, so, it may not be ideal, but at least you have food and shelter. You've got to develop a sense of responsibility. You've got to work hard. You've got to be honest and polite. You can't allow your self-indulgence to control you."

"Okay, well, I see this conversation isn't going anywhere. Good bye, Mom."

"Norah, I want you to find fulfillment in-- .Hello?"

My sadness about Norah was compounded by Tibby's problems. After high school graduation, she took a couple of courses at Ohio State. By the spring of 1990, she moved to a cheap apartment, working a dead-end job and seeing a guy who seemed hard and mean. I didn't want to imagine what went on between them.

I thought about the girls. People used to stop us on the street to exclaim about Tibby. Blonde with golden-brown eyes and a smooth, classic cast to her features, she was shy and sensitive. From the get-go, Norah was tougher, socially-motivated and pugnacious.

Both girls were artistic and inventive. When they were four and seven, they devised a game called "Sis." "Let's play Sis," one of them invited, and the game would begin. They bustled around their bedrooms, tending to imaginary children and talking about their husbands, phantom brothers called Keith and John. I listened to the banter, the comical give and take. I thought how great it was that the girls were clever and healthy and interested in life. Their futures seemed bright.

Now, like so many other parents throughout time, I felt blindsided. I couldn't pinpoint when things started to go wrong. I'd made thousands of mistakes along the way. I'd rarely been the mother I wished to be--graceful, competent, and serene. But I'd done my best, whatever that means. Didn't the girls know that? Didn't they know that my short fuse had little to do with them and everything to do with the turbulence of our lives? It was one howling mess.

After Vin flunked out of Ohio State, we floundered in our campus apartment for a while. In 1972, his mother remarried and we moved into her vacant house in northern New Jersey. Tibby was two and I was pregnant with Norah. Back in his home state, Vin worked on and off—truck driver, janitor, wannabe car mechanic, his income supplemented by pot and hashish. He'd hunch over the kitchen table, picking out seeds and divvying up the stash into dime bags. He put the sealed bags in a cupboard over the refrigerator. A darting cockroach would have been no less repulsive to my eyes. And with a bug, you always have the chance of trapping, squashing, flushing.

One late summer morning after Vin departed for a joy ride with his friend Frank, five undercover policemen banged on the door. A typical hippie mother in a long cotton skirt and bare feet, I opened the door in surprise, six-month old Norah riding my hip. Barging in, hands on holsters, the cops threatened to shoot our barking dog unless I removed her. They marched upstairs and rummaged through my underwear drawer. They poured out a 50-pound sack of brown rice, scattering it as they searched for evidence. Then they zeroed in on the kitchen. In a minute, they found the hiding place.

The lead detective turned to me. You'll have to come with us, he said, and the kids are going to Children's Services. As they raided my house, I'd been silent, heart pounding. Now I protested. It's my husband's stuff, I said. I have nothing to do with it! So they left me and the little girls and lay in wait for Vin. He was spared the inquisition I'd endured, and a few weeks later, he got off with a minor fine and six months' probation.

The following winter, I took a job as a switchboard operator at a company that made metal drums for warheads. Vin was still between jobs, collecting unemployment. I tried to construct a work wardrobe—a few pairs of bell bottoms from Vin's sister, two or three wide-collared shirts, polyester. It was mainly for the girls that I took the switchboard job. They needed things. Shoes. Winter coats.

While I worked, Vin slept. When I came home for lunch, he was still in bed, curly black hair disheveled on the pillow. "Get up, Vin!" I shouted on my way out. "Get up! I'm leaving." He didn't.

While he lolled in dreamland, our young children were left to their own devices. One day in February, four-year old Tibby decided to walk to my office, a mile over railroad tracks and a busy turnpike. Wearing untied tennis shoes, lavender sweat pants, and a white turtleneck with red hearts, Tibby somehow found me. I was doing my job, plugging the lines into the board, talking briskly, when my peripheral vision detected a little face outside. I grabbed her up, hugging her to my chest, sick at what might have happened. Wrapping my cardigan sweater around her, I felt embarrassment as my co-workers watched. They were witnessing the by-product of neglect, of serious dysfunction. Using the switchboard, I called home—no answer. Which meant that eleven-month old Norah was on her own.

I detested leaving the kids with Vin, and hated my job at Industrial Metal Finishing, such an ugly little office. During that desolate stretch, I cut back on food to buy the girls a few upscale toys: a solid wood gym house for indoors and a blue and white geodesic dome for the yard. I pictured the people who bought such pricey toys—stable people, happy people. Their children were on the fast-track to success. Vin didn't worry because he never thought about the future, but I feared what was in store. Well, I thought, at least the girls can play with the toys of prosperous people's children.

Make learning fun. That was the key. They just had to succeed in school. I knew what happens when you don't go to college after high school. I didn't want the girls to follow my path, toiling at dumb jobs for minimum wage. I didn't want them to wake up in their thirties, struggling to balance college with work and family, trying to make up for lost time but never overcoming the financial losses.

So I read to them. I talked to them about college and careers. If they dared to interrupt my homework, I'd snap at them. By the time we got back to Ohio in 1983, I'd thought it was clear: I'd bought the house in Worthington with its hefty property taxes precisely because of the solid school system.

It had come to naught. I'd raised the girls with an eye to filling the gaps in my own upbringing, but any way you sliced it, my influence hadn't worked, and the time for controlling them had long passed. I told myself that we'd all been victims of Vin's betrayals. Anyway, I had other things to occupy me. My marriage, job, academics, and Ethan let me turn from the sorrow. I pushed the girls to the back of my mind, making room for the parts of life that were still salvageable.

In September, José, Ethan, and I went to Texas for 48 hours to visit Rachael. En route to Houston, Ethan hollered, "Waitress! I want my lunch!" Driving through Houston, he noticed the horizontal design of the traffic lights. At the top of his lungs he demanded, "What's wrong with the lights?" Later that day, he said reassuringly to his grandmother, "Everybody gets old, Grandmother Rachael." Eating brunch at a restaurant next morning, he told her, "Your face looks like the stepwoman's." Like the evil stepmother in *Cinderella,* Rachael had upswept hair and a sharp chin. She only smiled.

José and I sighed with relief as we flew out of Houston. Arriving in Chicago at 7:40, we found that the Columbus flight would be delayed. Dragging our bags through O'Hare, we tried to restrain Ethan. He broke away, darting between people and in and out of gates, delighting in his power to make us run after him. Toddlers always run in a slightly stiff-legged fashion, but Ethan was

127

fast and nimble. When we caught him, we tried to soothe him with M&Ms, sunflower seeds, and peanuts. He drank apple juice and ate Fig Newtons.

Finally, we were airborne. On the Columbus flight, he would not accept a seatbelt, kicked the chair in front of him, spat on a traveler, and threw a magazine over the seat. José hissed in exasperation. "C'mon, you little Bozo Brains! Settle down!" We tried reading to him, drawing pictures, and talking, but even the in-flight meal was a terror. We got home at 11:45 p.m. Next morning, work.

My Datsun died right after Christmas. Now, we had no means of personal transportation. "We should get a new car," I urged José. "With a used car, you never know what you're getting," I said, thinking of the inert Rabbit in the garage. My credit was okay, so we purchased a dark grey 1991 Dodge Colt station wagon. For the next five years, I'd owe just under $200 a month.

That was a cold winter. Our pipes froze and the toilet wouldn't flush. We couldn't afford a plumber. For days, José got our cooking and bathing water from Dulles Hall, parking the Colt at the loading dock, filling 20 empty milk jugs, and bringing them home, a ritual that he repeated for days, until the pipes unfroze naturally.

We were more than ready for spring. In March, from scrap wood, José built a bi-level bird feeder. He painted it dark green. When the thick enamel was dry, he hung it from a long chain in the silver maple. We stood back and surveyed his masterpiece.

"It looks like a picnic table for squirrels," I said.

"Okay, smartass."

But after grading papers and sitting at his computer all winter, nature was the best medicine. He was expanding the vegetable garden that he'd started the summer before. The tiny plot in the southeast corner of the backyard had grown to 10 by 24 feet. During the winter, José sent away for gardening and seed catalogs, and he devoured *New York Times* articles about soils, crop rotation, unusual hybrids. The real work started in late March. With a spade and tined fork, he turned the soil and amended it with peat, sand, and manure. Unlike the lonely intellectual struggle, gardening offered an instant payoff.

In April, he ordered an elephant-sized mound of topsoil. I was stunned by the black avalanche covering the driveway, but José got right to work. When the wheelbarrow was heaped high, he pushed past me, arms and back rigid, legs moving double fast.

"But, why do you need so much, dear?"

"I need to build up the beds, dear," he said, breathing hard. "Raised beds are good for the plants, improving drainage and air circulation."

He wore an old pair of chinos, a ragged grey tee-shirt, and cracked sneakers. It took a week of shoveling and transporting, but all the soil ended up in the vegetable garden. José used abandoned railroad ties to contain it all. The leanness of his form took on a hard edge with the labor. He seemed healthy and new, sweating and tanned. Somehow, the dirt on his cheeks and arms emphasized his refinement.

Through the warm months, José peppered his conversation with tidbits about gardens and plants. "Carrots love tomatoes," he'd say, referring to the wisdom of positioning complementary crops side by side. He planted marigolds to repel insects. And if the crops weren't picked by a certain moment, they would bolt.

"Do you love me?" I asked one night. I was cutting his hair. I'd learned how to do it, to save money. As usual, he sat on the den floor, his back to me, legs stretched out. I sat on the couch, leaning forward and scissoring away. In a repeated motion, I held the sections of his hair between the fingers of my left hand, cutting with my right. I tossed the cut hair onto the carpet. He'd vacuum it up afterwards. José liked his hair as short as possible during the summer.

"Yes, dear, I love you," he said.

"What would you do if I died?"

"I'd weep tears if you died."

I thought about that. One of us would have to die first. One of us would abandon the other. The survivor would never be able to express the sorrow to the one who was gone. That would happen someday to one of us. It was surreal and appalling. I finished cutting José's hair and brushed the clippings from his shoulders. I held open the collar of his shirt and blew a few short puffs down his neck to dislodge the strays. He stood up and looked at himself in the mirror, turning his head right and left. "Thank you, dear." He ran his hands over his smooth head. "It feels wonderful."

His academics continued to percolate. Now that he was finished with his courses and general exams, he mapped an outline for a dissertation that examined the French experience of pandemic influenza during the Great War. With his mother's help, he'd travel to France for primary research that summer. In April of '91, for networking purposes and to improve his résumé, he joined the

Society for the Study of French History. When his check bounced, he wrote a letter of apology

30 April 1991

Professor Malcolm Crook

Department of History, University of Keele

Keele, Staffordshire ST5 5BG

Dear Professor Crook:

My bank informed me this week that they returned my membership check. Sorry about that—I've enclosed another. As I am a graduate student, you probably ought to get my money into the bank as fast as possible.

I shall travel to France this summer to continue researching my dissertation on the French experience of Spanish 'flu (1918-1919). I plan to visit the ADs in the Var and the Vendee, along with (necessarily) brief stops at the AN and BN, and the SHA in Vincennes.

Again, sorry about the check. And thanks for your note.

Sincerely,

J. Talbert

***

That summer wasn't as hot as the one in 1988, but we sweated through more than 30 days of 90-plus temperatures. Nor did we get much rain, and the city imposed sprinkler restrictions, which wasn't good for José's garden. Raccoons finished the job, harvesting the corn before we could. "Very efficient animals," José said, examining the bare ears.

He couldn't get to France that summer after all. When he was offered another teaching job at Ohio State, he took it. We needed the extra few thousand dollars of income. The research trip would have to wait. He'd also lined up teaching jobs for

the fall. He'd teach a Western civ course at Otterbein two nights a week, and a similar one two mornings at a local seminary, the Pontifical College Josephinum. He'd teach an additional section of European history at the prison in Marion, Ohio. And in September, he interviewed for a Program Officer job at the Ohio Humanities Council. He thought he had a decent chance at it—they were desperate for someone who could write Queen's English, he said. During the interview, the man told José that he could have two weeks in December to go to France. So it would have been an ideal job. But he didn't get it.

That fall, we watched the Clarence Thomas confirmation hearing. Anita Hill, a law professor, testified that Thomas had committed lurid acts in the workplace. Threatened with losing the appointment, Thomas responded with outrage, saying that the hearing had turned into a high tech lynching. Yet a Black woman was doing the lynching, and in the end, no lynching took place, unless you consider the brutal way Hill was treated by the political right during and after her testimony. José and I were convinced of the truth of Hill's allegations.

When Clarence Thomas was confirmed as an associate justice by a slim majority in the fall of '91, José was incensed. For the second time, he reacted to what he saw as grave injustice, punching the laundry room wall before slamming out to the garage for a smoke. Later, I repaired the hole with a leftover piece of drywall and spackling compound.

At the time of the Thomas hearings, José was teaching inmates in Marion, most of them doing time for burglary, battery, or drug deals. Some were white and some were Black. José held the idealist notion that, if given a chance, some disadvantaged people would become eager readers and learners. A college course would add order to their lives, and maybe some hope. When he accepted the prison job, he wanted to test his hypothesis. He found out that the inmates appreciated the history lessons.

"To a man," he told me, "they're apt, serious students."

The prison guards, though, weren't supportive. They resentfully escorted José through the steel doors to the classroom, conveying their view that prisoners shouldn't get the time or attention. Too many tax dollars were already being spent on incarcerating them; educating them at tax-payer expense was a perk they didn't deserve, unfair to law-abiding people who struggled to educate themselves and their children out of their own pocket.

"Well, have at it," one of the guards said with a shrug as José stepped inside the locked corridor with his books and notes. "More power to you, if you think it'll do any good."

After he'd been teaching a few weeks, another guard made a point of telling José that one of his students wouldn't be in class anymore.

José asked, "Is he sick?"

"No," the guard said. "He's in the hole."

After the experience at the Marion prison, José thought that the guards were as hardened as any of the inmates. His doubts about the purpose of prisons and his misgivings not only about capital punishment but about punishment altogether were stronger than ever.

A couple of weeks later, one of the department's doctoral students, a Black man, was accused of cheating on his general examination. A committee reviewed the evidence. It was agreed that there had been extenuating circumstances. Candidacy was approved. A few years later, the student's dissertation likewise came under scrutiny for its poor writing and sketchy citations. But the student graduated, and afterwards landed a tenure-track job at a decent institution. At the time of the scuttlebutt, José and I talked about affirmative action. I asked him whether he thought it was fair to people who might have higher qualifications. White people like himself, I implied.

"Yes, I think you have to have Affirmative Action," José said. "It's most important for the children of the minority group; they need to be immersed in the advantages of middle class life, and in such an environment, they'll theoretically succeed. It doesn't happen overnight."

Years later, when the former student was chair of his own department while José still struggled along as a T.A., I thought about the poorly written dissertation and the cheating charge. I hadn't found out the particulars, but the idea of a Black person being railroaded was only slightly more abhorrent than the thought of a Black person being given an unearned pass. Compassion for other people didn't come as easily for me as it did for José.

We celebrated Ethan's fourth birthday on December 13, 1991, the day I got my master's degree. Mom attended commencement at St. John Arena. Afterwards, we had a birthday party at Ethan's school, and another party at Mom's. A week later, just before Christmas, I spotted a flyer in the halls of the math department announcing basset hound pups for sale. I pleaded with José, "Oh, let's just take a look! Basset hounds are so adorable!" "Okay, dear," he said with a shrug. I made some excuse to leave the History Department midday.

José and I drove to a rundown house. In the corner stood a lopsided Christmas tree with wrapped presents underneath. Three puppies wrestled and romped. Six weeks old, six pounders, six inches high at the shoulder, their ears hung nearly to their paws. Thick little legs and bodies. The homeowners seemed oblivious when the puppies urinated on the bare plywood floor. One pup was white and black. Another was white and red. The third was tri-color. José and I watched them. I got on all fours and pretended to be a mommy dog. The puppies ambled toward me, biting with their sharp baby teeth.

We decided to get the tri-color, paying $200 for our new family member. José had brought a corrugated box, knowing that we'd never be able to "just take a look." We called our new baby Molly. Ethan couldn't be contained. He ran nonstop with Molly, screeching as she chased him down the hall and through the den. He squealed with delight when she stole his socks or piddled in the house. José and I must have been extreme dog people--the racket didn't disturb us in the slightest.

A few months later, Ethan and I were watching *Peter Pan* for the umpteenth time. It was evening. Molly slept on my lap. José was

on the driveway, smoking and catching a breeze, when he heard a faint cry. It was coming from our neighbor's house. For decades, Myrtle Johnson had lived alone in the white house with black shutters. Short and plump with glasses and curly white hair, she puttered around her yard, tending her peonies. She sat for hours in a plastic chair on the front porch, observing the neighbors. José heard Myrtle call out again. He tried to open the front door. Locked. At the sound of the twisting knob, Myrtle's voice became more insistent. José went around back, pushed open the kitchen window and boosted himself in, clearing the sink. He found Myrtle on the living room floor, moaning faintly, her hip fractured. By the time he called the squad, she'd been lying there for several hours.

I was unaware of the commotion and José didn't mention it. He wasn't like my father, who belonged to the Masons, attended Christ Lutheran church, and regularly gave blood. Back in 1966, my dad started Reynoldsburg's Tomato Festival, which became a big moneymaker for the town. My dad was a good citizen, but he was

136

also tactical about his activities. He wanted everyone to recognize his civic-mindedness. That was good for business. But José kept his good deeds to himself. He didn't mention Myrtle's accident and I didn't find out until the next morning, when her daughter Carolyn came over to thank José.

Carolyn said, "You know, José, my mom didn't know what to think of you before this. Well, she sure is your biggest fan now. We can't thank you enough."

It was true—because he spoke little and kept to himself, some people thought José was cold and humorless. Myrtle was no exception. When the girls and I first moved in, before I even knew José, Myrtle had been impressed with Vin. When he was in town, Vin flattered Myrtle and joked with her. To those who didn't know him, Vin was a likeable raconteur. But I thought of that line in *My Fair Lady*: "Oozing charm from ev'ry pore, he oiled his way around the floor."

In mid-July of '92, José finally went to France. For the next several weeks, I'd be responsible for all of the household tasks. Another reason for my nervousness was that, while José was away, I'd be acclimating to a new job: after seven and a half years in History, I'd accepted a promotion in the College of Social Work, more responsibility and a higher paycheck. But my new boss hovered, trying to direct the most mundane aspect of my work. Nor did I enjoy the vibe--after the intellectualism and wit of the History Department, Social Work seemed lowbrow. So when José left for France, I felt doubly lost. The new job seemed like a mistake, and my husband was gone. His letters helped.

Sunday afternoon, 7/12/92

Dear Sharyn & Ethan (and Molly),

I hope you are all feeling well and behaving. We arrived at Orly at 6:15 a.m. and I was in the city by 8:30. The room in the Hotel des Allies is as the guidebook promised—small (8x12), clean, simply furnished (twin bed, scarred wardrobe, table and chair, and a basin large enough for laundry and spit baths).

On Wednesday-Friday, I was at the Archives Nationales. So far, I've struck out. I won't panic just yet. Yesterday I scouted out a few places: the Bibliotheque historique de la ville de Paris (rue Pavee), the Bibliotheque et Archives de l'Assistance Publique a Paris (rue Minimes), and the Army Archives at Vincennes. None was open, so I'll have to go when I get back to Paris. Vincennes is an unlovely pile of stone. They are renovating and cleaning the place now (remember the scaffolding in Prague?).

This a.m. I browsed around the Ile de la Cite and Notre Dame (another unlovely pile of stone—I prefer Chartres). I was looking for an English-language bookstore—I've almost completed Three Cheers for the Paraclete.

If the garden turns into a jungle, don't worry—it's there for interest and fun, not guilt. I will happily spend hours in it when I return to chez nous.

On the bright side, there is the coffee, the bread, and the markets. I've never seen such blood red, unblemished tomatoes and peppers. The coffee is wonderful and the breads better—I intend to bring home two or three panettes. These together with the availability of a real newspaper make for a vast improvement over Prague.

Ethan, I hope school is going well. And yes, I <u>will</u> get you a surprise (I have already gotten one for Mommy). Since there's a store just a few blocks away called Le Home du Chien, I'll probably get surprises for Molly, too. Sweetie, do what Mommy says. I love you very much.

Dear, I hope the job is going okay. If any of your co-workers take liberties, just tell them I would be happy to catch the next flight and kill them in cold blood. Hope that the tax man and my creditors are keeping their distance. If you do have a money crunch, call Mom—she understands that my casual, occasional employment is the reason we're so poor.

And would you do me a favor dear? Would you call me at the Hotel des Allies on Saturday August 1ˢᵗ at 9:00 a.m. (your time)? I worry about you guys and for your sanity—not to mention my own. I'd also like to hear your voices, and it's much cheaper to call here than to call there. Just ask for me by name. (Tel: 43-31-47-52).

Love, José/Daddy

P.S. Happy Birthday, dear. I hope the rose arrives in one piece, alive and not too puny.

P.P.S. Yes, Ethan, I saw an old man on the Rue de Rivoli doing wee-wee against a building. I also stepped in dog duty on my way to the A.N. on Thursday. They have to sluice the gutters and hose down the sidewalks every morning.

Wednesday nite 7/15/92, Grenoble

Dear Sharyn & Ethan (& Molly),

Remember the commercial from last February's Olympics, "They won't accept American Express"? Guess what Grenoblois will still not accept. Not even Am Ex traveler's checks in French francs. Quelle surprise.

They agreed to let me stay at the hotel tonight, even after I left for an hour to find a bank that was still open (no go) or a merchant who would cash a traveler's check (of course not).While out, I got lost (I haven't quite enough cash to buy a city map). I see why historians so rarely go on research trips.

You would not believe the number of young Americans in Lyon who could speak no French at all. What are these kids doing here? I speak 4-year old's French, but can at least get past the ticket agent in the railway station.

The trip down from Paris was great—the Train et Grand Vitesse is amazing, but I got bumped from my seat when we got to Gare de Lyon. I did not realize I was riding standby. So I stood for the last leg of the trip.

Grenoble is striking, and the mountains surrounding it are beautiful. After I change money and get something to eat tomorrow, I'll hunt down the archives. I hope you guys are feeling okay and that the two little guys who are not the boss are behaving themselves. I enjoyed the phone call the other night. I miss and love you all very much.

Love, José/Daddy

Monday Evening, 7/22/92, Grenoble
Dear Sharyn, Ethan & M.—

Hope your weather has finally cooled off. I heard a rumble of thunder shortly after I got back to the hotel late this afternoon but I think the storm dissipated. It's still very warm here and the hills

140

around look a little parched—I don't think Grenoble gets much rain in the summertime.

I had a better day in the Archives today—I still found precious little, but at least I was not harassed and scorned. I'll try again tomorrow. I've located the dossiers of a number of teachers in the department, and quite a few came down with the 'flu, but as yet haven't discovered one who died on the lectern.

I'll write again from Bordeaux on Wednesday morning. Take good care of yourselves. Give each other a hug. And give Molly a Snausage.

Love, José/Daddy

PS – Happy Birthday again, dear. I'm looking forward to escorting you to the Worthington Inn —you must wear something stunning.

PSS—Have just finished "The Mysterious Stranger," and also knocked off "The Man that Corrupted Hadleyburg." Not bad, eh?

Thursday morning, 7/23/92 Bordeaux

Dear Guys—

Yesterday was a long day. I caught a 7:20 train out of Grenoble and arrived at Tours just after 2:00 p.m. There I changed to a TGV to Bordeaux, and I got here just after five o'clock. I'm glad to be out of Grenoble—the archives there were a bust. On the last afternoon, I did find some bundles for the 1889 epidemic, but the records for 1908-1930 are missing. Tough beans.

It was even nicer to leave behind the dumpy Hotel de la Poste. My back was feeling the effects of the worst bed I've ever slept in—the springs were so feeble it was like lying across a ditch. Still, the landlady was nice. She made my train reservation—this would have been tricky in a 100-degree phone booth, and especially so as going east-west on the French rail system is more complicated than north-south, where every trip is "Paris-to someplace else."

Along the way I got to see a lot of France. The countryside is beautiful—hundreds of acres of sunflowers, and of corn. I knew that Europeans grow corn, but I didn't realize how much. And, of course, gardens everywhere. And cows and sheep. But I still have not seen a basset hound or a Great Dane.

The arrival in Bordeaux was extraordinarily smooth. The city is sunny and warm (not nearly so hot as Grenoble), and sprawling. And many Bordelais(es) wear sunglasses, unlike the places I've been. I bought a map in the station (très chere—28 ff) and found the bus headed for the "Place Gambetta." When I asked the bus driver where I could buy tickets, he said "Ici" and <u>smiled</u>. I almost fell down--the first smile I've gotten from a petit-fonctionnaire. Anyway, I found the Hotel la Boetie without trouble, and what a hotel. Shower and toilet in the room (both spotless!), firm bed with bright reading lights over the bedstead (another first), TV and telephone.

There is a patisserie right next door and a laundromat 50 yards down the street. Only four small, medieval blocks from Place Gambetta, and only about ¾ mile from the departmental archives. I will go there this afternoon. In fact, I'll take the bull by the horns and talk my way in without speaking to the director—my downfall in Grenoble. Then I can just go through the catalogues myself and request help if needed. Fingers crossed.

I hope you all are doing okay. And that Grandma and Grandmother R. are feeling well. Thanks for the call the other day

142

in Grenoble—I was pretty blue and you cheered me up. Hug each other for me and give Molly a treat. I love and miss you all very much. Will write again this weekend.

Love, José/Daddy

PS—Dear, have you ever read Twain's story, "The Invalid"? I started it on the train out of Grenoble yesterday and laughed so hard I was in tears. People began to stare, so I put it down and finished it later. The French never seem to read and laugh at the same time. J.

Sunday afternoon, 7/26/92 Bordeaux
Dear Guys,

I hope this finds you well and enjoying cool weather. I'm fine--even did my laundry yesterday morning, and this is always good for morale.

In matters of research, I seem to be on a see-saw. I either get next to nothing, as in Grenoble, or too much material, as I've found here. Too much, because they permit <u>no</u> photocopying. Apparently by 1988 they became overwhelmed with copying requests (especially from people doing genealogical research) and simply discontinued it. Their microfilming service is expensive, requiring eight days.

So, I transcribe with my pen. Twenty-six pages on Friday— not bad considering the turn-of-the century script. Find an Americanist and push him off his bicycle for me. At the rate I'm going, I'd need a month here. Still, I shouldn't complain. At least Bordeaux has the records I need. And they're open 8:30-6, with no break.

I miss you guys very much and can't wait to get home. I finally got rained on Friday morning in a terrific thunderstorm on the way back to the archives.

I'll write you again when I get back to Paris. I'm looking forward to hearing your voices. Take care of each other, and you two little guys obey the boss. I love you all very much.

Love, José/Daddy

PS—I watched the Tour de France last night and this A.M. on the TV. What a snoozer—I'd rather watch bowling. The commentators keep slobbering over French athletes. How un-American. J.

Wednesday Evening, 7/29/92, Paris

Dear Guys—

I arrived back in the City of Pretense and Rudeness before noon today. The train made no stops and was only one-third filled—altogether a pleasant, air-conditioned ride. I really hated to leave Bordeaux—pleasant town, weather not too hot, nice hotel, courteous archival employees. Now, if I can get some good materials out of the military archives at Vincennes, I think this will qualify as a successful trip for a bumbling first attempt. Of course, that's a pretty big "if"—even Thorndyke admitted that the staff at Vincennes are "uncivilized."

I trust that the two little guys are listening to the big boss—I'm looking forward to the phone call on Saturday. And I want to come home. Take care of yourselves. I love you all very much.

Love, José/Daddy

PS—I feel pretty good—drinking less and eating more. J.

Tuesday Evening, 8/4/92

Dear Guys—

Today was the first cool day in Paris since I got back— temperature was around 70-75 degrees and even some clouds to cut the sunshine. This is important if you work at Vincennes, as Vincennes is a dump. The little grass inside the chateau is brown— they had the sprinklers on this morning, but I suspect it was too little, too late. Few trees. What a desolate place. Yesterday morning, three dust devils 20 feet tall blew around the courtyard. I got a good view of the dust storm because I was stuck outdoors—the sign said the hours had been reduced, but did not say what the new hours were. So successive waves of scholars and even tourists (these folks must have been hard up for something to look at in Paris) stopped at the door, read the sign, and asked me what was going on.

Like I should know? I pretended it was natural to loiter in a hot, dusty courtyard. A professor from the University of Rabat struck up a conversation (if I may call it that), who told me he was researching the Moroccan army in the 19th century. Of course, I did not know they <u>had</u> an army in the 19th century. I wasn't sure whether he was researching French colonial troops or crazy, unwashed guys with very sharp weapons.

As my French is not sufficient to probe this distinction, and even if successful, might have given offense to the descendent of aforesaid crazy, unwashed guys, I grunted approval of his life's work and let the exchange languish. He thought I was German. A young woman who accosted me later on the stairs must have thought I was French. She started babbling; I think she said she was a journalist and wanted to know the hours of the archives. I apologetically shook my head. She smiled at me the way one smiles at a strange dog.

Speaking of dogs, on the way back to the hotel I stopped at a café for a beer. A short-haired pointer had the run of the place—I think he belongs to the owners. He apparently liked the way I smelled, attempting to eat my trousers, crotch seam first. It is difficult to drink a beer, maintain one's studied, Parisian sangfroid and have one's clothes eaten at the same time. I scrunched up to the bar and he lost interest.

Well, since Vincennes is closed on Wednesdays, I'll go to the boutique at the A.N. and buy Thorndyke his new A.N. guide, and double back to the library at the Institut Pasteur. I doubt I'll find anything.

I imagine this will be my last letter. Only eight more days— I've been counting since I lost sight of Long Island. I love and miss you all very much. Just think of this experience as if I had gone to the Duper for five weeks.

Love, José/Daddy

José came home mid-August, worn out but in great humor. He'd photocopied reams of material that he'd use to prove his case about the French military's export of influenza in 1918.

He'd been semi-successful in his research, and I'd done my part at home, finding time to strip the bathroom of its ugly fern wallpaper. The walls underneath were uneven, so I used joint compound to texturize. When it was dry, I painted the room with cream-colored enamel. Now our bathroom had a slight Mediterranean feel. Almost like France. I was proud. I'd kept up the lawn mowing and the household chores. Ethan and Molly were thriving. All of our work, I thought, was for the family's good.

The joy of being home again colored José's outlook for weeks. Radiating a new vitality, he rose before five, brewing a pot of coffee and starting the day's laundry. While the clothes agitated, he sat on the washer in his green bathrobe, leather slippers on his feet, sipping hot coffee and reading either *The New York Review of Books* or something for his dissertation. Feeling safe and unburdened, I slept until 7:00. José brought coffee to my bedside, waking me with a soft kiss. He weeded his overgrown garden and reclaimed the grocery shopping. With bursts of mindless joy, he chased Ethan and Molly around the back yard and played hide-and-seek inside. It was a reassuring commotion.

Together again, José and I discarded the tight wariness that comes with being alone. We touched and kissed more often. As I sat on a bar stool reading, he slowly caressed my neck under my long hair. When he was busy with some household task, I'd lean close, running my palm along his tan arm with its sparse golden hairs, feeling the warm denseness. We let our eyes rest languidly on a pleasing feature, an endearing movement. We paid attention to the simple statements that were thickly coded with the message of love.

After the European excursion, we faced unpaid bills, so José was again forced to rely on the benefactress. As usual, Rachael promptly responded, and her check squared José with all the creditors. That same week, he got a letter from an old high school buddy. Lex brought José up to date on the doings of their peers from the late '60s.

. . . B. lives in New York and is a fairly well known casting director. J. is a photographer who's had several shows at the MOMA. P. is a film producer. A. was working for a long time on Capitol Hill, a trusted assistant to a congressman; she married an assistant to Walter Mondale. J. is a veterinarian living and working part time on Cape Cod and spending time tending to race horses. C. is a doctor in Boston who practices medicine half time and also helps administer the MIT HMO. Along with the M.D., he also earned an MBA. He married the daughter of one of the wealthiest men in America, so C. spends much of his time in New Mexico on his father-in-law's ranch.

Lex wrote on, casually documenting the successes of the Greenwich crowd. And here we were—me a Civil Service employee, and José still a T.A. and adjunct lecturer. In his free time, Lex sailed off Cape Cod with his brilliant British wife; we lived in a tract house with hardly any free time. Somehow, José was never envious, and his lack of envy took away some of my own. I thought about the lustrous lives of José's school chums. Maybe José will have his own claim to fame after his work is published, I thought. The project would necessarily demand mastery of general modern European history, military history, and the history of science and epidemiology.

His research materials would require space and organization, so José zeroed in on what had been Norah's bedroom. One weekend in September, as I made the beds and cleaned the bathroom, I listened as he tap-tapped on his computer in the new home office. Photocopies from France were stacked in piles on a long table. A tower of library books included *Social Revolutions in the Modern World* by Theda Skocpol and *The Selfish Gene* by biologist Richard Dawkins. I also saw Thomas Kuhn's famous work, *The Structure of Scientific Revolutions*. I'd heard about paradigm shifts, and knew that Kuhn had coined the term, but the phrase was used too loosely in graduate school. It seemed like a cliché.

"What's this about?" I asked, thumbing through.

José stopped typing for a minute, collecting his thoughts. He sighed, not in exasperation, but luxuriously.

"Well, dear, I can't really answer that question in one or two sentences," he said, rolling his head from side to side to stretch the neck muscles. "Painting broadly, Kuhn argues that big science happens when the frameworks of earlier discoveries are discarded-- always a hotly contested process. Science doesn't proceed by accretion but by irreconcilable rupture, and that's what Kuhn calls the 'paradigm shift.'"

I stood behind him, rubbing his shoulders. "Sort of like when you dump one spouse and marry another?"

He extended his neck and looked at me upside down, rolling his eyes good-naturedly. "More like when the Ptolemaic system of astronomy is dumped in favor of the Copernican system," he said.

"A-*ha*," I breathed.

I kissed him and looked at a handwritten list on a legal pad near his elbow. He'd laid out some of the big questions he'd wrestle in his dissertation:

How did France and the French people react to influenza in 1918-1919?

What were the traditional responses to, and remedies for, influenza?

At which level of government was the flu first noticed in 1918?

Did reactions change between spring and autumn of 1918?

After effects in professional medicine, the universities?

What conclusions will this study offer on the perception of disease?

5

AMBITION

There is a great deal of human nature in people -- Mark Twain

While José was in France, Tibby shared some news. It was July, my 42nd birthday. I'd just started the Social Work job, and was about to begin my doctoral program. I'd figured it out: I'd complete the nine courses by spring of '94. My general exam would happen a year later. With everything on my mind, I didn't see it coming: Tibby was six months pregnant.

My eyes traveled to her middle—yes, I saw. At five feet eight, she easily hid it. I just hadn't been looking. Her wide-eyed expression confirmed her dread in telling me. Well, she was right to be worried: the father was the thug-like person I'd seen sitting in his car, either too ashamed or insecure to come to the door. The two were living in a tacky apartment.

It didn't make sense. Tibby, headed for single motherhood after watching me struggle along that same road? She'd been a child of poverty and dysfunction--how could she want that for her own baby? Clearly, I'd failed at motherhood. I'd failed to guide my daughter. I was dying to tell José the minute he got home, but kept the secret a few more days. Finally, I blurted it out. "Can you believe it? Can you just *believe* it?" I was trying not to cry.

His eyes were wide and soft. "These things happen all the time, in every kind of family, dear. Let's give Tibby the support she needs right now." Speechless beyond a cluck of surprise, I stared at José. My husband—so wise, so good. José's words neutralized the sting.

In September, Tibby's co-workers from the hair salon planned a baby shower. Mom was invited, but she refused to attend. "I will not condone Tibby's decision to have a child out of wedlock," she stated with finality. Elsbeth and I did go, joining twenty young women, joking and gabbing in Tibby's small apartment, along with the mother of the boyfriend. Our words were brief but gracious.

On October 9th, my boss asked me to destroy the dossiers of faculty applicants, five years' worth. The shredder wasn't working, nor did we have a paper cutter, so he told me to cut the files into little pieces with scissors. When he left, I muttered, "Forget *that*! Here I am, a person with a Master's degree, and you're asking me to cut up two hundred dossiers by hand? Good luck, you cretin!" When his office door was safely closed, I hefted armloads of files down three flights and into the parking lot. On tiptoe, I shoved the intact folders into an open dumpster. I was wiping beads of perspiration when Tibby called. She was in labor. That evening, I went to the hospital.

Distressed from the trauma and anesthesia, Tibby wouldn't be comforted. After a time, I went to the nursery to see my grandson. His hard legs were drawn over his belly, his face scrunched in a scowl. But he didn't cry. Tibby would call him Devlin.

My incorrect first husband Vin phoned from California that night to find out about Tibby and Devlin. As I dutifully told him about the baby and Tibby's state of mind, José relaxed on the couch. The sleeves of his white shirt were turned back, showing tanned forearms. He held a can of Busch beer. The Braves and the Pirates were on TV. But José wasn't paying attention to the score. He was listening to my side of the conversation. A slight smile played around his mouth.

When I hung up, José lifted his head, and with a dancing motion of hand and wrist, encircled his thumb and forefinger, making a hand horn—a little habit, used to emphasize the most delicious of life's ironies. Now he placed the hand horn to his lips and called out: "Yo, *Grand*-pa!"

Okay, so despite his smug certainty about his Italian sex appeal, Vin was a grandpa. And that made me a 42-year old grandmother. Really? How could it be? José and I were rising in our studies. Our family life was just beginning. Ethan wasn't yet five years old. We were still feathering our nest, one twig at a time. I might have been a grandmother in the technical sense, but . . . .

In December, I finished my first doctoral course, modern British literature. In class, I'd felt inadequate. The younger, full-time students were astute and clever, so quick. Feeling muddled and dim, I was mostly silent. But I read everything and thought I had a decent idea for the paper, which I called, "On Bathrooms and Vico:

Metaphoric Cycles in *Possession*." The following spring, I was given the nod for the English Department's best seminar paper.

That winter, José and I worked and studied. We drove Ethan to child care in the mornings and picked him up after work. We looked after Molly and took care of the house. José shoveled the driveway and sidewalk, and did the grocery shopping. Most weekends, I cared for Devlin while Tibby worked at the hair salon— Tibby needed all the help she could get. José grappled with his grading chores and, when he found a bit of free time, his dissertation writing.

Another dog was the last thing on our minds when in March of '93 Mom called to say that "the Cat Lady" was on the radio, searching for a home for an abandoned basset hound. We decided to make the trip to Citizens for Humane Action. Just to look. When we arrived, the basset was being adopted. We saw other worthy dogs, but steeled ourselves and headed back to the car. At that moment, a canine in an outside pen captured my attention. He looked like a skinny polar bear—pure white with a beautiful smooth head. He stood with his paws on the fence. He barked energetically. I realized that he was actually talking to me, looking into my face with good natured intensity. We ignored his plea and left him there.

That night, I cried for the lanky white dog. He had nothing and yet seemed so deserving. We had a lot to share—a house, a yard, and a deep affinity for dogs. I called the shelter and learned that T-Rex had been roaming the streets in the dead of winter, icicles hanging from his ears. He'd languished at the shelter for more than two months.

"It's because he's so big," the volunteer told me. "Nobody wants him."

The next day, with José's lukewarm approval, Ethan and I went back and got him. We renamed him Mr. Petey, after the stray I'd wanted when I was a little girl.

Petey was loving and gentle. He and Molly got along. We were happy to have him. But in May, he got sick. In the yard, I watched him cough violently, stagger, arch his back, and collapse. We rushed him to Ohio State's veterinary clinic. Along with pneumonia, the vet students diagnosed myasthenia gravis, which meant that Petey's nervous system was damaged. The disorder had led to another problem called megaesophagus, which meant that his food wouldn't stay down. Breathing food into his lungs had caused the pneumonia. Petey almost died. His care came to $1500.

Talking to José's mother, we let it slip about Mr. Petey. She was aghast. "Do you mean to say that you don't have enough money for your light bill, but that you'd pay that amount for a *dog*?"

Yes. Petey recovered from the pneumonia, but he'd always have megaesophagus. For the rest of his life, he had to be fed in a vertical position. So we set his food on the counter, and he'd eat with front paws on a chair seat. Afterwards, during a ten-minute span, José or I would stand guard, one hand on Petey's collar, the other on his back. Petey's digestion had to be underway before he could be released. When the time was up, we'd say, "Okay!" He'd jump right down.

Weighing 84 pounds when we got him, Petey filled out to an impressive 102. He had a tendency to bolt and roam, but he was loyal and whip-smart. Dinner was an occasion for profound gratitude. Whenever he was pleased or excited, he tilted his head skyward, and with deep musicality, expressed himself: "Woo-woo-WOOO!" When I sat on the floor to watch TV, Petey rested next to me, his front leg possessively over mine. When in repose, his ears flopped upwardly. Then José would say, "Donkey ears." We were a happy family of five.

On October 5th of '93, our seventh anniversary, José presented me with a second wedding ring—twice as thick and heavy as the original. Now I could admire two golden wedding rings on my finger, one narrow, the other double thickness, a constant symbol of José's love. It was a promising time. And sometimes, surprising. With rare candor, José said he needed to finish his dissertation by the following March. And sure enough, he began to work on it every day. Good, I thought. Goal-setting! Meanwhile, my doctoral courses were almost finished. It was then that a startling notion began to crystallize. Is it possible, I wondered, that I can beat him to the finish line?

March '94 came and went. José hadn't made much of a dent in his dissertation. Whenever he found a spare hour, he sat down to his scholarship, but he couldn't give it the time it demanded. Our days were strictly scheduled. Up before dawn, José satisfied his caffeine and nicotine habits and read in the quiet house. I got up a few hours later. After walking the dogs, I ran to catch the 7:20 bus. Meantime, José supervised Ethan's attire and breakfast. After dropping Ethan at child care, where he was now a kindergartner, José headed for the stadium lot. In 168 Dulles, he read and graded. Two days a week, he taught his course. Late afternoon, he picked up Ethan and headed back home. He started dinner and fed Petey and Molly. When I walked in at 5:45, dinner was ready.

After dinner, José watched PBS News Hour while drinking a beer. When he brought home a cheap six-pack, he'd stand over the wastebasket in his button-down shirt and belted trousers, cutting the plastic dividers apart, so that wildlife wouldn't get stuck in the holes. At night, after we put Ethan to bed, José prepared his next lecture, and he read for the dissertation.

When summer rolled in, I took a deep breath. Ohio State calmed down during the summer, giving me time to study even though I was technically there for Social Work people. It was a good time for José, too, rejuvenating himself in his vegetable garden. One Saturday, I sat in a lawn chair and watched him hoe through weed roots, turning over the black soil, pinky-beige earthworms wiggling out of moist clods. I liked it when José worked outdoors, his strong and graceful form repetitiously bending and chopping. And with both hands full, he couldn't smoke.

Something twanged in my heart. Knowing I was about to dash the bucolic perfection, I asked again, "When will you quit smoking, dear?" He kept hoeing and answered lightly, "I'll stop someday, dear." As always, noncommittal. He straightened, took a few breaths, and flashed a shy grin. He turned back to his work. I thought, "Someday." Maybe José meant that he'd quit right after his dissertation defense. Or maybe he meant it in the terms of a historian: everything quits at some point, sooner or later.

Along with his gardening, José taught a class that summer at Otterbein College. On the hottest days, I used vacation time to take Ethan to the local pool,

where he taught himself to dive. Occasionally, José and I watched TV, including *Travels with Rick Steves*. We enjoyed Rick's forays to Eastern Europe and France. We liked his broad if shallow historical background. Observing the genial, fair-haired host, José dubbed him, "the Golden Retriever of Men." And that summer, we sat hypnotized as O.J. Simpson's white Bronco led a strange parade along the Los Angeles freeways.

Ethan finished nearly six years at Ohio State Child Care in September, starting first grade at Colonial Hills School. After school, father and son ate muffins and watched a movie. Movie-averse José had come to enjoy a few kid-friendly videos--*Clash of the Titans, Jason and the Argonauts, Young Sherlock Holmes*. These they watched, time and again.

We ate together every night, and discussed a lot of things, including the meaning of words. One evening, José used the word "presume," and six-year old Ethan asked what the word meant. José told him, and Ethan said, "I thought that's what 'assume' means."

In January of '95, we took Ethan to a friend's birthday party at a Chuck E. Cheese pizza place. I wasn't thrilled about venturing out in the cold. Heavy snow began to fall before we left the driveway, and in a few minutes we were stuck in a blizzard, hemmed in by rush hour traffic. We sat silently, snow thickening against the windshield. It was thirty minutes before we started to move again. "And here we are," José remarked lightly, "on our way to Sharl Fromage."

I held up a finger. "Sharl *Ew* Fromage!"

***

He was usually good natured, but tight finances, the lack of progress on his dissertation, and a heavy teaching and grading load took their toll that winter. Instead of poking fun at his own missteps, he turned severe. Some of it was my fault.

Ethan was seven, leaving young childhood. He needed a desk. The sale-priced model from a Scandinavian furniture store would occupy a corner of his room, seeing him through high school and beyond. But the desk came unassembled, arriving in eight big boxes. One cold weekend, José had to put it together. For two days, instructions, hardware, and heavy flat pieces of wood were spread over the floor like a giant Lego project. As José worked, Molly and Petey stepped on the pieces. He didn't complain, but he didn't seem happy.

Next we got a gas bill, in José's words, of Biblical proportions. The furnace died shortly after; we sat bundled in coats and hats, unforeseen problems delaying the new installation. My adored African violets perished. To relieve our frozen fingers and feet, we drove to the mall, where we walked in silence. I spied a French bistro with warm lights and cozy tables. A delicious smell wafted out. I imagined eating a dainty snack in an upscale environment. "Let's go in!" I cried.

"Trop cher!" José retorted.

There was never enough in the bank and always too much scrimping. I felt the resentment rising again. I'd been patient. I had a right to be irritated. So when José postponed his dissertation completion date for the umpteenth time, I sighed. "Aren't you sick of this treadmill? Aren't you sick of being poor?"

"I don't like it any better than you do, dear. You can put the blame on me, where it belongs."

"Well, when you finish, you can move on to something more--lucrative. But you have to finish first. Gads, I mean, it's almost as if you want to be a T.A. forever."

Looking me dead in the eye, he responded, "I will never have money." The words were bad enough but the flat, brutal tone was insupportable. José was deliberately closing the door to possibility.

"Why do you think that way? Explain it to me!"

But there would be no more dialogue on the subject.

Oh, the expectations we bring to marriage. I had married a scholar, and by now, he darn well was supposed to be making a name as a scholar. He was supposed to be earning a decent living as a scholar. The nose in the book eventually has to translate into financial security. Well, it hadn't happened, and José's words felt like a rupture. He's used our marriage as a self-indulgent retreat, I fumed. I didn't talk to him for a while.

It boiled down to a strange absence of assertiveness. It was scarier than laziness. He was like the most brilliant gem, yet in the depths there waved a threadlike fissure. It didn't matter that I was no gem myself. All I knew was that I was weary. Whatever his problem is, I thought, the bills just keep coming. I went back to my editing--the dissertation of some Chinese sociology student. They never get the articles right, I snorted, angrily adding "the" and "an."

It hit me then that I'd played a role in our financial difficulties. Shortly after our marriage, I divided the household expenses. "We'll keep our separate checking accounts," I told José. "I'll take care of the mortgage, the property taxes, and the car and house insurance." I'd also end up shouldering the child care, the monthly payment for the Dodge, and the bill for the new furnace.

José would buy the groceries, and I transferred the utility bills to his name, too: electric, gas, phone, water. The yearly income taxes would also be his responsibility. This was the sore point. To boost my paychecks, I'd been claiming 10 dependents since our marriage, a shady strategy that resulted in a hefty IRS bill every April. When I devised the plan, I'd thought our situation would stabilize in short order. Then I'd fix things and once again become an honest woman.

Well, fast forward nine years. In March of '95, José was as usual grimly anticipating the taxes we'd soon owe. He sulked about it for weeks. He just couldn't ask his mother, not again. But there was nothing extra in my bank account, and I thought I was doing more than my share. Sensing his despair, I thought, "The second he opens his mouth to complain—*pow*! And, does he really need a *New York Times* every morning? He doesn't skimp on his caffeine, nicotine, and beer habits, either," I thought meanly. "Just add up those items, and, there you go! --our yearly tax bill, paid in full!"

But I quickly remembered that José got me a dozen red roses every year for my birthday. Every Valentine's Day, he gave Ethan and me our own heart-shaped box of chocolates. He bought us gifts and little treats all the time. I looked at him as we drove to work, as he helped Ethan with his homework, as he patiently fed Molly and Mr. Petey. I had to admit that he'd never been lazy. He was never one to sit around. He didn't sleep much. He was always helpful and thoughtful and engaged, neat and respectful. He'd always anticipated what had to be done around the house and yard. He was a dogged reader and razor-edged thinker. And he had always been desperate for a steady professional job.

Things inevitably worked themselves out; adjustments had to me made, either in attitude or in buying habits. I had no appetite for conflict, and gratefully embraced the sweet if fragile balance that returned to our family. Anyhow, I told myself, José wasn't the enemy. Academia was to blame. Universities discriminated against hiring older Ph.D. candidates. The vitality of academia's revenue depended on a ghetto of T.A.s to teach the survey courses, while tenured professors were rewarded for their research.

Like my old friends, the military historians Ray and Kip, most T.A.s didn't complain about the system. Yes, their pay was low, but their fees and tuition were paid, they were young and unencumbered, and they'd get their Ph.D.s in five years and move on to bigger and better things. That's what Ray and Kip did. But some of them, the older ones with family obligations and certain hang ups, endured low pay and no benefits, year after year.

Meanwhile, I was just marking time in the College of Social Work. The high intellectualism of the History Department was absent in Social Work, so I kept watch for another campus job. But I did like my unofficial role as resident grammarian. I'd often edit faculty articles and students' dissertations, for a fee, under the table.

And Social Work faculty would constantly ask my advice about style and usage.

During a faculty search in the spring of '95, the Social Work dean and a few faculty members wondered about the proper way to spell out "C. V." on a résumé. Should you use "Curriculum Vita"? Two people thought "Curriculum Vitae" was correct. No, just plain "Vita" is okay, others thought. They asked me, and to make sure I got it right, I asked José, who'd made a serious study of Latin--four years in high school and several terms in college. He jotted down this information, which I shared with the Social Work people:

- Vita means "life." It is singular.

- Vitae means "lives." It is plural.

- However, "curriculum vitae" means "course of life," and in this case, "Vitae," a feminine noun, is the object of the preposition "of," and so takes the letter "e" at the end. This is the genitive case, whereas "vita" alone, as subject, is the nominative case.

- Therefore, "Curriculum Vitae" should appear at the top of the résumé. The plural of "C.V." is "Curricula Vitarum"—as in, "We sure are gettin' a bunch of curricula vitarum these days!"

In an aside for my ears only, José remarked that only a bi-syllabic moron would put "Vita" at the top of his academic résumé.

That summer, I wrote the prospectus for my dissertation. It would be an ethnography focusing on identity formation embedded in the words of Civil Service Employees at Ohio State University, female workers who held advanced degrees. In a nutshell, my dissertation would be about myself, a rigorous, narcissistic joy-ride.

As I studied in the hot den while classical music played, José took Ethan to the Worthington pool, or to Columbus Clippers' games--at one of these, Ethan caught six stray balls. Meantime, I carried a book everywhere, and between family requirements, during every spare second, I tried to cram as much information into my brain as possible.

In early September, I passed the general examination. The first two chapters of the dissertation were counted as the written portion. And then came the oral. Sleep deprived, I stumbled over the first three questions. But I regained my balance and ended the two-hour defense with my credibility intact.

By the early months of 1996, I decided to join José's secret club: he wouldn't tell me how slow he was going, and I wouldn't tell him about my breakneck speed. I'd show him how to kick ass. Organized and motivated, I sneaked out of the office many times a week, tape recording my respondents in their campus offices. I read folklore scholarship, discourse analysis scholarship, ethnography scholarship. I studied meta-narration, feminist theory, post-modernism. I wrote, quote mined, and synthesized well into 1996. And I did a lot of writing on the job, no one the wiser. By late July, I had a five-hundred page document. I set the dissertation defense for August.

When it had all been arranged and I was simply fine-tuning the manuscript, I dropped the bomb. We were doing dishes.

"Well," I said with cool nonchalance, "I've got my defense scheduled."

In a sideways glance, I spied the shock, but kept right on drying silverware, the pieces falling into their proper slots. Clink, clank, clunk. After a few seconds, he said, "Oh?" It was not a frivolous "Oh," as in, "Oh, I see." It was the incredulous "Oh?" you'd get when you told someone you'd just won the lottery. Score one for the middle-aged mare who came late to the race.

Yet I wasn't home free. Three of my committee members had been enthusiastic about my dissertation, but for months I'd been worried about the loose cannon, the one with a sociolinguistics background. She called herself Beech Silverwomon. We'd talked about that unusual name. "You didn't want a 'man' in there anywhere, did you?" I asked.

She agreed. Now, as my dissertation defense approached, I was sure that Beech hadn't read my study. I kept calling her to get a sense of her position. She kept putting me off. "Well, I don't see how we can get together any time soon," she pointed out. "My ex is coming to town this weekend, and I haven't seen her for a while."

In all the months I'd been sending my chapters, she'd never said anything good, bad, or indifferent. So a few days before the oral defense, I called her again and asked if we could meet. No, she said, crying. She was having a "crisis."

"All I want to know is, do I have anything to worry about?"

She replied, "You do not have anything to worry about."

Early on August 12, Mom left a message on my answering machine at work.

"I *believe* in you, sweetie! Be the best. Expect the best. Because you *are* the best." She kissed the phone noisily.

The defense turned out to be a celebration rather than a trial by fire. Beech Silverwomon took a shortcut. "Sharyn," she said, "choose one text in your dissertation that is especially indicative of identity formation, and parse it using the techniques of linguistic discourse analysis." She hadn't even picked a passage or formulated a specific question. But I complied, choosing a passage and talking about its modality and its paralinguistic and meta-narrative devices. My discussion satisfied her.

My advisor and the expert in qualitative research asked probing questions, many of which were unanswerable. But I knew why they were unanswerable and, in explaining why, vindicated myself. The outside reader was a young Turk from the astronomy department who had actually read my study. He specialized in cosmology, the beginning of the universe. Oh my God, I thought. So totally symbolic! This is big. This is the beginning!

Just before the defense ended, José and Ethan arrived in the English Department. They waited in the hall. During the defense, Ethan kept peeking through a skinny window in the door; José asked him, "Is Mommy nodding her head or shaking her head?"

After the defense, I stepped out so the committee could deliberate on my performance. In a minute, my advisor came striding forward with an outstretched hand. Typically, doctoral students have to revise and rewrite portions of their work before the committee signs off and the document is submitted to the Graduate School. But mine was approved then and there, without any correction. My advisor said that he'd never seen such a meticulous dissertation. Urging me to send the manuscript to university presses, friends from Social Work started to come, joining José and Ethan in the hallway. There was champagne, and as I finished shaking hands with my committee, the cork blew. I hooted breathlessly, "Oh no! I thought it was a random act of violence!"

No random act of violence could touch us now. We were safe. I was really finished. The only thing left was choosing the blouse that would look most fetching under my black robe on graduation day.

Commencement was held at St. John Arena, a pristine September day. My long-lost child Norah was back in town. Both girls took me to breakfast and attended the ceremony. Everything was straightening out. I'd climbed as high as I could go academically. Tibby and Norah were on my side and at my side. Mom was there, too, grinning ear to ear. Despite her arthritis, she said she'd crawl to the ceremony if it came to that, so proud was she of her daughter's achievement.

I was upbeat for a while, but the thrill of completion soon waned. Yes, having a Ph.D. in your back pocket is a good thing. But I was still a lowly civil servant. And José, in early middle age, was still a T.A., leaping at every temp job that came his way. He wasn't alone in his struggles. Even friends who had landed tenure-track jobs were miserable. Joyce had found employment at Cleveland State as an assistant professor of modern American history; she hated the cold vibe. My friend Kathleen, armed with a new Ohio State Ph.D. in modern European history, complained about her tenure-track job at a college near the Mexican border. She despised the dusty town with its Wal-Mart and fast-food restaurants. She recoiled from the aggressive insects in her apartment. And she was beyond dismayed by her students' lack of preparation. "My God," Kathleen moaned, "--the mascot is a *javalena*!"

I commiserated with her. "You'll die a slow death there, Kathleen."

José disagreed. For him, a tenure-track job was the end-all, be-all. Eleven years before, his hand-written statement of purpose summed it up: "I wish to pursue an M.A. and Ph.D. in European history to secure a university teaching position." Back then, I'd admired the bracing clarity of that sentence. Now, as we drove up High Street after work, he talked about his plans.

"When I finish my degree," he said, "I'll take any tenure-track job I get, even if it means a part-time family life." I was dumbstruck. I wanted progress, yes. That had always been my mantra. But I didn't want to lose my husband. A part-time marriage for the sake of some tenure-track job at some second-rate school?

We stopped at a red light. A battered brown car pulled up next to us. We observed the vehicle—rusted out, dented. A rear window was fractured. The muffler, about gone. On the door, a hand-painted sign: "Humera Taxi Cab Company." Oh gosh, how pitiful, I thought. But with arched eyebrows, José employed the artfully eloquent voice he used when he made fun. "Manuel Humera, CEO and driver."

We broke into chortles that meant, "Boy howdy, things could always be worse!" But I couldn't escape my ambition. I couldn't escape my desire for the American Dream. José was impervious to the false promises of the American Dream, which to him was propaganda that stoked the country's economic engine. Comparing his balance sheet to anybody else's did not occur to him. True, he denigrated the extravagance of the rich and bristled at the corruption of the powerful. He even made fun of middle-class neighbors who used a "lawn service," which he thought was both a waste of money and environmentally bad. But he didn't keep score like I did.

168

One evening, something shifted. I was cooking and José was working on his dissertation. "Dinner's about ready, dear," I called.

"Okay, dear—I'll be right out."

He slid back into the matrix of his scholarship. I stood in the hall, looking at him. A small ink stain marred his right cuff. I took in the broad shoulders, the graceful hands, the fingers tapping as he strived to create something out of nothing. He'd been working all day, but in a minute, he'd sit down, joking with Ethan and me. Afterwards, he'd drink the usual beer while we watched the usual evening news. He is, I thought, so humble, so uncorrupted.

In the kitchen, I tossed the salad and poured Ethan a glass of milk. It hit me. I spent most of my time planning. I was always trying to be "pro-active"--a term José despised. Doesn't sitting back and waiting for things to happen end in disaster? José didn't think so. Despite his ingrained skepticism and despite being a historian, he knew how to live in the moment. He had his worries, but they receded in the face of a good read, a good joke, a good meal.

That night, I told him about my students and their quirks. Some of the male freshmen openly flirted with me; as a 46-year old grandmother, I thought that was hilarious.  But José still disliked the topic. So we talked about grading. I wanted to be fair, I told him, but I also wanted the students to like me. "You aren't their friend," José said seriously. "And don't ever inflate your grades, dear. Doing that not only deprives the students of a chance to grow and learn. Grade inflation devalues your own discipline." Yes, I thought. He's right. The life of the mind is what counts. The life and health of integrity.

After that simple conversation, I resolved to find value in all I had, rather than longing for the things I didn't. It was slowly congealing. I wanted to be like Nabokov's mother, who reveled in contentment when she came upon "a small bird's cuneate footprints on new snow."

6

THE BRIGHTEST HOUR

Be a football to Time and Chance--
--Ralph Waldo Emerson

My friends go to church," Ethan said one day as he ate his grilled cheese sandwich and tomato soup. "Why don't we?" He wasn't complaining, just curious. Ethan's remark took me by surprise. I didn't tell him I'd rejected Catholicism as a teenager. When I forgot my hat, I bobby-pinned a Kleenex to my head. Did God prefer a Kleenex to a bare head? The priest sang out, "Let us proclaim the *mys*-ter-y of faith!" What does that even mean? I cast a sideways glance at Mom. Her pursed lips didn't offer a clue. I thought about millennia of religious warfare,

171

still going full blast. The snubbing of women, the barbaric stance on birth control. No, I wasn't religious.

Yet I could never deny Ethan a learning experience, so in December of '96, I started taking him to Mass. Catholic Church was all I'd known, so we went there. After a few weeks, I decided we'd be going regularly. I pushed aside my faintly intellectual objections. My studies were complete and I was wondering about new things. Why did normal, trustworthy people talk with such certainty about such fanciful notions? Drilling down into a faith community might offer insight on that score. Going to Mass would be a valuable experience for Ethan, too, if only to show him first-hand what I assumed he'd ultimately reject.

On the surface, I got the rhythm of the Mass. The liturgy was pleasingly symmetrical. First, the congregation talked to God. With the Epistle and Gospel, God talked to the us. Then, in the *Confiteor* and the *Our Father*, we talked to God again. Of course, God had the last word, bolstering and admonishing the faithful until the next Sunday.

The literary aspects also interested me. I liked the Gospel readings, parables with didactic turns. The epistles were historical wonders, studded with sexism and references to one's slaves and camels and asses. I also liked that a greasy mechanic could sit next to a dapper professional—true democracy. Most of all, I enjoyed the sense of calm.

After a few weeks, Ethan lost interest in church. He tried to persuade me that he was too tired to get out of bed. In the pew, he squirmed and hissed, "Is it *over* yet?" But I was thinking it was time for Ethan's formal religious instruction. José was skeptical. He'd

172

been raised a Baptist, but from the age of reason had rejected religion. Once he said, "Maybe I can conceive of some power creating the universe, but the divinity of Jesus?" I'd felt the same. In fact, I was even skeptical of some behind-the-scenes intelligence orchestrating the big bang. But I still wanted to enroll Ethan in CCD.

"What's CCD?" José asked.

"I don't know. Christian Doctrine."

"What's the first 'C' for?"

"I don't know—Coherent Christian Doctrine?"

"How about Crock of Christian Doctrine."

Along with the toe-dip into religiosity, 1997 was also the year Ethan and I started a tradition: mother and son road trips. That year, I climbed a little higher on Ohio State's job ladder. And 1997 was also when José turned to his dissertation writing with a vengeance. His vigor came from I knew not where, but he was focused and consistent. He typed steadily, piles of documents and maps and books all around. The dun-colored hair curling at the nape of his neck was threaded with silver now.

In January, I walked over to the History Department and put a copy of José's first chapter in Thorndyke's mailbox. I was thrilled, but José didn't know whether Thorndyke would still be willing to advise him, after so many unproductive years. Two months later, José was still waiting for a response from Thorndyke. Silently bearing the fact of being ignored, he was also putting up with the same old cycle of grinding, temporary teaching jobs. He was always drained. No benefits, no security. Combined with his own psychological struggles and self-doubt, academia had cornered José.

On my end, things were looking up. In February, I told the Dean that I was looking for another job. He countered, offering me a 15% raise to stay. My job title would also be reclassified. I went for it. More money, less stress, and I could keep teaching English courses for a second source of revenue. In my new role, I'd continue to manage the doctoral program, the annual Symposium on Doctoral Research, and the annual Night of Excellence. And now I'd be writing the Dean's speeches along with a biannual newsmagazine called *Intervention.* My résumé would get a makeover.

With the job situation settled, my restlessness spilled onto the home front. In early 1997, I thought about selling our Colonial Hills house for a two-story in a posher neighborhood. But, no. I owed less than $40,000, which I could wipe out in three years. I thought of all the work we'd put into our place, the painting and refinishing, the vegetable garden and shrubs and perennials. I considered our safe, quiet neighborhood, the good schools, the proximity to stores, work, library, and St. Michael's church. That was only part of it. The whole drama of life had unfolded in the house. José and I had courted there. Ethan had known no other dwelling. The house had become a true place. Abandoning it would be like abandoning a faithful canine.

The winter of '97 drew its final breath. At my old friend Peggy's urging, Ethan and I would drive to South Carolina at the end of March for a week-long visit. I pored over the road map, got the car serviced, and signed the leave forms at work.

José stayed home with Molly and Petey. As Ethan and I drove, the weather grew milder and the surroundings, more dramatic--Ohio to Kentucky to eastern Tennessee and into the

Carolinas. A Blue Ridge breeze floated through the open window. José had teasingly warned against rednecks and filthy bathrooms, and said we'd only be able to get buckwheat pancakes. What a smart ass, I thought, smiling. I pictured him, enjoying the solitude, writing and reading, drinking coffee, and scratching the dogs' chests.

With its combination of modern and quaint architecture, Greenville seemed affluent—I had never seen so many BMWs. Peggy's carriage house appealed with its plantation shutters, vaulted ceilings, mirrored walk-in closets, and wet bar. A sole bathroom and bedroom, but a space perfectly suited to a single woman with grown children and no pets. Peggy worked at General Electric, designing wiring plans for turbines. Her salary far outstripped mine, and she treated us to the best of everything.

It was balmy and sunshiny, flowers bursting with color. On day two, we enjoyed coffee and snacks at a darling café, and a seafood restaurant that evening was a good choice because nine-year-old Ethan loved fish, the ocean, and shells of all sorts. The people in the booth behind us were half finished with their meals. As Peggy and I chatted, Ethan whirled around and inserted his face between two adults. He asked, "Could I please have your shells when you're finished eating the creatures inside?" Peggy howled. She loved children's antics.

We explored the Biltmore Estate near Asheville. We drove down to Savannah and luxuriated in a four-star hotel. The breakfasts were complementary—anything we wanted, omelets made to order. Eating in the airy restaurant, we met a middle-aged couple. The man stuck out his hand, stating, "Syracuse!" I wondered, do you identify yourself while on vacation by announcing your point of origin?

We visited Tybee Island and, when his skin pruned, physically removed Ethan from the cold Atlantic. We took in pro-slavery Senator John C. Calhoun's house in Charleston, and enjoyed a carriage ride. We ate nonstop: ice cream, pecan pie, crab chowder. Peggy was hooked on cappuccino, so we drank a lot of that, too. On the last day, we went to a beach south of Charleston, called Isle of Palms. As Ethan body-surfed, Peggy and I gossiped. Friends from fifth grade onwards, Peggy and I talked on the phone at least once a week, but we hadn't seen each other for years. As always, we tried to gauge the truth about one another's lives.

Peggy asked, "Do you really like being married?" She was twice divorced. The first husband was a serial abuser. The second was a nut job. To say that Peggy was sour on marriage, and on men in general, didn't come close. I wasn't going to rub it in, so I just nodded and said, "We enjoy each other. We enjoy Ethan."

"Don't you ever feel claustrophobic?" she asked.

"No," I answered honestly. "We're comfortable in each other's company. And, you know, we depend on each other. We like each other. We laugh about the same stuff."

After a few seconds, she asked, "Do you feel like you're, I don't know, subservient?"

"No, oh no, Peggy. No. José believes in marriage equality. He lives it. He always has."

For a time, Peggy stared at the ocean. "Well, I mean, do you ever have to pick up after him? –his socks? His dirty dishes?"

"No. José is tidy and organized."

"He must have some fault, Sharyn."

I wasn't going to mention the dissertation rut, or the smoking. I asked, "Well, what about you? Are you ever lonely? Do you ever feel the need for a partner?"

"*No!*" Peggy said, laughing at the idea. "Oh God, no! I'm just where I want to be, the master of my own universe! I love, love, love my freedom!"

I didn't want freedom from José, but on that trip, Peggy taught me a few things. Driving back to Ohio, in between Ethan's imaginative romps, including a long-winded story about "Prince Ethan the Third," I thought of Peggy's unrushed manner of doing things, from applying makeup to swiping her credit card to purchasing gasoline. Thin hands and long fingers tipped with polished nails, she performed these mundane tasks with slow, pleasurable deliberation.

"The best way to approach a vacation," Peggy insisted, "is to follow a general itinerary but to stay flexible and relaxed." I thought Peggy's recipe should be applied to life itself. It dawned that I'd always been in a rush. Peggy's example encouraged me to cultivate calm and mindfulness. Like Peggy, I tried to luxuriate in every little movement, reading the morning paper in bed until 7:30, drinking my coffee slowly, breathing deeply as I walked the dogs. I tried not to care when I was late for work. After all, the Dean himself had told me to take time off during the lulls.

Back in Ohio, nothing was in bloom yet. But Ethan was a blooming Catholic by May, baptized at the Newman Center near the campus. He also received First Communion that day. Afterwards, when Ethan was no longer a pagan but a true child of God, we enjoyed a cake reception at home. As I got things ready, I hugged José. He'd been gracious at the ceremony I'd forced on him.

After his baptism, Ethan better tolerated the Mass--getting in line for communion broke up the hour-long trial. I continued to enjoy it, too, suppressing troubling questions about hierarchy, bureaucracy, sexism, and ultimate reality.

A few days after Ethan's baptism, a kid in his class tried to pick a fight with him.

Ethan said, "Scott, I was just baptized, okay? I don't want to fight."

May was the month when José returned to the solace of his garden, tending to his vegetables and the explosion of red carnations with spear-like foliage lining the fence. He was also busy in the garage, trying to inject life into the long-dead Rabbit. He'd hoisted the engine out; it hung precariously on a triple-thick chain and giant pulley. José was teaching himself about auto repair; several manuals were spread on the workbench. One at a time, he'd purchased the tools needed for the overhaul. But the car still wasn't running.

Around this time, I began to feel a vague foreboding about José. He looked drawn and grey. I dismissed those feelings. Now that the strain of winter was past, he was busy and cheerful--grading, working on the dissertation, mowing the lawn, fiddling with the car, doing the laundry, weeding the garden. I pushed away the disquiet to deal with my own problems. One of them was Mom. Out of the cosmos, when I least expected it, Mom lobbed a grenade.

On an ordinary Friday in the spring of '97, I called to ask her and the dogs to come on Sunday for our usual movie and lunch. I had to call every Friday--a standing invitation wasn't good enough.

178

"Well, we won't be coming this week," she said, "and just ask Ethan the reason why."

Mystified, I asked her what he did or didn't do. She refused to say.

After we hung up, I asked Ethan. He didn't know. But when he thought about it, he remembered that his nephew, four-year old Devlin, had been over. They'd been roller skating on the driveway when Mom drove up. Ethan said slowly, "Well, maybe I didn't talk to Grandma as much as I should have."

At my insistence, Ethan called his grandma to apologize. Afterwards, José got on the phone. "I'm sorry if your feelings are hurt," he said sympathetically, "But Ethan isn't sophisticated enough to deliberately snub you, Betty. His attention had just been on Devlin."

Mom loved and respected Saint Joseph. Yet despite his coaxing, Mom did not come that weekend, and she harbored a seething grudge against Ethan for weeks after.

In June, Mom had a hip replacement. The night before the operation, I hosted an awards event in Social Work, getting into bed after midnight. I left the house the following morning at 4:00 a.m. to take Mom to the hospital. The procedure went well, but she was in pain for days, not eating and throwing up her water. She couldn't sleep despite pain meds.

While Mom was hospitalized, José and I took care of Mom's dog. Without Jenny the Great Dane, Mom was desolate. One morning before dawn, knowing I'd be sleeping, she called José to ask if he'd drive Jenny to the hospital, "to reassure her of Mommy's whereabouts."

Sure enough, later that morning, José happily drove downtown with Jenny. He and Jenny strolled into the hospital. He took her into the elevator and up to the fifth floor, where the nurses and physical therapists showered attention on the big black dog. José and Mom had a special bond. He was always eager to please her. But I was mad that Mom called José behind my back, asking him to make the extra effort when we were already doing what seemed like a lot.

Mom was a troublemaker in the hospital. She got into a tiff with the nurses about the food, which she couldn't eat anyway. She lectured me, José, the nurses, and her roommates about the perversity of meat-eating, and about whole foods versus processed foods. I didn't disagree with that, but her tone was so high-handed.

"Can you believe they serve white rice instead of brown? -- in a hospital? --where people are trying to get *well*?"

Looking at the menu, she spat sarcasm. "What's a 'vegetable medley'? That's got to be from a can."

And, "If you can't find me a simple baked potato in this whole hospital, I just give up."

In Mom's slipper, the nurses found a cache of contraband—vitamins, minerals, and herbs. The pharmacist had to analyze everything. This process started another brouhaha, when Mom got on her soapbox about the ineptitude of the FDA and the dangers of hospital drugs. She fought anybody who tried to give her a sponge bath.

One day, a nurse took me aside.

"Can I ask you something personal? Does she drink?"

I stared back. "No, Mom isn't a drinker."

The nurse shook her head, baffled. She said that Mom exhibited the "typical, confrontational, compulsive behavior of an alcoholic."

I was relieved to hear an objective bystander come to that conclusion. It wasn't me. It was Mom. The hospital staff must have been glad to see her go, six days post op. I'd always loved my mother, but, like the nurses, I experienced her unprovoked ire with disorienting regularity. It was like stepping in the dark on a stair that isn't there. I never got used to it.

Things did start to return to normal. A month after the surgery, Mom drove over with Jenny. She and I ate lunch and watched the 1992 film, *The Fugitive*—she loved Tommy Lee Jones. She got all tense during thrillers, and I chuckled silently at her reaction.Meanwhile, José was in the home office, working on his dissertation.

In August, I took a week off work.I wanted to relax, read, watch videos, listen to books on tape, and go to the pool with Ethan. But José didn't rest. In between his reading and writing, he was now looking for any sort of administrative or professional job at Ohio State--academic advisor or something similar. We both knew that he needed more than the part-time teaching job at the seminary. His funding in the History Department had dried up.

One hot day, as Ethan and I left the pool, our arms full of towels and books and sunscreen, I spotted a naked baby bird next to a brick stairway. Its skin was impossibly delicate, a peachy blue color. It was alive, its head wobbling on a stem-like neck. I picked it up.

The bird lay almost motionless on my left thigh as we drove home, tiny naked wings and yellow claws, whisker thin. I interrupted José's dissertation work to show him. Immediately taking over, he lined a food storage container with a piece of soft fabric, and set the little bird into it. It lay very still, but the tiny rib cage was moving. José ground peanuts into a fine gruel, added a bit of water, and with an eyedropper fed the bird a drop or two. The creature seemed to rally. For a couple of days, it eagerly swallowed. Even so, I thought it was hopeless, and was sorry that I'd interfered with nature's plan. But José hovered over the nestling. He called him "Speedy." Despite his efforts, the bird lost strength, and on day four, it stopped moving. José kept watch until the little body gave up its warmth. He put the lid on the plastic box. With Ethan's help, he buried the bird near the vegetable garden.

Summer and fall of 1997 was a time of equilibrium. I was even starting to enjoy my newly-framed job in Social Work. Relieved of the burden of my studies and making a decent wage, I thought, all jobs have a downside—heck, even tenured faculty have to put up with bureaucratic nonsense and department politics. I felt fortunate, on an even keel.

In October of 1997, I planned a weekend trip to Put-In-Bay on Lake Erie. José was coming. It would be our first family vacation in ages. I reserved a fishing cabin at East Point Cottages. It sounded so romantic. The accommodations, the proprietor promised, were "as nice as your own place." The cottage had a fridge and microwave and stove. All we had to do was bring food, sheets for the beds, and towels for the bathroom. It would be too cold for Ethan to swim, but there was a dock near the cottage, and he could fish with poles that had belonged to José's dad. We'd bring food and firewood--the innkeeper said there was a fire pit outside the cabin. I pictured a mini-Hyannis Port.

We loaded the Dodge Colt with our stuff and with Molly and Petey, and set out. We crossed Lake Erie on a ferry and drove onto the island. In half an hour, we pulled up a rutted driveway next to the lake. We entered a small office. Next to the desk stood an old rounded refrigerator with a hand-made sign: "Milk, Cheese, Bait." A wizened, tattooed fellow with black fingernails gave us a key to our cabin. We opened the door and breathed in damp mustiness. We stared at the bare linoleum with raw, unsecured edges, the broken-down couch, the sagging double bed with stained mattress. So we got a clean, bland, dog-friendly motel room, ate dinner at a family restaurant, and laughed at my romantic longings.

The next month was November. On Thanksgiving, I cooked. Mom, Tibby, Norah, and Devlin joined José, Ethan, and me. The night before, I made three desserts: homemade pumpkin and pecan pies and a cherry cheesecake—the crust made of pulverized walnuts, butter, and brown sugar. I roasted a 21-pound bird and fixed all the other good things along with fresh cranberry orange relish and a sherry reduction gravy.

The usual catastrophes ensued: After dinner, Molly the ever-hungry basset hound decided to see what remained of the meal. Her claws got stuck in the lace tablecloth, and the sugar bowl, creamer, and candlesticks ended up on the floor. I also cut myself on aluminum foil.

At Christmas, Vin was in town again to see the girls, but his real hope was to worm his way into my house. It was José who asked him to come for Christmas dinner. "Otherwise, dear," he said, "Vin will have to spend the day alone in Tibby's apartment."

In the face of such heart, I couldn't object. "Well, but what are we going to tell Mom?" I reminded him that Mom had hated Vin for years, and not without reason. She often spoke ill of him in front of the girls. Now, Mom and Vin would both be coming for Christmas dinner. José wasn't concerned, even though Vin himself expressed his trepidation about seeing Betty for the first time in ten years.

"Geez, I dunno, José," he said sheepishly. "I mean, Betty might not be too thrilled."

José said that he'd handle Betty.

On Christmas Day, Mom came earlier than everyone else, and after she sat down, José told her about Vin's imminent arrival. "Now be *good*," José admonished her with a twinkle.

Vin showed up wearing a tuxedo. The get-up suggested both his immaturity and his wish to show how much he appreciated the invitation. Tibby and a date named Tom drove up in his Jaguar. Devlin was polite and hungry, and Norah was back in Ohio again, too.

Mom behaved admirably at Christmas, but by early January, she was up to her old tricks. On one of our Sunday lunch and movie dates, she brought a toy horse for our big dog, Petey. The buff-colored horse whinnied, which appealed to five-year old Devlin, Mom's great grandson, who was spending the day. Devlin carried the horse into Ethan's bedroom, but Mom was watching. She loudly remarked, "I hope those little kids aren't playing with that horse. I brought it for *Petey*."

Nineteen-ninety-eight was a productive, happy year. In January, José taught at both Ohio State and the Josephinum. But he still seemed careworn. It wasn't anything specific, and I brushed aside the feeling. After all, he was teaching several sections of European history and busy writing his dissertation. Who wouldn't look a little peaked? He'd completed three chapters by now, putting each new installment into Thorndyke's mailbox. But after 15 months, Thorndyke still hadn't responded. José didn't know whether his advisor had even begun to read his work. "Bastard," I thought.

My mind drifted to a sultry Fourth of July a few years earlier. Dana, my boss-friend, invited us to a cookout, with fireworks afterwards. After saying no many times before, I thought we shouldn't wriggle out of yet another invitation. José acquiesced, but he had no interest. He hated the heat, and a barbecue in that weather would be torture. He despised being trapped in situations where he couldn't smoke. And then there were the strangers. José was always shy around people who might force shallow chatter on him. From the get-go, he'd been prejudiced against Social Work. He'd never figured out just what it is that social workers do. He was skeptical of the legitimacy of their academic inquiries, and was dubious about their methods of scholarship.

Now he sat in a lawn chair on Dana's patio, dark green polo shirt open at the neck. Wearing lightweight trousers and leather sandals, a hot breeze lifted strands of his hair, but I could tell he was suffering. Bart Brown told a joke and everyone burst into merriment. The chatter escalated and overlapped. As she filled glasses and flipped burgers, Dana erupted into peals of laughter. Everyone was game except José. When he smiled, it was stiffly. When a pleasantry came his way, he was supposed to shoot one back. His heart wasn't in it.

He picked at his baked beans. What a waste of time, he was thinking. The unexpected tidbits that one uncovers in historical research were calling. That very morning, he said he was finding curious incidences of 1918-era French soldiers cursing the big cheeses on the General Staff. "--calling their superiors '*cochons*' and saying '*foutre* this' and '*foutre* that' can mean only one thing," he said. He paused as another idea occurred. "--maybe it's true that one skewers in French, but hammers in German and English." With so many leads, José was not happy at a cookout, nor was he looking forward to the fireworks. But after dinner, he had to march right along with the rest of us, across High Street and over to the Park of Roses.

Acres of people were already there, relaxing on folding chairs and camped on beach towels. The display wouldn't happen for a while; it was only just twilight. The air was oppressive. As we sweated, Dana energetically led the way, muscular legs pumping. We followed obediently. She dodged and forged, herding us as close as possible to the blast-off point. For José, it was like the Bataan Death March. We kept going, ten minutes. Fifteen. Twenty. Suddenly, José's eyes fell on the last person he wanted to see. On the grass to our right, in the middle of a sea of others, lounging on a tan blanket, was Professor Thorndyke.

There was no mistaking him. The Francophile nose that went on forever, the short goatee, the head with its fleshy underpinnings. In baggy shorts and a black tee that hugged his bulbous middle, he propped himself on an elbow next to a supine blond male. Their faces were close. Thorndyke's eyes riveted themselves on the companion, and the young man listened to whatever Thorndyke was telling him. For a split second, we took it in. Then José trained his eyes on the backside of the social worker ahead of us.

The firework display went on and on. After 11:00, we headed home, starting and stopping and starting up again as the traffic dispersed. José said he hoped that Thorndyke hadn't noticed us. He muttered, "Golly Ned!" Now, two years later, I thought of the man lolling on a blanket. I thought of his disregard for my husband, not taking even a minute to call or email about the chapters that had regularly appeared in his mailbox. I was furious and disgusted with Thorndyke. But part of me was glad that José had seen Thorndyke and his pretty young boyfriend. Now he knew how his advisor was spending his time.

The year 1998 flew by, warp speed. We looked after Ethan, who had homework, Cub Scouts, rugby, and violin practice. There was always laundry, grocery shopping, yard work. José and I shared carpooling duties, often taking Ethan to a friend's house or a birthday party. José cooked dinner many nights, frequently making his specialty, "Fireman's Chicken." Chicken breasts and sage dressing, covered with mushroom sauce and sherry, and topped with melting Swiss cheese. José and I enjoyed the dish, but Ethan always whined, "Oh no, *not* Fireman's Chicken *again*!"

I walked the dogs, but José routinely fed them. "Presentation is everything," he'd say, adding choice leftovers to the dry food. He mixed it on the countertop and announced that night's fare. "We haaaave: roast chicken, giblet garni, and chow! Come on!" Molly and Petey didn't need more urging.

That summer, I began to plan a three-week cross-country camping trip. In bed at night, I pored over the road atlas, mesmerized by the names of faraway western places: Sweetwater Station, Wyoming. Shoshone, Idaho. Hungry Horse, Montana. So vivid and dramatic. So far removed from Worthington, Ohio. I loved to think ahead and plan for all sorts of exciting contingencies. Ethan and I would depart in late July; I'd rent a car, leaving the Dodge Colt at home for José. He'd take good care of Petey and Molly.

As I planned the excursion, Jenny the Great Dane died. A few weeks later, Mom decided that she needed a new Great Dane pup. Dogs were her religion. Once she mentioned that the word "dog" is "God" spelled backwards, as if that proved anything. I was against Mom's decision to get a puppy. At age 76 and with her physical limitations, I thought Mom was crazy to take on another Great Dane. But as usual, she got her way.

José, Ethan, and I drove her to a breeder in Powell, Ohio. Inside the kennel, she hobbled ahead of us, swinging her cane. A few bitches with distended teats lay here and there, lethargically lifting their heads as we passed. As they took nourishment, the wriggling whelps looked like bizarre appendages. In the back, a big fawn male barked. Ugh, I thought. Like the world needs more dogs.

At a safe distance, José and I followed Mom. Her right foot turned at a right angle; her back was hunched and twisted. Stopping at the pen holding older puppies, weaned and ready for sale, Mom and the breeder discussed temperaments and personalities. Watching the unfolding spectacle, I whispered to José. If anything happens to

Mom, I said, the new dog will end up with us. "Yes dear," he whispered back. "I know."

After lengthy consideration, Mom chose a merle female, eight weeks old. The puppy's ears had already been cropped and taped, like mini-antlers. That was another practice I detested. "There should be a law," I thought as Mom officiously signed the papers and picked up the breeding certificate. Now the dog was Mom's. Jody was her name, after St. Joseph.

A few weeks later, we gathered in Mom's backyard, watching the big leggy puppy gambol around. My cousin Valerie was with us that day, and something caught her eye. Mom had arranged a dozen giant plastic balls, bright turquoise-blue, in a pyramid shape in the corner of her yard. Propped against the fence, the ball structure was eight feet across and six feet high. The purpose, Mom had explained, was to combat weed growth. So far, that plan wasn't working. Valerie hadn't been warned, and at the sight, she stopped in her tracks.

With a smile, José remarked, "Valerie, your aunt has balls."

In June, long-anticipated construction work on the house began. We were adding a master bath. We also updated our sad little kitchen with new cabinets, floor, and countertops: after ten long years, the ugly circular burn would be history. The week after the renovation began, I caught wind of a job opening in West European Studies, something to do with program planning. They were looking for a person with a background in European history. When the announcement came across my desk, I called José right away. After some convincing, he emailed his résumé to the Program Director.

He got the job immediately, sight unseen. After that, he joked, "I only get jobs for which I don't interview in person."

His title would be Assistant Director, West European Studies Program. Or, as he privately said, "Factotum." He started his new job the next morning. It was a wonderful turn of events. But a nagging worry about José kept surfacing. Something wasn't right, my gut told me. Again, I dismissed it—with everything going on, he was sure to be anxious, I thought. The new job, our home improvement project, and Ethan's and my cross-country trip.

On July 31st, Ethan and I headed off. José didn't pretend to be disappointed that he wasn't coming—he'd never been infatuated with the idea of "the open road," and he was neither a camper or a physical adventurer. Where I'd see wonder in a vast expanse of nature, he'd see a wasteland. While I'd enjoy small-talk with local strangers, finding out about their culture and viewpoints, he'd cringe at the idea. At heart, José was a city boy. The bigger the city, the better. It wasn't only the cultural and architectural riches. José disliked the nosy surveillance of small town neighbors, preferring the sophisticated anonymity of Manhattan or Chicago. He thought Columbus barely big enough. In José's mind, small western towns were "miserable little outposts of commerce." We wrote to him from those miserable little outposts almost every day.

7/31/98

Dear Dad,

I am in Illinois and I am really excited! I will bring you back something nice. Our rental car is working well. It has air conditioning. One time Mom got lost and I read a book to her, to cheer her up.

Love, Ethan

Dear Dad,

We are in Nebraska. And we just crossed the Mississippi. Now we are staying in a nice motel. It is fun! I wish you could be here. The town we are in is called Kearney and it is pretty cool! The motel has a pool. How are you feeling? I'm OK. At first Mom wanted to spend the night in a dump. And we saw a plane dusting a field.

8/1/98

Dear,

Most of the day was spent traveling through Iowa. From the east to the west, Iowa is farmland –there's always a farm on both sides of the interstate. And very well cared for places with silver-topped silos—I didn't see one shack in five hours. Rolling hills, bluffs, and the trees are different: they grow in clumps, shorter, scrubbier.

Nebraska--. It's incredible how adjacent states can exude such different qualities—N. is not only flat, but its cities (from what I've seen) are flea bitten and depressed. On to Wyoming.

We were going to stay at the youth hostel in Lincoln, at the University. When we looked at the beds w/o sheets and linoleum floor, we immediately thought of "East Point Cottages" at Lake Erie! Ethan said, "This is a dump, Mom." So we drove on, another 120 miles west, to Kearney, NE (where we're going to church tomorrow morning). Got a room at a Best Western motel with 2 pools and a sauna--they provide a free breakfast.

Forgot to say that we've seen hundreds of bikers on their way to Sturges, SD in the Black Hills. At a rest stop, a female biker said that the convention draws about 400,000 from around the globe; she says the traffic jam there is something to behold. She claims it's a blast.

Please give Mr. Petey a hug and kiss—and tell him I'm coming home. (Kiss Molly, too.) -- Are you eating and sleeping well? Please take care of yourself for me.
Ethan and I love you, lots.
S.

Day 3, Kearney NE to Laramie WY 8/2/98
Dear,

After a cup of coffee, I woke Ethan and we left for St. James' church for the 8:00 Mass. I got us there, in an unfamiliar town, right at 8:00. Modern structure, no live music, parishioners are generally old timers, probably farmers. The lector actually wore one of those Western string ties. They have a gifted priest, a young guy with great stage presence, a subtle and compelling speaker.Ethan was glad it lasted only 45 min. They also had whole wheat communion wafers, which he dislikes. So he drank the wine.

Kearney NE is a plain-as-a-post town, clapboard houses in need of paint, the usual motel and fast food chains. Glad to live in Worthington.

We're back at our motel now—ate a "free" breakfast which was not memorable. Now Ethan is swimming and trying out the

192

whirlpool, sauna, and weight room. I told him he could goof around for an hour after breakfast before we take off for Laramie. More later today . . . . (Oh, I bought the local Sunday paper, The Kearney Hub-- ! I'll bring home.)

8/3/98

It's Mon. morning. Ethan is sleeping in the Best Western Gaslite Inn in Laramie, Wyoming—it's 6:30 a.m. but I've been up since 5:30. Our routine is falling into place: I get up, wash, put in my contacts, do my makeup, get dressed. Then I search for coffee: in this case, there's a little electric pot on the sink. As I drink my daily 2-cup allotment, I take stock of the money situation, decide when to depart, and sit down to write to you. This is a much appreciated solitude; as you know, going anywhere w/ E. can be demanding. So, I'll let the little guy sleep, and will fill you in on yesterday.

Back 2 days: We had been exceedingly disappointed in Eastern NE—grey, flat; Lincoln is a sad, gritty little Midwestern city w/ a rather embarrassing "downtown." The Univ. of NE was deserted; only about 1/10 the size of Ohio State, and the stadium seems to be in the process of being constructed—it's only half there. Yesterday, as we went west from Kearney, we were underwhelmed for 4 more hours. (It takes 8 hours to drive thru NE.) But as we approached the western edge of the state, we began to see dramatic cliffs. The trees disappeared almost entirely. Farmland turned into ranchland.

About 4/5 through the state, we had to get gas. Only 1/8 of a tank. We passed several exits—nothing. Finally, a little sign w/ a gas pump on it, so we took the exit. Talk about emptiness—we drove 3 mi. east to a place called Lodgepole. This was truly a ghost town. We not only couldn't find any gas, we couldn't find any people. A deserted fire dept., a little "sundries" store without activity. Zero. I was getting worried when I spied 3 old guys shooting the breeze in front of the Linger Longer Lounge.

They said I'd have to drive 18 miles to Sidney for gas, but recommended using the 2-lane S.R. 30. So we headed west on the deserted country road. I let Ethan steer to get my mind off the gas troubles, and to give him a thrill. So he unbuckled, hopped next to me, and helped me steer for 5 miles as I worked the gas. He did a good job. We made it to Sidney, I gassed up, and everything turned out.

Well, western NE and eastern WY are pretty neat. Ethan has been raving about the "huge, awesome mountains." I gave him his camera, and he took several "sweet" pictures yesterday afternoon.

We got a nice motel room in Laramie, and luckily there's a Safeway and a K-Mart next door. We've been eating out of the cooler--o.j., milk, cereal, fruit, peanut butter, crackers, cookies, hero rolls, sliced turkey, and two kinds of cheese. Yesterday, Ethan ate Frosted Mini Wheats dry in the car, and drank milk out of the quart-sized milk jug. No spills, and it kept him busy. In a minute I'm going to wake him up—it's 7:00, time to roll up to Dubois, high in the Wind River mountain range, 300 mile trip, mostly on 2-lane roads. We'll see what happens! We cross the Continental Divide today.

Love you lots, S.

Day #4, Laramie to Dubois, WY

Dear,

We left Laramie at 8:00, a drab little town but a surprisingly handsome university. When I opened the motel door this a.m., I was shocked at how cold it was.

Driving through the mountains, with sporadic showers and bursts of brilliant sun, was surreal. During our 5 hr.+ drive through stretches of empty sagebrush-covered prairie, we felt ourselves constantly rising—ears popping. Gorgeous cloud-festooned mountains covered with pine forests, fantastic rock formations, and enormous red buttes that look like castles with a hundred wings. We saw a spectacular reddish-wine canyon, set back from the silver-green prairie, just as the finale of Beethoven's 9th came on the CD player. Tears came to my eyes.

The trouble with all this rapturous beauty is that Ethan became frustrated. He wanted to park the car along this skinny little berm so he could climb and explore. I pointed out that there were fences everywhere, meant to keep people out. He grew sullen. At 11:30 we pulled into a little town called Lander, and headed into a McDonald's to use the bathroom. I spoke to an Indian woman, a social worker for a reservation. I asked her where we could go for Ethan to safely run around. She said, Sinks Canyon State Park, about 15 minutes away. We headed there, found it with no trouble.

A most beautiful place. We had the place to ourselves. I put together a picnic, but Ethan was too excited to eat. He dashed here and there—the Wind River, complete with deafening rapids, bordered the picnic area. On top of that, there was a mammoth rock formation he wanted to climb. He didn't get very far, luckily! And, he found a snakeskin. I made him put in a Ziploc bag. He was in 7th heaven, and in a great mood the rest of the day.

Now we're in the Black Bear Country Inn, which isn't too bad. I was dreading a repeat of "East Point Cottages." Because it's not a chain, it's sort of funky--an old RCA TV with no remote; frayed washcloths; stained walls; a microwave and refrig., but neither works – (oh, and the tub's "cold" and "hot" knobs are reversed, making for a zesty bathing experience). We got here at 2:30, and had a delightful day—the Wind River is right behind the motel. I watched Ethan play there for 40 min. After that, we walked all over this little western place. We saw people on horseback, a prairie dog and the corresponding holes, and we climbed a rocky outcropping and sat looking at the action below. The topper: two rainbows—a startling sight, framed in mountains, patches of bright blue sky interspersed with thunderheads.

Well, it's nearly 7:30 p.m. Tomorrow, up at 4:30 to get to Grand Tetons by 6:00 so we'll get a campsite. I'm a bit nervous about camping—wish you were here. Miss you tons. How's the kitchen coming? You're probably going cuckoo. More later.

Love, S.

8/3/98

Dear Dad,

I am in Wyoming and we went to Sinks canyon and it was awsom! I really hope you are feeling good and me and Mom climbed a mountain and it was great even though Mom wasn't so brave.
Love, Ethan

Day 5, Dubois WY to Grand Tetons 8/4/98
Dear,

Woke up at 3:15. Had a wakeful night, listening to car doors slam, motorcycles pull in and depart, people's loud voices through thin walls. I had to get up early anyway, for a chance at a decent campsite--first come, first served. So, bleary eyed, I packed the car, got myself ready, and woke Ethan. The plan was that he'd sleep in the back, but of course he didn't.

We left at 5:00 a.m. I mailed your letter in the Dubois mailbox and proceeded through the deserted town. Only the faintest trace of light behind us, at the world's eastern edge. We had to travel up a winding mountain range—the park is 50+ miles away. In the darkness, and with dense patches of fog, I gripped the steering wheel, dreading a collision with an animal. As the day brightened, we gasped out loud when we saw the enormous teeth-like mountains in the distance. Bathed in the pink light of dawn, it's just unbelievable. Whatever I say will be a cliché—but I did not expect such a place.

We didn't get our hoped-for Jenny Lake campsite, but had to drive north to Colter Bay. Made a bunch of wrong turns in the meantime, so it wasn't all peachy. But our campsite is very nice. We *had only a little difficulty pitching the tent. There's a picnic table, tall pines giving privacy; the air mattress seems to work. We pitched the tent and ate some Golden Grahams with slightly sour milk, dutifully locking the food in the car. Bears are everywhere—black and grizzly. We tried to walk down to the water but there was only a steep precipice. So we got in the car, drove 5 min. to the Jackson Lake marina, and rented a canoe. $8.00 for one hour. Ethan in front, me in back. Despite the life vests, I was terrified—my precious camera was in my fanny pack and, with every little bobble, I was sure we were capsizing. But Ethan was fearless, a really excellent seaman! He said, "Ok, Mom, you paddle on one side for three strokes, and I'll paddle on the other. I'll say 'change' and we'll switch sides. OK, one, two, three, change!"*

After a few minutes of only the sound of oars hitting the water, Ethan piped up again. "Should we do battle speed or ramming speed?" I cracked up. Here we were, in the middle of a huge, glacial lake, framed by the most magnificent mountains. Weather—80 degrees, brilliant day. We saw a bald eagle circle above and land in its eyrie atop a 50-ft. pine. At the end of the canoe ride, I felt pretty comfortable with it.

The crowds aren't bad—in fact, when we returned to our campsite ("N Loop, Site 310") for lunch at 1:30, there wasn't a bloody soul around for 2 hours. After eating, we drove to Jenny Lake where Ethan went swimming in icy, crystal clear water. I spoke to a nice Jewish couple from Connecticut. Next, we took a long hike.

Now I'm sitting in the tent, writing this at 8:45 p.m. Ethan is poking the embers of the fire he built. He roasted a few marshmallows. He must be tired—as I surely am—because despite our most exciting day and complete delight with this paradise, Ethan complained several times about not being able to climb the Tetons. I miss you horribly and am pretty homesick. Hope you're getting along with the dogs and their walks—hope work is going well, and that the renovation is coming along. Tell my Mom I'm thinking of her. I'll call you tomorrow night from Gooding, Idaho.

Love you always, S.

8/4/98

Dear Dad,

This trip is very fun but I do miss you and Molly and Pete. I am in the grand Tetons. They are the highest montins I have ever seen! We went to Jenny lake and it was very fun plus the water was very clear. And we went canoeing and Mom was very scard! How are you doing? It must be pretty boring back in Ohio! Mom got lost trying to find the campsite. Well I better close this up now or never.

Love, Ethan

Day 6, Grand Tetons 8/5/98

Dear,

Well, we survived our first night in a tent, lows in the 40s. Now, at 7:00 a.m., my fingers are so cold I can hardly hold the pen. The restroom is about 50 yards from here. Just got back, opened the thermos, made instant coffee w/ lukewarm water, and washed my face w/ the rest of it. Sleeping in a tent isn't that comfy, although I did get 7 decent hours of rest. But it's amazing to wake up in the middle of the night and gaze into the starry sky through the mesh roof. No bears yet, but this place is teeming with wildlife—big horn sheep, buffalo, elk, coyotes, even wolves. I'd love to see a moose. Yesterday a darling little prairie dog kept coming into our campsite—it was especially interested in the CD player. We depart for the hostel in Gooding, Idaho, about 325 mi. from here, in about 90 minutes. Hoping it's acceptable. I'll do laundry tonite. More later.

Dear,

It's now 10:00 p.m. A hot day, 102. The southern part of Idaho is barren. On our way, we visited Craters of the Moon—a black, desolate field of lava, 20 miles in length. Gooding's a tiny town with a feed store and a whistle stop. The B&B is fine, not opulent but pleasant, and a pleasant proprietor. I was able to wash and dry 2 loads of clothes here ($.50 per load). We ate at a Wendy's, had a lemonade, and later, Dairy Queens. Tomorrow we're heading to the coast. I'm not sure I can do it in my present state, but I'll try. Will mail this tomorrow. Keep a stiff upper lip w/ all the remodeling. Love you, S.

8/6/98

Dear Dad,

Now we are staying in a bed and breakfast. It is really nice. I am now in Idaho. We have decided to go strate to the ocean in Oregon. I spend most of my time playing with a bouncy ball. How are you and the dogs doing?

Love, Ethan

Day 8 Oregon Coast and Northern California 8/7/98

Dear,

We've driven 2,930 miles, and so far, I've spent $98.37 on gas. Sorry the last part of the last letter was so rushed. I was exhausted at 10:00 p.m. after driving all day in 100 degree heat through the wasteland of south central Idaho. But my exhaustion didn't result in a quick slumber. Ethan and I were restless in our twin beds: he dropped off after 11:00 p.m., and it took me til after midnight to conk off.

The place wasn't bad—a few old guys in red shirts watching TV in the common room. Two young college girls from Wisconsin, a red-headed man traveling to Las Cruces, NM. Everyone was quiet and minded their own business. The hotel is over 100 year old—4 bathrooms on the 2nd floor. No a.c., but we used a ceiling fan, which was fairly effective. You could get to our room two ways: via the front door, up two flights of stairs, down two long halls. Or, you could take the outside staircase from the side yard. The evening we arrived, I hung wet beach towels on the "balcony" with badly peeling paint, and it was by this stairway that Ethan and I made our silent getaway at 6:00 a.m. this morning.

Ethan actually slept for two hours, till 8:00 a.m., as I drove toward the Oregon State line. It's not fair to condemn a place as big (and presumably as lovely) as Idaho based only on a brief drive through one of its most desolate parts. Still, I loved Wyoming, and Idaho didn't feel right. I couldn't wait to get to the coast, and some semblance of civilization.

So yes, we actually drove 650+ miles yesterday, from central Idaho, through Boise, through the whole state of Oregon. And me with only five hours' sleep the previous night. As I mentioned on the phone, I just wasn't up to driving to Crater Lake and camping there. Although driving to the coast would be an even <u>longer</u> drive, I thought it would be great to get to the ocean for Ethan's sake, and I also thought the route would be easier than the one to Crater Lake. I wasn't prepared for what we encountered.

There's just no way to avoid the Cascade Range when traveling east-west through Oregon. And when you have mountains, you get winding roads. The first small problem occurred in eastern Oregon, about 100 mi. west of the Idaho line. Ethan decided to lie down, and got extremely on 30 minutes of hairpin turns. I pulled into the Blueberry Muffin Café, a teeny shack on Route 26 West. The locals looked up and stared at us, as if we'd just landed from Mars. I got Ethan a 7-Up with cracked ice to ease his car sickness. The cashier was upset when I handed him a $20. Anyway, after drinking the 7-Up and a cool cloth on his head, Ethan's eyes weren't so sunken.

We passed into the Pacific Time Zone and I whooped, gaining another hour. A good day for it, believe me. We went on and on and on—Oregon is quite beautiful, and becomes more so as you approach the Cascade Range. On Rt. 26, signs warned of livestock; Ethan spied a wild mustang peeking over a red butte high above the highway.

I decided to head towards the southern Oregon coast, and to do that, figured that we could take a mountain byway that would lead us to 126 West, which goes through Eugene and all the way to the ocean. Well, MacKenzie Pass won't be soon forgotten. Forty-five miles of turns so sharp you must have both hands on the steering wheel and a foot on the brake pedal at all times. The dense pine forest on either side of the narrow 2-lane road produced deep shadows, which along with sporadic bursts of brilliant sunshine made it nearly impossible to see the road. And the constant SUVs barreling along on the other side—. I prayed we'd come out unscathed—if Ethan had been sick to his stomach before, now it was my turn.

It was dreadful. Kind of a shame, because the place itself is fairy-tale quality. The trunks on these pines are red, smooth, and maybe 50 to 80 feet tall. Redwoods??

One thing that helped me get thru was listening to <u>Into Thin Air</u>, the account of the doomed 1996 expedition on Mt. Everest. Jon Krakauer. My problem didn't seem so bad compared to the empty oxygen canisters, frostbitten toes, pulmonary edema, deliria. Ethan also enjoyed this long book (we haven't finished it yet). And he was excellent all day. Very sweet guy. At 6:30. we got to the Chateau Motel in Florence, OR, a few miles from the coast. For 30 minutes, I tried to find the beach, but gated communities thwarted us. I hated to disappoint Ethan, who had been such as stalwart traveler. Now, nearly 9:00 Fri. morning, we are off to cavort on the beach by the

Pacific. It's very chilly (55 degrees), with bright blue sky. More tonight.

Friday, 8/7/98, p.m.

Hi Dear,

This morning, Ethan played for an hour by the sea just south of Florence, OR, Then we drove down the coast towards the California Redwoods.Stopped at a place that rents dune buggies; I was curious about the price. $20.00 for half an hour. But they didn't have two-seaters, so I told Ethan to forget it.... No way would I spend $40.00 for 2 dune buggies.

We drove to a cute town called Bandon, ate lunch, walked around, and Ethan played on a jetty next to the sea. He spent quite a while peeling barnacles off a log.

When we left Bandon at 1:30, I thought we should head straight down to Del Norte Coast Redwood Park, a 100 mi. drive. I knew I'd have to set up the tent. We were making good time when I spotted the most incredible ocean view at Port Ormond, OR. Turquoise water, huge rocky outcroppings everywhere—to make a long story short, Ethan ended up goofing around there till about 4:00. So when we finally got to the state park at 6:15, people were already camping in our site. I'd reserved the place in June and had a receipt to prove it. Even though the rangers had another site for us, I was pissed and decided to look for a motel near the beach. Figured Ethan might stop pestering me for 5 minutes if I let him play in the ocean.

What do you know?—in ten minutes, I spotted a youth hostel, a large house on a redwood-surrounded bluff, directly across from the Pacific Ocean. They had 2 bunk beds in a dorm-like room with an ocean view. Catch is that we had to share the room with 2 families of four people each. No privacy is no fun. Ethan was thrilled, though. We ran across Hwy 101 and Ethan frolicked in the frigid breakers from 8-8:45. He is unbelievably joyous in the water, and impervious to the cold. Three women on the beach stood, admiring his bravado for the longest time. I was shaking in a t-shirt, flannel shirt and windbreaker. I had to force him out of the water after the sun disappeared, and got him right into a hot shower and into his p.j.'s. Well, now I'm sitting on a bunk, writing this and wishing I were elsewhere, as strangers keep milling in and out. But the price--$18.00—really can't be beat.

On to Mendocino tomorrow. I'm driving very carefully. Please don't worry about us. We'll be home before you know it. I confess I'm very homesick—a wave of homesickness hit me this afternoon, and I miss you seriously. As I drove Hwy 101, even w/ the beautiful Pacific crashing on my right and the majestic groupings of Redwoods on my left, I nevertheless wished you were close enough to kiss.

Love, S.

8/7/98

Dear Dad,

We are in California. It is very fun! We are staying in a hostel. It is not so bad and we are sleeping in the same room as two other families. I went to the beach once and it was very cold! And I

*learnd how to body surf. I wanted to rent a four weeler. But Mom
said no because it was not a two seater.*

Love, Ethan

Day # 9—Northern California Coast to Mendocino 8/8/98

Dear, Before I forget, a few facts:

> *Speed Limit in WY and OR: 75 m.p.h.*
>
> *No tax on clothing in OR.*
>
> *You're not allowed to pump your own gas in OR.*
>
> *I didn't see one black person in Idaho or Oregon.*

*Now, to recount our experiences on Sat., Aug. 8. We sneaked
soundlessly out of the Redwood Hostel at 6:00 a.m. Only a 200-mile
drive to the Mendocino Coast, so I thought we'd get there by noon
or shortly after. Saw some gorgeous, endless redwood forests; and
50 miles into northern CA, spotted a herd of magnificent antlered
elk. We ate a good breakfast at Adel's Restaurant in Eureka.*

*We sort of expected a beautiful day today like the one going
down the Oregon coast yesterday. Nope. Weather was the worst
we've had: 55 and overcast. Strong, stinging winds along the coast.
Worst of all, we took another hideously winding path from Hwy. 101
to the coast: 22 miles of hair-raising twists and turns without
respite. When we finally reached Highway 1 (after again nearly
running out of gas—in tears), I was shaking, gasping, nauseated, in
a cold sweat. I can't handle those roads: it's like reading in the car,
multiplied by 100.*

*I thought we'd be better off on Hwy 1, but it was more of the
same for another 50 miles to the campground. I was a mess, nearly
threw up at Elk, CA, 10 miles short of our destination. We finally*

made it, and Ethan, who had been really sweet and reassuring in the car, was thrilled to see children riding banana bikes in this packed Kampgrounds of America. I let him ride one for 30 min. = $3.75. Meanwhile, I pitched the tent. Mid-afternoon Ethan and I trudged 2 miles through sand dunes to the beach. Freezing cold, and rough, menacing waves. The beach was loaded with driftwood, entire trees included.

I was dizzy and cold the rest of the day, so disconsolate that I washed my face when we got back, and didn't reapply my makeup, just a hermit, unwilling to poke my head out of the tent.

We ate Chunky Soup; Ethan roasted a few marshmallows. We brushed our teeth inside the tent, with a cup and a jug of spring water. Time for another few chapters of _The Ghost Canoe_ by lantern light. At 9:30, lights out.

8/8/98

Dear Dad,

We are in Mendocino. It is nice. We are right by the beach and we just went there. Mom doesn't like the roads. The roads are very rough and have hair pin turns. Now I am in the tent eating sour gummi bears. How are Devlin and you doing?

Love, Ethan

P.S. Dad now it is Sunday and I love San Francisco!

Day #10, To San Francisco 8/9/98

Dearest,

Slept til 6:00! We were off at 7:30. Had to grin and bear 1½ more hours of twisty roads as I retraced my tracks up the coast for

17 miles to get to Hwy 128E; this latter was better, but had its share of stomach-churning curves. Beautiful, beautiful redwood stands and grape orchards. Reached Hwy 101 at Cloverdale, where we ate breakfast at a nice place. Off to S.F.

Today was as wonderful as yesterday was dreadful. Weather 70 degrees—cloudless blue skies. Crossed the fabulous Golden Gate Bridge at about 11:15. This city is so splendid. I adore being here, and could easily imagine living in such a charming, cosmopolitan place. We instantly found at room at a Days Inn on Lombard Street. $85.00. But what do you expect?

Ethan and I walked around from noon to 7:55 p.m. Had a great, great day on Fisherman's Wharf, Ghirardelli Square—so much going on, live music, people with their dogs. The Wharf was teeming with people on this sublime Sunday. I heard many accents: Russian, French, Irish, and of course Spanish, Indian, Japanese. We splurged on lunch, sharing crab cannelloni (wonderful, $14.00)— Ethan tasted it and solemnly pronounced it, "Magnificent." I ordered a glass of Cabernet Sauvignon, which I drank with intense pleasure. $4.50. But you told me to get a drink, I needed it, and one is rarely in S.F.

After that, we went to the Palace of Fine Arts and the Marina. I sat and gazed at a large flock of pelicans flying south, toward the Golden Gate as the sun set behind it. Ethan frolicked in the water-- too cold to swim, but he got his feet and legs wet, and picked up clams, and also busied himself by throwing sand in the water and so on.

Now I must get Ethan to bed. Hope the remodeling is going OK. <u>Wish</u> I were there. I love and miss you so much. Can't wait to see you, dogs, and the house.

Love, S.

Day #12 8/11/98

 I have to tell you about yesterday before I can describe today's events. It was a sound idea to go to S.F. and spend 24 hours, rather than try to maneuver down hellish Hwy 1 to Point Reyes for yet another camping expedition. So it set me back over $100.00— who cares? The city is enthralling.

 Our motel on Lombard St (Days Inn—nothing fancy) was close to everything, but one can walk just about anywhere in SF.

 When Ethan and I arrived on Sun., we made our way to St. Mary's Cathedral. Hoped to be able to go to church, but it was 12:30 and the last English mass had been at 11:30. (They also have a Gregorian Mass.) Although the Spanish Mass was scheduled for 1:00, Ethan persuaded me to skip it. At least we made the attempt. The cathedral is exquisite—ultra-modern, with a vaulted ceiling made in four huge pieces. Stained glass in the form of a cross connects the four sections. In the center of the cross, a shower of silvery metal threads hangs down over the congregation. Ethan was so impressed—asked if it was "better than St. Peter's" in Rome.

 In an earlier missive, I described what we did on Sunday (Fisherman's Wharf, the Marina). But I didn't tell you how much fun it is just to walk through the city's hilly streets. The houses are mostly stucco and connected to their neighbors, much like NYC brownstones are attached. The garages are underneath the second story.

The landscaping is so lovely—bougainvillea, velvety shrubs with horizontal branches—I think maybe hinoki cypress?, square  *privet hedges artfully growing around domed boxwoods. The houses are of pastel colors which glow and sparkle in the sunlight: bright white, tan, sky blue, ivory, shell pink, pale yellow, grey. Most have ornate white cornices and trim around the windows and doors; many have black wrought iron details--locked gates to gardens; widows walks; grilles on the lower windows. Abundant terra cotta roofs. Picture all this with the azure bay in the background, coming in and out of focus as you walk.*

Yesterday, Ethan and I spent 3 additional hours in S.F. before heading south. This city is too wonderful for such a short stay. You and I must come back and spend a week.

This morning, 68 degrees and cloudless sky, we drove through roller-coaster hills toward the North Beach area;parked and put change in the meter at 8:45 a.m. We got a bite to eat at a corner café and ate in the fresh air, watching business people in their suits and dresses scurry around. Ethan had delicious freshly-squeezed orange juice ($2.25) and a chocolate croissant. I had a slice of some of the most delicious banana bread I've ever tasted, and coffee. (I overheard a young Japanese woman raving about the b.b., so decided to try it.)

After that, I decided we'd mail some postcards and try to locate a cable car. Took us 40 minutes of hoofing, but we did it. The cable car was packed, so we had to stand on the running board. I made Ethan grip the rails with both hands, put my arms around him and also the pole. The car jerked up and down some steep hills, right into the heart of downtown S.F.

Bye bye, cable car: the end of the line. Ethan and I jumped off. At this point, we were about 2½ miles from the rental car, and the meter was about to run out. Fearful of a tow, we walked double time all the way back; couldn't have found the car had I not been clutching a map of the city. (I'd drawn an X on the spot where we'd parked, so I wouldn't forget). No ticket, everything great. We headed south, sorry to have missed Nob Hill, Chinatown, and more of North Beach.

Getting to the 101 Freeway was somewhat scary, driving through throngs of impatient S.F. and Bay area natives without knowing what I was doing! But it worked out fine.

Took us four comfortable hours to get to Cambria, a lovely, Murder, She Wrote-like town on the central coast. I am thankful we stumbled upon the Cambria Pines Lodge. It's utterly charming. We're in a supposedly "rustic" cabin behind the main lodge—surrounded by manicured, winding English gardens, footpaths, herb beds. About one mile to the sea; after we unpacked yesterday, Ethan and I headed right down to Moonstone Beach, 5 minutes away.

It was 3:45 p.m., flawless skies, 75 degrees. He played in the powerful, sizeable breakers, and in the secluded tide pools, til 6:30. By then, after having eaten only the banana bread and a few pretzels all day, I was famished, so I dragged the future marine biologist from his research and we went back to the motel. Cleaned up, and had a delicious dinner in the main lodge restaurant: Ethan had baby back ribs, garlic mashed potatoes, fresh veggies, sourdough rolls, onion soup, and of course a Shirley Temple. I had grilled salmon, garlic potatoes, fresh vegetables, onion soup, and the rolls, plus another glass of Cabernet Sauvignon. What a day. But it was when we were sitting in that beautifully appointed, atmospheric restaurant, savoring our dinners, that I missed you so keenly. You should have been with us.

Well, I've spent way too much $ over the last 2 days. Told Ethan to expect a diet of bean burritos and peanut butter here on out! It's now 7:55 a.m. Today, more tide pool explorations; a complimentary breakfast here at the hotel; an excursion (5 minutes away) into Cambria to wash laundry and sightsee; then, at 1:30, our tour of Hearst Castle. More later.

Day #13 8/12/98

I'm sitting in a nice Best Western in Atascadero. We're about to drive over to my little house on Magdalena Avenue, the house I'd loved so much and abandoned to return to Ohio. I'm scared. I'm sure that not a trace of me or the girls remains. It's almost like life itself—you live and work and carve out a niche for yourself, then you disappear. If you could return, you'd find that you made no dent, no impact. Nobody remembers you. It's as if that lifetime (or, in the case of the Magdalena house, that 2 years and 8 months) didn't happen at all.

A quick recap of yesterday before I launch into any more morbid philosophizing. We ate an enormous buffet breakfast at

212

Cambria Sea Pines before leaving for Hearst Castle. But early in the morning, from 8:00-9:30, I took Ethan back to Moonstone Beach for more body surfing and tide pooling. The place is magical—the rock formations seem to cause the breakers to explode in high cascades, fans of spray 10-12 feet high, again and again. A perfectly heavenly early morning walk on the beach. I folded the beach towel on a high rock near a tide pool and sat contentedly for 45 min., watching Ethan feed clams to starfish. Surf just thundered away. Big breakers. A sparkling 90 minutes.

Met a nice 50-ish woman w/ 2 dogs on the beach. She had a Yorkie and a retired racing greyhound; the latter naturally became the subject of conversation. She told me we'd never regret adopting one, that they are the sweetest and smartest of dogs. This one had the softest fur. A brindle. The woman said that she and her husband sold their home in Sausalito for $550,000 and moved down to Cambria, population 3,600. They bought a 5-bedroom in Cambria for $275,000—paid cash with the proceeds of their Bay area sale. The husband was recently laid off, so they bought a chocolate store. She says they're doing very well. Went to Hearst Castle. At 3:30, Ethan and I headed to Morro Bay, where he played for 2 more hours. We saw 3 dead seals. Arrived in Atascadero at 6:30. Ate Cheerios for dinner.

Love, S.

8/12/98

Dear Dad,

Sorry I didn't write to you for so long. We just went to Morro Bay. It was great! So far my favrit beach was Moonstone Beach!
Love,
Ethan

Day 14 8/13/98, 8::30 a.m.
Dear,

Well, I'm ready to come home. This trip seems to be going on forever. Ethan and I departed the slick new Best Western yesterday and we did look at the town and at my old house. When we left in 1983, there were 16,000 residents; now it's 24,000. Many new shopping areas, and home construction seems to boom at the edges of town. But the expansion has been tasteful—nothing tacky in this still placid western town, which is still surrounded by the same mountains (hills), cloudless and warm in the summer. Not humid.

We finally found my old house. I couldn't remember how to get there, probably b/c so many new homes and other structures have gone up, obscuring the path. Proceeded down East Mall, Capistrano Ave., turned right on Mercedes, another turn onto Magdalena Ave. I wasn't prepared for all the new homes on the right side of the road, where previously there had been none. And I drove right past the building that had been my home 15 years ago.

The people who own it now are "really sweet young folks," according to an older woman who lives on the other side of the street. Where the carport used to be, an addition. The yellow siding I painted is replaced with grey vinyl. The trim around the windows

214

and doors is orange. The rose bushes I planted in the stone beds are gone, replaced with leafy shrubs. Next, we drove around back to the dirt road leading to Pine Mountain Cemetery. The mountain itself, which was free of housing when I lived here, has a few big homes now. I got sentimental and sorrowful—remembering the hoot owls and deer behind my little bungalow.

After the sobering trip thru Atascadero, we drove down to San Luis Obispo. Had breakfast at the Apple Farm, a landmark restaurant where I bought two jars of their famous boysenberry jam. We walked around town, visiting the old mission, and looked in a few shops. This is the greatest place; I'd love to retire here. Home prices in S.L.O. are high, though: a modest house in Atascadero is $180,000, while the same in S.L.O. would go for nearly $300,000. But you feel such a charming, cosmopolitan air. I wish you could be here with me.

We took off at about 11:30 for the Santa Barbara area. Pulled into Refugio Beach State Park at 12:45—stayed til 5 p.m. Ethan body surfed and ran wildly for hours. We both got sunburned. Refugio is a long beach, but there is only a narrow ribbon of sand on which to sit and sunbathe. The tide was rising, and shortly after we came, it rushed up and soaked our towel and sandals. So I had to get a sheet out of the back seat. But it was a relaxing time; about 75 degrees; cloudless skies. Flocks of business-like pelicans soaring in perfect tandem overhead.

We got to the Sandman Inn in Santa Barbara at 5:45. At the desk, the clerk gave me a note: my old friends Cathy and Ben would be arriving at 6:00 rather than 7:00. And here I am with tar all over my feet, face and hair a fright. We somehow got ourselves presentable by 6:05, which is when they came driving up.

Got into their Ford Taurus station wagon, and drove around the city. We ate at a Mom-and-Pop Mexican operation (tacos and burritos). Cathy gave us presents: Crabtree and Evelyn shell soap for me; a lighthouse sculpture for Ethan; and a little ceramic basset hound modeled after Molly! We had fun reminiscing and catching up; Cathy works for a Catholic charity and Ben has been a substitute teacher for years. As I've mentioned, Cathy is the mother of six children. She's so jolly and kind. She spoke very warmly to Ethan, and Ben also spent time telling him about the ocean and the surroundings.

After the Mexican food, Ben drove us out to the Santa Barbara Pier. We took a stroll and got some ice cream. It was dark and getting chilly and Ben had us back at the hotel at 9:15. We slept well—I woke at the luxuriant hour of 7:00 a.m. Today, a drive down to L.A.—lunch with Nancy (Cathy and Ben's 25-year old daughter)—and more beach experiences.

Love always, S.

Day #15 8/14/98
Dear,

A little note before we leave for Disneyland. Yesterday was 25% fun, 75% frustration. The drive south from Santa Barbara to the outskirts of L.A. was fine. I'd forgotten one has to go up so many steep grades along the way. The traffic patterns became more congested in the Valley, and it came to a virtual stop north of

Hollywood and Beverly Hills. We took 110 to 10, 10W to the Santa Monica Pier. Finally got there at 11:30. Walked around a bit.

Then Ethan begged to be allowed to get wet. We were to meet Nancy at her office at 1:00, so I hesitated to let Ethan bodysurf. But I figured, who cares? We're here once in a blue moon. He'd just have to be sandy during the early afternoon. So he played til 12:30, at which time we drove east to La Cienega Blvd. in Beverly Hills.

As Ethan moaned in his wet, sandy shorts, trying to peel them off and replace them with dry clothes in a moving car and despite his seatbelt, I knew we'd have a time of it getting to Nancy's office. The traffic is unreal—not only dense but disorderly and unpredictable. My heart was in my throat during the 50 minutes it took us to drive 6 short miles.

Finally located Nancy's workplace--the Academy of Motion Picture Arts and Sciences. She'd left a note with a security guard, letting us know that she was eating at Philly Pizza half a block away. I hadn't seen her since she was 9 years old. Two years ago, she finished her history and English degree at UCLA summa cum laude, on scholarship. I know this because Cathy told me. Nancy didn't mention it. Anyway, we had a delightful, short lunch. Ethan had a lemonade and we shared a great meatball sub.

Nancy gave us a tour of the building, fashioned on the outside like a Spanish mission, but sleek and new inside. We saw the "Cecil

B. DeMille Library," the "Kirk Douglas Stairway," and the "Karl Malden Reading Room." Examined a few Oscars. Looked through John Huston's leather-bound movie scripts. Saw Mack Sennett's typewritten letters referencing Charlie Chaplin. It was really interesting. Nancy likes her job, but she's going back to UCLA this fall for a Master's program. Her husband Chris, a philosophy major with some computer training in grad school, now works for Disney, designing web pages.

We said goodbye to Nancy and went to get the car. Can you believe, we had to pay $4.75 for 65 minutes! That's Beverly Hills. After more traffic hassles and a missed off-ramp, we finally got to our dog-eared Howard Johnson's at 4:30. A whole day of stop-and-start driving. I tell you, the quality of life plummets as you approach L.A., and I suspect this is true of all things south of L.A. I wouldn't want to live south of San Luis Obispo.

Ethan had been so sweet in the car all afternoon that I decided to brave traffic again and drive on surface streets to Huntington Beach, 15 miles away. We ate dinner at Marie Callender's (got my wonderful boysenberry pie!), and at 6:45, to the beach. He frolicked in the biggest waves yet til sundown.
More later. Love you. S.

Day 16 8/15/98
Hi Dear,

Well, Disneyland was a huge hit with the little doober. We were there from 8:45 a.m. to 10:15 p.m. yesterday. Walked our little doggies off! Admission for an adult and a child under 12 is $66.00 . . . . . Parking, $7.00. Lunch—a modest one: $16.00. Drinks and *snacks, plus a couple of hot dogs later in the day came to more than $20.00. So we got through it for about $110.00. No toys or souvenirs of any kind. The place was packed. Can you imagine how much they rake in on one summer day?*

But all-told, the cost was justified. Ethan had a splendid time. As usual, he approached amusement park rides with great trepidation, asking ten thousand questions about the velocity and angle of the vehicle we were about to embark on. Afterwards, he begged to go on the ride again. This wasn't always practical, since there's a 45 min. wait for many of the attractions. We lucked out on "Pirates of the Caribbean," though: serendipitously got there just as they opened. We were the first people on the first boat on that wonderful ride.

We skipped the Matterhorn Bobsleds, where the abominable snowman leaps out as you hurtle down the mountain; the Splash Mountain log rides; and Space Mountain. These were all too scary. But we hit most of the really fun rides. Nevertheless, we experienced only about 1/10 of what Disneyland offers.

We had a mint julep, lemonade, croissant, and biscotti at the Mint Julep Bar; we split an order of pot roast, potatoes, and carrots at the Carnation Café; had a latte, a roll, and a lollipop at the Blue Ribbon Bakery; and wolfed down hot dogs, chips, and lemonade at the Plaza Inn on Main Street U.S.A. Also, popcorn, candy, milk. It makes you hungry to walk around for hours. At 9:30, fireworks and wonderful live music. At night, the whole place is lit up: gas lamps in Main Street U.S.A., torches in "Africa," and so on. The Sleeping Beauty Castle is awash in pink light, and all the trees and shrubs are covered with tiny white lights. You hear music all day long, each "land" with music specific to itself. Plus, there are many live musicians: in Old New Orleans, a Dixieland jazz group.

You can probably tell I like Disneyland myself. It's crowded, and annoying to wait in the lines. It's also a massive capitalist racket. But it's an amazingly efficient place, and perfect down to the last detail. In Old New Orleans, behind the Mint Julep Bar, in the back of everything, I spied a pulley reaching from one building to another. On this pulley was a clothesline on which hung a lady's pink blouse and a pair of ruffled bloomers!

After a day of delirious enjoyment, we found the motel in the dark with no trouble. Today, off to AZ. I'm now going to be coming closer and closer to you.
S.

Dear Dad,

I just went to Disney land it was so cool!!!!!! I went on an Indiana Jones ride it was very scary. I wish you were there
Love
Ethan

Day #17 8/16/987:20 a.m.
Dearest,

Hope the dogs aren't driving you to drink. Cannot wait to see you. Can you believe I've used up that entire spiral notebook, writing letters to you? I had to bum this paper off the Indian (East) woman at the desk of the Courtesy Inn here in Williams, AZ. This morning, after 8:00 Mass, we're going to head up to the Canyon, 58 miles north. Let me tell you about yesterday.

I woke up early in Fullerton—a miracle after the previous day's odyssey through The Magic Kingdom. Cleaned up the car (sand all over the inside), got gas, woke Ethan. We left southern California and drove east through awful smog and pretty heavy traffic. This was a Saturday—just imagine the weekdays. Got to Riverside at 10:30, ate a big breakfast, and continued east toward the Mojave Desert.

The temperature had been high in Riverside. When we got to Ludlow, smack dab in the desert, the intense heat almost physically knocked me over as I got out to use a gas station toilet. A few days earlier, five Mexicans perished in conditions such as these: no water, no shade. It's fierce. The line to the bathroom, by the way, showed that this was indeed the last outpost before Needles, about 100 miles to the East.

I was scared I'd tax the engine so put the a/c on the lowest setting. We just kept at it—blistering, desolate wasteland. Got to Needles, bought more lemonade, and soon after, crossed into Arizona. The desert conditions persisted for a time. Then we began to climb. By 3:00 p.m., a thunderstorm, 5,000 feet above sea level! Temp. in the low 80s!

Reached our little Grand Canyon outpost, Williams, AZ, at 5:30. Unexpectedly cute western town surrounded by mountains. Many shops. Ethan and I explored—he wanted a knife, I said no. A staged gun fight in the center of town took place at 7:00 p.m.—4 locals, two of whom are real cowboys, took part in this hokey display of trading insults and firing blanks. Their names were Barnes, Muley, Red, and Catfish.

We ate burritos at a good Mexican restaurant in town (walked there); this is a party town for sure. Talked to a local who owns a jewelry store: says that, in winter, they get 150" of snow here.

Love, S.

Santa Rosa,, NM Tues, 8/18/98, 6:25 a.m.

Dear,

Just a brief note, the last one I'll write. Sunday the 16th was Grand Canyon day, as you know. When we spoke, I must have given you the impression that I was underwhelmed with the Canyon. It's true that I prefer a place with visible water, but the sights on Sunday, and early Monday morning, were unreal. At Yavapai Point, we spent quite a while gazing, and hiked along a faint footpath leading to Mather Point. The view became more phenomenal as we went along—the other rim, the north rim, is 10 miles away, and a thunderstorm complete with lightening streaks unfolded right in the middle of the Canyon. We were still standing in the sunshine, but cool gusts came our way. The tiers and layers of canyons within the Canyon were alternately illuminated by sun or veiled by the rain. It was pretty darn breathtaking.

I managed to keep Ethan from falling 2400 feet to his death. We made veg. soup (in your grandma's pot), peanut butter crackers, and also ate a whole jar of pickled beets for dinner. A bit down market from, say, the Cambria Pines Lodge, but what the heck, gotta clean out the food bin. It was fun, and I amazed myself with my campsite efficiency, down to washing dishes in ½ bucket of water.

We went to a campfire talk given by a park ranger, and to bed by 8:30. Read Ethan more of <u>The Ghost Canoe</u> by lantern light; we're almost done. I slept very badly—felt as if I was on an incline. Relieving one's bladder in the dark, stumbling on pine cones, isn't the most pleasant experience, either. But when I heard coyotes and their pups howling in the dead of night, I felt part of a hidden world.

Packed up and left our campsite at 7:00. Got a final glimpse of the majestic Canyon; rays of morning sun filtering through purple and red crags.

Yesterday, Monday the 17th, was tedious, driving well over 500 miles from the Canyon to Santa Rosa, NM. Ethan and I stopped only twice, very briefly. He was a superb, uncomplaining traveler. I thought we'd never get where we were going—of course, my fatigue from the previous day didn't help matters.

Finally arrived in Santa Rosa at 5:15; lost an hour when we entered Mountain Time. Our room in Days Inn is nice—two queen beds with excellent mattresses. We ate Cheerios, juice; I had an orange; we each had a box of Crackerjacks. Watched "Cosby" and a movie called <u>Trading Moms</u>; caught a few snippets of Clinton's embarrassing confession about his activities with Monica Lewinsky. Maybe our era of economic prosperity will come crashing down as a by-product? Can't wait to hear your views.

Well, today we're off for Oklahoma City. The following day, western Illinois. Thursday, I get to kiss you again.
Love, S.

Ethan and I came home invigorated. The dogs were delirious with joy. Despite looking a little wan, José seemed centered and engaged; he'd been busy, giving his all to the new job. Not to mention the remodeling, still in progress. The bathroom addition was nearly finished, and the kitchen had a new floor and pristine cabinets with white china knobs. New surroundings and a new frame of mind.

The euphoria lingered. We looked again and again at the photos from the trip. Even our contractor stopped his work, peering at a shot of the Grand Canyon at first light. "Whoa, just look at that!" he whistled. José liked the sparkling image of Ethan's first encounter with the Pacific Ocean. On a deserted beach near Florence, Oregon, I'd caught our ten-year old in profile, hands on his hips, inhaling in amazement, the dark blue expanse and whitecaps unfolding as far as eyes could see. As José silently studied the photo, I knew that he was caught in the spell of a crystallized moment, a moment he hadn't shared.

Now we were together again, wearing the routine of life like a familiar garment, every day embroidered with its unique variations. We were content even when, in the late summer of '98, after seven years, José's Pontifical College Josephinum teaching job ended abruptly and I thought cruelly. The new policy stated that only practicing Catholics could instruct the seminarians in the subject of history. But José's Ohio State job bridged the gap. We were being buoyed aloft a current of well-being that we hadn't felt since the early days.

Most of the time, we saw eye to eye. We talked about Bill Clinton's sexual indiscretions. We agreed that Clinton was arrogant and reckless to have done it in the Oval Office. How insulting. And when confronted, he should have told the truth.

"But why," I asked, "did FDR and Eisenhower get a pass, and not Clinton?"

"Well, there's the First Amendment, dear." José responded. He didn't look up as he stirred the split pea soup simmering on the stove.

"I know, but this thing's getting way too much coverage."

"I can't disagree," José admitted. "The important stuff's getting lost in the shuffle."

Still, José was less forgiving than I was of Clinton's shenanigans. He'd always been disgusted by the inability of powerful men to keep themselves buttoned up. Early in our relationship, he called JFK a whore. That verdict took my breath away for its lack of nuance. José the historian tried to rise above his narrow vantage point. But as we talked about Bill Clinton's libido, José put aside his scholarly burdens. The lopsided power dynamic bothered him—a naïve young woman being pressured by the most powerful man in the world. "C'mon," he said, without a trace of a smile.

Later that day, we were attentive as presidential historian Michael Beschloss assessed Clinton's historical legacy. José called Beschloss "the Ken Doll of Historians," but despite the guy's glossy image, we listened. Clinton, Beschloss said, would be remembered for the longest economic expansion in American history. Clinton's name would be linked with Dow Jones, not Paula Jones. And for sure, the economy in the late 1990s was galloping. Even our finances had stabilized. But we still lived simply, enjoying the quotidian pleasures, and an occasional free-of-charge outing, just as we'd been doing all along.

7

BELOVED SCHOLAR

Death takes us piecemeal, not at a gulp --Seneca

In late 1998, José began listening to Mozart's *Requiem.* He slid the disk into the CD player and surrounded himself with the music almost every evening as he sat reading in the white brocade chair. The strings rushing toward crescendos, the dark, liquid warning of bassoons, the thunderclap of tympani--and the silken adagio, a yearning of heavenly voices. José had always been attracted to the Romantic composers. I was the one who adored Mozart. I wondered why he'd become so obsessed with the piece.

"Why the *Requiem* all of a sudden, dear?"

His voice was gravelly as he responded, simply and reverently. "It's . . . so beautiful."

It was about this time that a back molar went bad. José knew that we couldn't afford out-of-pocket dental expenses, so, ignoring my protestations, he allowed the abscess to run its course. No painkillers except Ibuprofen. At night, he sat patiently on the couch, leg crossed and foot dangling, hand to cheek, silently enduring the torture. Eventually, the tooth fell out.

The new year, 1999, was upon us. José was spending at least 50 hours a week at his job in Oxley Hall in West European Studies. He was also teaching a history course on the main campus, and another, two nights a week in Mansfield, 60 miles north. In early January, he struggled with the commute--five feet of snow on the ground, single-digit temperatures. Our Dodge Colt had 120,000 miles, and the transmission was failing.

That winter, I fed the dogs and took them out at 5:30 for a ten-minute walk in the cold, driving to campus before daybreak. After parking in the lot, I picked my way over rutted ice and snow on the fifteen minute hike to the office. I had just enough time to organize my materials before class started at 7:30. I was also under the gun in the Social Work College: the newsmagazine was about to go to press. Meanwhile, the Worthington schools were closed early in January because of dangerously frigid weather, and for a few days, 11-year old Ethan was home alone, unsupervised.

Ethan had grown tall and lanky—over five feet tall and 90 pounds. His baby roundness was long gone. I'd arranged for him to see an orthodontist, and as usual, I made the final decision: he'd get a full set of braces in April. The process would be prolonged: the braces could come off in three years, but Ethan would need to wear a retainer at night until after college. My dental insurance would cover only $1000 of the $4700 treatment.

Ethan's teeth needed to be straightened, and his bedroom needed a makeover. He was approaching adolescence, and even with the new bookcase-desk combination, the room was too juvenile. So I took a vacation day, enlisting José's help that morning before he left for work. In his overcoat, he helped me rip out the stained, cream-colored wall-to-wall carpeting. When we were done, José stood to one side, panting softly. He rested briefly before leaving for campus.

My attention was on the warm oak under the carpet pad, tongue-in-groove planks, and in pretty good shape. Amazing! We'd been living in the house for fifteen years, but hadn't ever seen the original hardwood floors. I was as proud as an archeologist as I pried out staples and nails and filled the holes with wood putty. When the floor was finished, I sanded and repainted the dings in the baseboards. Next, I painted the walls. A few days later, with some of my teaching money, I bought a red and navy braided rug, clean and practical.

José continued to look drained. His face was gaunt, and his eyes, hollow. His hair seemed thinner than ever, but I thought, who wouldn't look tired with his schedule? All through that winter, he hefted 50-pound sacks of dried corn to feed the ducks on Mirror Lake near his office in Oxley Hall. That had been his habit since he started his West European Studies job. Every spare second at home, he worked on his dissertation, his shoulders rounded, his fingers typing rapidly on the old computer.

One evening in early March, we joined the West European Studies director and staff for dinner in honor of a visiting military/diplomatic historian who had given a lecture that day at

Ohio State's Mershon Center: "The Age of Nationalism and the Causes of the First World War." The golden, up-town feel of the restaurant contrasted with the bleak end-of-winter greyness outside. Sitting around an oval table, we all joined in the light yet one-sided conversation--nothing but history. That suited me, but the only thing I was able to contribute was the last name of Churchill's mother: nobody else could remember "Jerome." We had a memorable free meal of crab-stuffed Portobello mushrooms and teriyaki salmon.

March turned to April. The snow melted. Suddenly it was sunny and in the mid-50s. José was working on new tasks in Western European Studies: publishing a newsletter and planning a British Studies Seminar. But his selection of art for the flyer got a negative response from a professor in the History of Art Department, who wrote to José's boss:

If you're going to use an illustration, you shouldn't be so cavalier in your choice of image. What does a 19th century lithograph by Daumier have to do with 'Building, Burying, and Collections, 1600-1670?' Surely you could have done better than that.

José's boss forwarded the huffy message, and José emailed it on to me, prefaced with his own comment:

Golly Ned, some people! Remember, dear, this is a forward! Love, J.

Another new responsibility in Western European Studies was the creation of a website. José accepted the challenge with grace, but he wasn't the least bit familiar with HTML or other aspects of web creation. So I knew the web design would not be pleasant. My computer-challenged husband was juggling so many things.

He was wrapping up the penultimate chapter of his dissertation. By now, Professor Thorndyke had been stockpiling José's chapters for two years. After thousands of hours of work in fits and starts over a decade, José still had not heard from Thorndyke. Not a phone call. Not an email. I thought about my own doctoral advisor, prompt and helpful.

"Listen, dear," I said, "Thorndyke is being paid. It's his job. It is his job to supervise doctoral students' work. Why won't you rattle his cage?"

José didn't answer. Instead, he turned back to his computer. One afternoon, as he smoked in the garage, I looked at the screen.

> *Narrative history has been discounted partly because it imposes a context, a viewpoint, a perspective—white, European, male—upon the past, implying that this hegemony is born of nature.*

In grad school, you find out that scholarship isn't so much about answering a question as joining a conversation. José had been doing just that with his study on pandemic influenza and its effect on the French military and the French people. But it takes at least two to make a conversation. Thorndyke's neglect contrasted with José's diligence—his dissertation was nearly finished, and he was pushing himself to the limit, prioritizing the various job tasks, anticipating what to do next.

As Assistant Director of West European Studies, José was one of several Assistant Directors, each of whom handled the business end of things in their realms: African Studies, East Asian Studies, Latin American Studies, and Middle East Studies. José was particularly friendly with Will Roper--years before, Will had also been a T.A. in the History Department. A historian of Russia, Will was now Assistant Director of the Slavic and East European Studies Program. Will remembered José's approach at assistant director meetings: "Extending his arms, shoulders raised and fingers spread, José dramatically tiptoed to close the door when the discussion became too rousingly critical of the powers-that-were, who might have been lurking outside."

In the spring, José's load lightened. He was teaching only one course while working full-time in the West European Studies Program. As usual, I was teaching English composition. Meanwhile, Ethan had gotten his upper and lower "devices"—the top one expanding his palate and the bottom one bringing his lower jaw forward. The stainless steel contraptions in his mouth must have felt miserable.

On her usual Sunday visit, Mom criticized the decision.

"You didn't fall for those orthodontists' tactics, did you?"

Ethan silently took in the discussion.

When I assured Mom that it was the right thing, she countered, "Oh, he's too young for braces! He doesn't *need* braces! Joseph had teeth like that when he was a child, and he grew into them!"

Despite Mom's sniping, Ethan would be getting the full set of braces in May. It would cost us, so I tried to save in every way I could. Maybe I could save on bus fare. José was working long hours in the West European Studies Program, so he needed to take the car, leaving early with a heavy thermos of coffee. Meantime, I'd gotten used to riding the bus. But I didn't like to pay. Since Ohio State students could ride free, and since José was technically still an Ohio State student, my idea was that I'd just borrow his student ID. I'd flash it really fast, so the bus driver wouldn't notice that the photo was not of me.

I emailed my husband about my plan, asking if I could borrow his Buck-ID so as to carry it out. José responded:

Dear,

I'd have to nix your "Free" COTA plan, for three reasons:

1. *I've seen many drivers check Buck ID's carefully, just to catch deadbeats ("Ma'am, why are you carrying a man's ID?").*

2. *You are a "mature woman," so you're sure to be busted. Particularly as most COTA drivers would want a second look at your ID just to bask a little longer in the glow of your bwaana.*

3. *I'll tell the bishop.*

So you see, this little ruse is bound to fail. You should drive the car home. It's parked at Pavey Square. I'll take the late Crosswoods bus and see you at 11:00.

Love, J.

That night when José came in, I was lying awake. He sat on the edge of the bed. I could feel his weariness, but he was in a good mood and wanted to tell me a story about a co-worker, another Assistant Director, the one in East Asian Studies. On a break together, the man told José that he'd accrued hundreds of vacation hours, and he'd either have to take twenty vacation days very soon or forfeit the time. So he asked his director if he could take the twenty days.

The man's director said he'd think about it. After a few days, the guy had to remind his boss. The boss replied, "We're kind of busy around here right now. Instead of taking twenty full days of vacation, how about taking forty half days?"

José and I chortled. "Wow," I said. "That plan would work really well on a cross country trip--in half a day, I might get as far as Indianapolis." We tried to imagine a faculty member's reaction to such a scheme. José said, "Well, I hope I won't face that kind of roadblock in September."

"What's happening in September?"

"Back to France, dear," he said, "—to finish up my research."

The next day in Littleton, Colorado, two high schoolers in long black coats shot several of their classmates and teachers. Recently out of high school themselves, my stunned freshmen picked the massacre as the subject for that day's in-class essay. Columbine left an acrid taste for days. The shock of the thing seemed to be reflected in José's exhaustion and colorlessness. But again I swatted away the jittery feeling. He was keeping his stride at home and work, and I'd heard no complaints.

Soon enough, I'd find out that he'd been feeling sick and run down for months. Much more worrisome, he'd been conscious of a pain in his chest for several weeks. "Denial." That was how he explained it when I asked why he hadn't immediately seen a doctor when he felt the bad thing: he was "in denial." He'd never used a cultural cliché before. But denial was the only way to describe his response to the nagging ache. If he didn't think about it, it would go away. It didn't.

Finally, on May 27th, without telling me, he visited the doctor. An x-ray revealed a mass in José's upper chest, level with his left collarbone. José didn't tell me about that, either. At least not right away. As usual, he came home from work just before dark, walking through the front door with a smile and the usual,

"Hi, guys."

"Hi, dear," I called out.

When I looked up from my cooking, I was struck. José seemed altered. His face seemed shrunken, almost as if the skin of his forehead had been manually pulled back at the scalp. His smile didn't match the look in his large eyes. Later, he admitted that when the doctor told him about the tumor, he knew he was a dead man. But that night, he didn't say anything.

The next morning, a Friday, he told me only that the doctor had spotted something, and that he was going back to get a CAT scan. I sat, speechless. It was too soon to cry. I went to work under a cloud of shock and dread. Between students, I called Mom. She said she was sure it was nothing, and not to worry. Her voice was hollow and distant.

José spent that morning at the doctor's office, and after getting the scan, went to the thoracic surgeon, whose staff couldn't find either the scan or the x-ray, which were supposed to have been forwarded to them. So, nothing accomplished, José took the bus home, coming in the door at about 6 p.m. No beer that evening.

We were sitting silently in the den at 9:00 on Saturday evening when José's doctor called. He'd conferred with the surgeon. The tumor was at the top of José's left lung, two inches by two inches, the size of a golf ball. Along with the lung, a rib was involved. The doctor told José that the thoracic surgeon assumed that the cancer had already metastasized. The strategy: José would undergo chemotherapy and radiation for a few months to shrink the tumor before surgery to excise it later in the summer.

I listened to José's side of the conversation. Barefoot, I sat in a white nightgown, rocking slowly. The windows were open and a breeze filtered through. The conversation was going on too long. José's voice was too measured and too focused. It was almost dark. I could see the outline of José's form, the shape of his light shirt. I couldn't see his features. Hot tears filled my eyes but I didn't wipe them because I didn't want José to notice the lifting of my arms or the dabbing of my hands. Unblotted, the tears fell onto my chest. I gulped once or twice, but kept the sobs inside. As he took in the doctor's blunt news, José was quiet.

A few hours later, Tibby and Norah came over. I took them into another room and broke down as I told them what was happening.At first, they didn't seem to understand that the diagnosis of lung cancer is dire.

A few days later we got a copy of the official assessment of the x-rays and CAT scan:

CLINICAL HISTORY: A 48-year old male with left-sided pleuritic chest pain.

FINDINGS: There is a large mass at the left apex with erosion of the inferior aspect of the left third rib; we can definitely see rib erosion and the destruction of the posterior third rib and a large pleural base for this tumor which extends from paraspinous location to a point 5.5 cm lateral. The mediastinum appears intact. Pericardium and heart I believe are normal. No spinal involvement is appreciated. Looking through the rest of the bony thorax at bone windows, I do not identify any metastatic lesions to the spine. Liver window images fail to show any intrahepatic lesions. Spleen, stomach, pancreas and adrenal glands, as far as we can tell, appear normal.

IMPRESSION: Left apical tumor mass about 5 x 5 x 5 cm arising in the posterior apex, eroding the posterior left third rib, without causing pleural effusion. This should be considered a resectable tumor until proven otherwise.

As with all such assessments, the human being is reduced to a collection of parts. The things that made José unique weren't part of the ratio: his wit, his brilliance, his humility. The intangibles were not measured. But the cancer was.

The last sentence implied that we should hang on to hope: "This should be considered a resectable tumor until proven otherwise." Maybe it was just a large, self-contained tumor that could be removed. Maybe, maybe, maybe. The movie that came to mind was *Out of Africa*. When Meryl Streep, well, Karen Blixen, finds out she has syphilis, she speaks in a measured tone, oddly dispassionate.

" . . . this is not what I thought would happen to me now."

I automatically related shocking events in my own life to dramatic moments in films, giving me a template of how it might be possible to react. Now I tried, unsuccessfully, to copy Meryl's dignified response to terrible news.

Monday, May 31st was Memorial Day. José was fatigued. Carrying a folding chair, we walked slowly up to High Street to watch the parade. Ethan would be on a float in his Boy Scout uniform, and we wanted to be there for him. But as we approached, the crowd was dispersing. We'd missed the parade. I'd been preoccupied, grading papers and worrying, losing track of time.

On June 8th, José underwent a needle biopsy. He got a topical anesthetic. Under the supervision of a radiologist, a resident guided a needle into the chest just under the left shoulder blade. When they plunged in the hollow needle, the jolt was like a gunshot. José wasn't prepared for that. Afterwards, he went back to work, and in the early evening, he took the bus home. Next day, the doctor called. The biopsy revealed squamous cell carcinoma.

José went to work the next morning, but I took a vacation day. Numbly, I drove Ethan to the pool. I spread the beach towel and sat down. Vaguely aware of the smell of chlorine, of the sun burning my shoulders and forearms, I realized that our lifeboat had capsized. José's prognosis was terrible enough, but on top of that, I feared treachery from Ohio State. When they found out about José's cancer, I was sure they'd fire him. They could do that. He was only a temporary employee. I sighed and turned my face toward the sky. The glare brought smarting tears, invisible under my sunglasses.

I didn't move on the towel. My black thoughts were incongruous with the hot, bright day and the joyful screeches. I was surrounded by laughing families, coolers of food, plastic pool toys in too-bright colors. Mothers, fathers, young children. But they didn't really exist. Nothing existed but the ruthless beat of my heart.

Later that day, I called Mom, telling her the results of José's biopsy. Half an hour later, the radiologist's secretary called to say that she'd tried to reach José the day before, because he had missed a radiology appointment. No one had told us about the appointment. The radiation was (re)scheduled for June 16th. Then it was changed again to Tuesday, June 15th.

On Monday, June 14th, José went to the James for his chemotherapy appointment, which had been on the schedule for the preceding two and a half weeks. They put a bracelet on his wrist and forgot about him. After an hour and a half, he stood up, removed the bracelet, put it on the desk, and walked out. The charge nurse didn't look up from her pulp fiction.

On June 15th, José went to his radiation therapy appointment at 10:00 a.m. This time, a smiley, perky nurse asked, "Where's your cancer?—both lungs?" They drew a big black X just under his left collarbone in preparation for the treatment that would begin a few days later. In a span of three hours, decisions were made about his radiation and chemotherapy. The radiation would span five weeks, beginning June 17th. The chemo would be done every day from June 21st through June 28th, and from July 12th through the 19th. Surgery was tentative, but they thought it might happen in August.

On June 16th, José told his boss about the cancer and upcoming surgery. The boss was kind, and told him to simply "take off during the month of August." He later emailed José: "I appreciate your candor; be of good cheer."

On Thursday, June 17th, José began radiation therapy. No pain or discomfort, he lay on a raised bed beneath a rotating machine, which aimed at the tumor from both front and back. I was at work while all this was happening, unable to focus on Social Work stuff. I was consumed by what José was going through.

As my heart jumped with anxiety, a co-worker came in. Ronda was talking in serious tones, something about a voluntary life insurance plan. I looked at her, standing in doorway of my office, small and redheaded, somehow concerned for me. Her words didn't register. My head buzzed in desperation. Why couldn't I be more like Ronda? She'd endured her own tragedies, but it didn't show. She was someone who always seemed to be paying attention, someone who was able to balance her powers of observation with an easy, playful wit and democratic friendliness, traits that made her popular with everybody. After several seconds, I understood what Ronda was telling me, and I also grasped the real meaning of her words. By mentioning the life insurance, she was showing her kindness in the most practical way possible.

"If you're interested," Ronda was saying, "you'd better get yourself on over to Human Resources right now, because today is the last day to enroll."

In a stupor for weeks, I'd been oblivious. Of course, we didn't have life insurance, and since José's diagnosis, I'd bitterly regretted it. Now, blood pounding, I ran to Human Resources and signed the application form. A $63.00 deduction would come out of my paycheck every month, and in return we'd have coverage: $100,000 in case I died, $40,000 if José died, and $10,000 if something unthinkable were to befall Ethan. Unlike regular insurance, the group life insurance required no medical examination.

Chemotherapy was approaching. We were worried: the systematic poisoning of the body. But José's wit didn't desert him during that long summer. We knew that chemotherapy usually makes your hair fall out, and while reading a hospital brochure, we learned that chemo can also change the hair's texture. At this, José said in a stupefied falsetto: "I have an AF-ro!"

The first session was uneventful. We watched for nausea and vomiting, but José drank two beers that evening and ate pot roast for dinner. A dish of chocolate ice cream followed. Next morning, a large bowl of raisin bran and a banana. I hung onto these tiny details.

I was trying to do my work in the Social Work College, but cared less than nothing about the deadlines. I thought about Queen Victoria, retiring from her duties for 15 years after Albert's death. But I couldn't afford to play the Victorian invalid. As I half-heartedly tackled my office chores, it occurred that vitamins might help José. So after work, I stocked up. I also got some herb tea ("kava" with ginger), which, the store owner told me, is good for suppressing nausea.

I lined up the supplements on the kitchen counter. José was skeptical. Not that he trusted the oncologist, either, but he wrote to him anyway.

23 June 1999

Doctor Oberman:

Will the attached list of nostrums interfere with my course of chemotherapy? That is, will any of these items diminish the effectiveness of VP-16 or Cisplatin, or interfere with the action of the anti-emitics I take, both during the chemo sessions or by prescription? My wife came up with this regimen, and I told her I'd run it before you first. You can reach me at any of the numbers above, or leave a note for me at the 2nd floor Oncology desk. Thanks.

Joseph Talbert

West European Studies

That evening, he was depressed. I lay on our bed and he sat in the brocade chair. As usual, the *Requiem* was playing. He was talking about buying two cemetery plots, one for himself and one for my mom. "She's family, sort of," he said. "Anyway, you and Ethan will be in California." I lay in a dumb torpor, unable to respond. Oh, so Ethan and I would happily relocate to California. But not him. As if I was the one who was going to desert the family. I'd always detested his smoking. Now maybe he thought I was thinking, I told you so.

After a second, José continued: "We both know this is going to end badly."

The night before, I hadn't slept more than an hour. With José's brutal words, I covered my face and cried.

Next morning, he seemed better and apologized for upsetting me, but I felt shell-shocked. I had lunch with my friend Kathleen that day. When I told her the news, neither of us could finish eating

On June 21st, José began chemotherapy with a drug called Cisplatin. He took his anti-nausea medicine, and at first there were no ill effects. He didn't get home until 8:00, but insisted on taking the bus and walking the twelve blocks east on Selby from the High Street bus stop. The dogs and I walked to meet him halfway. He was fairly upbeat and ate all of his chicken, noodles, and salad. At his request, they'd left the IV needle in his arm, but it hurt him through the night, so he didn't do that again.

The first round of chemo was over that hot and humid weekend. José was sick. On Saturday night, he had serious heartburn; a cup of peppermint tea helped. On Sunday, he was profoundly lethargic—beads of sweat on his forehead. And his shoulder and chest were far more painful than before. The following Monday morning, he had a bowel upset.

That summer, Ethan was enrolled in violin camp at Ohio State, so he and I took the bus, leaving the car at home for José. I couldn't bear the thought of him walking long distances. Because of the cancer, Traffic and Parking allowed me to buy an "A" sticker so that José could park next to his office in Oxley Hall.

On July 1st, José was unable to drink his morning coffee or his evening beers. Nothing tasted good. He was weak and very hot. The radiologist told him that there was "no pleural effusion. Lungs are clear, and no lymph node involvement that we can detect." Despite the positive news, José was quiet and introspective.

That same day, José's job in West European Studies appeared in the Ohio State Human Resources "Green Sheet." There was no pound sign in front of the listing, which made me tremble: the pound sign indicated that someone already employed at Ohio State was being considered for the job. José should have been that person. The absence of the pound sign was ominous. Maybe they were trying to get rid of him, the sick temporary employee. They could forget about José and offer the permanent position to some healthy person.

In early July, the surgeon told José that he'd have to undergo bone and chest scans. "Because," the surgeon said, "if the cancer has spread all over the place, there's no sense in doing the surgery." The blunt delivery took José's breath away and when he told me, I fumed. Bone and chest scans might not pick up stray cancer cells, either. The surgeon hadn't mentioned that.

Surprisingly, José's appetite improved during the first week of July. Three squares a day. At the beginning of the week, he'd been down to 154 pounds, but by Saturday, the scale said 159. His mood was fair, and although tired, it wasn't like the week before. José told colleagues at work about his illness via email on July 10th. On July 11th, I told my dear friend Peggy. We cried together on the phone.

Meanwhile, José had to turn down upcoming teaching assignments. He hated to give up the courses, waiting until the last bloody minute, hoping against hope that he'd feel up to it. Finally he had to take himself out of the equation.

244

7/10/99

Dear Professor Garson:

I have sent you a copy of my "Dear Colleagues" email which will be self-explanatory. I had agreed to teach International Studies 210 in fall and winter. Now I'm afraid that I shall have to pull out. With my health under a cloud, it will be a stretch to take on the extra work.

If treatments go according to plan and are as successful as my doctors expect, perhaps spring or summer 2000 would be a possibility, but this seems far in the future and you ought to feel free to make other plans. Everyone in the International Studies Program office has shown me many kindnesses. I apologize if my short notice leaves you in the lurch.

By the way, I heard recently that the ISP website was up. It's beautifully done. I was wondering why so few centers mounted handsome old stuff for backgrounds. I have tried to do this for WESP—when it's up I'll let you know.

With warm regards,

José

During the third week of July, José had his second round of chemo and again had trouble eating and digesting. Swallowing was torture, nothing tasted good, and anything he managed to get down soured in his stomach. He didn't complain. One morning he lost a battle with a waffle, an uneaten bite on a fork tine, circling the syrup.

Even though José was feeling rough, we went to Ethan's violin concert. Ethan was first violin, and one of two violinists in a chamber quartet that played part of Haydn's *Surprise Symphony*. We watched Ethan, erect in his chair, in white button-down shirt and khakis. I smiled at the irony, musing, "I really, really need a good surprise about now."

Maybe it was selfish to think of going anywhere while José suffered physically and emotionally, but the surgeon remained noncommittal and I was climbing the walls, waiting to find out when the surgery would happen. Finally, I decided that Ethan and I could manage a few days away, so in late July, we flew to California for a week. There was nothing to be done at home. José was past the chemotherapy treatments. He was working and eating well. He'd be able to take care of the dogs.

I called him every day. The results of the bone and brain scan came back while Ethan and I were in Laguna Beach. We got the "Bogart Room" at the Hotel Laguna, where Bogie and Bacall stayed during their courtship, but I couldn't help recalling Humphrey Bogart's early death from cancer. As I spoke to José, I stared at the endless curl and shimmer of the Pacific.

He said that the surgeon had left a voice message. The cancer didn't seem to have spread—there was no discernible bone or brain involvement, and the tumor had shrunk by half. The surgeon went on to say that he'd be back from a six-week vacation in mid-September, and that the surgery would take place soon after.

"Okay, dear," I tried to sound upbeat. "At least we know how things stand with the surgery. And the news is good."

José didn't see it that way. "Well, the cancer's going to come back," he said. "But I'd rather die in my 50s than in my 40s."

We recounted the chronology: he'd been diagnosed in late May. He'd undergone chemo through June, and radiation from June through early July. Now, with surgery so far off, we worried that the cancer would begin to spread again. Was it wise to postpone the operation for eight long weeks? To our untrained minds, the sooner the tumor was gone better. Once again José had to ask his doctor, who explained that, after the final chemo, a waiting period of six to eight weeks is necessary, so the blood vessels can rebuild. The surgeon hadn't shared that detail.

Ethan and I came home from California, feeling a little better. That was a hot summer, and the dogs languished. José moved slowly, but his appetite was better than during chemo. We watched and waited and hoped. At the end of the month, we took in television coverage of the death of JFK, Jr., gone in a plane crash along with his wife and her sister. They'd been on their way to his cousin's wedding.

I dreamt I was in a black jungle, trying to clear a path. Just hacking away, hacking away. Something was brushing against my legs. I screamed and cried, but kept swinging violently and moving forward, an inch at a time. The dream stayed with me. Nothing would ever be right again. It wasn't work that subdued me now, but José's malignancy. The whole world felt malignant. Even the jokes that summer, few and far between, held a hint of the macabre.

One day in August as we relaxed together in the den, José and I observed our young, strapping next-door neighbor, Chad, as he worked in his backyard. Heaving dirt and hauling lumber for a new shed, he occasionally wiped his sweat-streaked face with a red bandana. Chad worked without a shirt, and his muscular body was hard to miss. After watching for a while, José pretended to be me.

Using the hand horn, he said, "Give me three months, Chad. I have him on shark cartilage." Shark cartilage was one of the non-traditional remedies for cancer patients we'd heard about. But if José had little faith in the medical establishment, he thought the alternative treatments were despicable.

Some of José's quips were light-hearted, but some pointed to the reality facing us. Contemplating his own burial, he remarked in late August, "Maybe they have some unhallowed ground at Resurrection Cemetery."

August passed. As September rolled out, José was eating well and had maintained his weight—staying at 155 pounds. Anybody could see that we were functioning normally, working on campus, taking care of Ethan, the dogs. The surgery clouded our minds but we didn't talk about it.

He went to work on the day before his surgery. During lunch hour, he walked across the street to the James Cancer Hospital for a blood draw. They also did an EKG. José was informed that he'd get an epidural as well as a general anesthetic. He'd be in the hospital four to seven days with a drainage tube in his side. I hoped they'd dope him up really well.

Wednesday, September 22nd, 1999 was the first day of autumn quarter. The campus buzzed with students, tens of thousands. The weather was mild and sunny. José worked that day from nine until five, when, without fanfare, he left his office in West European Studies and walked across Neil Avenue. He checked into the James. I soon joined him. Eleven-year old Ethan would be alone that evening, getting his own dinner and feeding the dogs. Surgery was scheduled for 6:30. They'd said several times that it would be a resection: the top part of the left lung would be removed, along with the one affected rib. With that information as our guide, we surrendered ourselves to the medical experts.

The surgeon was running late. For four hours, José lay on a narrow gurney, hooked to a heart catheter and an IV. Adding insult to injury, he wore a pink and white hospital gown. He was cold, so someone found a blanket. I tucked it in and slid my hands underneath, rubbing his bare muscular legs. I stroked his shoulder and back and talked soothingly. He was almost vibrating; his eyes were large in the thin face. He was very quiet.

Surgery began at 10:00. The operation was supposed to last three hours, so I settled into a comfortable chair with a book. I tried but failed to concentrate, nervously munching cheese crackers from the cafeteria. An hour later, I was surprised to see Dr. Ross striding. For an instant, I didn't comprehend. He stood over me and was direct and formal in his language. Two seconds after he opened his mouth, I knew it was a lost cause.

He said, "We got in there, and unfortunately, there are several small tumors throughout the lung. To remove the rib and top portion of the lung would be an unnecessary trauma to him. We're disappointed and frustrated, because all the tests looked so encouraging. But chemotherapy and radiation apparently have not adversely affected the tumors throughout the rest of the lung."

He paused for a second, watching me digest this information. He went on. "The situation is very grim: I'd say he has 12 to 16 months."

He said he was sorry and turned, walking energetically away in his green scrubs and cap, heading for the elevator. A bounce to his gait. I was shaking. My stomach seized. The overhead lights pulsed in my brain.

I looked around. The waiting room was empty. I thought I shouldn't walk alone to the car. I told the night nurse, who said she'd get someone to escort me. I waited for fifteen minutes. Nobody came. So I left alone, my steps echoing on the sidewalk.

I started the engine. High Street was almost deserted. Familiar landmarks took a strange cast. At a red light, I kept on sitting when it was my turn to go. A honk jolted me. After a while, I found myself in the driveway. I opened the front door. Molly and Petey wagged quietly. I bent to kiss their heads. I checked on Ethan, safely asleep. I took a bath without really washing, got into bed, and lay staring all night, saying out loud, over and over, "Oh, José. Oh, José."

Next morning, I showed up at my 7:30 course, the first meeting of autumn quarter. I handed out the syllabus, took roll, and dismissed the students. I ran across campus. I took the James Cancer Hospital elevator to the sixth floor, found José in a darkened room, rushed to the bedside, and broke down, my head against his forearm. He was just beginning to surface from the anesthesia.

Just then, the surgeon and a troop of medical students gathered at José's side. The students were there to observe the surgeon's business-like method of breaking the news of imminent demise to a lung cancer victim. In brisk and practiced words, the surgeon recapped what he'd told me the night before, about getting in there and discovering what they'd hoped not to find. In a huddle, the medical students listened with solemn expressions. José lay motionless, uncomprehending. After the lesson, the doctor and students filed out. I sat still, silent, a whirring sensation in the head. Occasionally a nurse drifted in, but otherwise we were alone. I sat for a couple of hours, stroking his wrist and hand, kissing his forehead and cheek. He was unable to stay awake, so finally I went home.

Petey and Molly were subdued; they sensed my numb shock. I moved through the house, zombie-like. I took out my contact lenses, and went barefoot onto the deck. Sitting in the sunshine, I stared into space, rubbing a swollen bee sting on my right thigh--I'd gotten it the previous weekend as I hung laundry on the line. Then I cried. It was Indian summer.

Several weeks earlier, José told Ethan about the cancer. They were walking. The sidewalk was marbled with shadows from the leafy trees overhead. José delivered the news in a matter-of-fact way. Ethan was stunned. Years later, he'd recall nearly going faint at those mildly spoken words, "I have cancer." The light tone of his father's voice was incongruous with the message. Cancer? That was bad, wasn't it? How could it be possible? Ethan's world was sheltered, predictable, stable. His father couldn't be in any real danger. Could he?

Now, on the 24th of September, as we went to the James, Ethan knew only that his father had just had an operation. Aiming to shield him from the prognosis for as long as I could, I smiled as we rode up the elevator together. "Dad will really like that 7-Up," I said. Ethan was carrying a six pack, which José preferred to the Sprite the hospital offered.

The dimly-lit hospital room was flatly quiet. Ethan and I bent down and kissed José and sat next to the bed. I asked José how his pain was being managed. Had he eaten? What could I do? Some water? Another pillow behind your head? I stroked his hand and kissed him again. He didn't kiss me back. Ethan's face was white and sober, eyes riveted on his father. I tried to cheer José, telling him that everybody was thinking of him.

"Only a few more hours and you'll be home, dear," I said with a lilt. The dishonest subtext was: when you're home again, everything will return to normal. We'll be young and happy and in love again. We'll watch our son grow again. We'll have hope for the future again.

On Saturday, September 25th, 55 hours after surgery, Ethan and I parked outside patient pick-up. By the entrance door, José sat in a wheelchair. He wasn't able to boost himself up, and I struggled to maneuver his limp heaviness into the Colt. We inched our way through the bristling masses of Ohio State football fans. Once home, José slumped on the couch. He slept off and on, and when awake, he looked blankly at the Buckeye game on TV. He wouldn't let me help him out of his clothes. He wouldn't go to bed. He wouldn't eat.

Finally, he made his way into the bedroom. I looked at the incision: 19 inches long, it started at the left shoulder blade and curved down his left side. José slept alone in our bed that night. The dogs and I headed to the couch, so as not to disturb him.

252

On Sunday night, his temperature spiked—102, back to 99, up again. I was about to call the hospital but he stabilized at 9:30 as we watched *Saturday Night Live 25th Anniversary*--a walk down memory lane and a brief diversion for José. He needed a diversion: on top of everything else, he was suffering through nicotine withdrawal.

We didn't plan to announce the prognosis. It was too painful, too intimate. Along with dropping the bombshell comes the expectation of revealing your reaction to it, either directly or involuntarily. And that would have been too much. Of course, the dean and my boss Dana had to know, so I could warn them that I'd be taking medical leave at some point. José's co-workers and boss had been informed. And Tibby and Norah knew. The girls cheered me with their concern and thoughtfulness that long summer. They knew what José meant to them.

I told my friends Peggy and Kathleen but kept the truth from my mother. She knew about the cancer, but we didn't tell her about the outcome of the surgery. When Mom called, I skirted the issue, saying that José had survived the operation, and that the stitches would be removed in a few weeks. Assuming all was well, Mom didn't ask about a prognosis. I also kept the whole truth from my other co-workers, my aunt and uncle, my cousins, the people from church, and all my friends, saying only that, "he's out of the hospital, recovering well, and we're hoping for the best."

José's mother was totally in the dark. Rachael still didn't even know about the cancer, four months after the diagnosis. She hadn't known about the chemo or the radiation, and she'd had no idea about the surgery. José hadn't wanted to worry her.I honored his wish and kept quiet that summer and early fall, but I thought she had a right to know.

We didn't discuss the outcome of the surgery at home, either. I knew that the cancer was terminal, but didn't want to bring it up. José didn't want to ask for the details. Requiring me to pronounce on something so unthinkable would have given me a terrible power. And it wasn't only the message. The way I told José would also wreak harm, no matter what my approach. If I told him with clinical detachment, it would prove the callousness he'd accused me of years before. If I told him in a flood of emotion, the emphasis would shift to my own weakness, my own fear, my own neediness. José instinctively chose to avoid both scenarios. By not asking, he denied me the terrible power, which protected us both for a while. But it was no use. The shape of our world had changed.

On September 28th, six days after the surgery, José went back to work, amazing his co-workers. He took the COTA bus. He continued to work steadily after that, but the surgical wound was painful, and the narcotics he took to sleep were killing his appetite. Then, he appeared to be bouncing back, seeming fairly robust by the first of October.

On the 8th, José went back to the surgeon to have the stitches removed. I knew he'd ask about the prognosis. I had to head him off at the pass. I emailed the surgeon and left a phone message, but he didn't respond. So I wrote a note of warning and hand carried it to the James. Giving it to a nurse, I stressed its urgent nature.

10/8/99

Dr.,

My husband Joseph Talbert has an appointment with you today at 1:30. Although I've told him about your findings during surgery on September 22, I have <u>not</u> mentioned the prognosis in terms of any concrete lifespan.

I'm sure he'll ask about his prognosis today. I would appreciate it if you would be as ambiguous and positive as the circumstances permit when he asks how long you expect him to live. To be told "12-16 months" will surely destroy his hope for any further productivity and pleasure in the life remaining to him. I don't know what medical ethics dictate, but please soften the news in any way possible.

Joseph does not recollect his brief meeting with you the morning after the surgery; he was too groggy to comprehend.

Thanks for your help.

At 1:00, I left my office and met José in front of the James. We sat silently in the examination room. The surgeon arrived, natty in his olive-green dress shirt and lizard skin boots.

At the doctor's request, José removed his shirt. Switching on a bright spotlight and sitting on a rolling stool, the surgeon looked at the stitches, which he said were healing well. José's shoulders seemed very broad, but he was thin. In one semi-circular motion, the surgeon scooted back around until he faced José. "Can I answer any questions for you today?"

Naked from the waist up, José asked about the outcome of the surgery. He still wasn't sure what had happened. I glanced at José as I listened to the surgeon's rhetorical smoothness.

"When we got inside," he said, "we found smaller tumors throughout the rest of the lung. That discovery has changed our treatment options."

Unflinching, José asked, "If the secondary tumors are the result of the main tumor at the top of the lung, why didn't you remove it? Wouldn't that have been a good idea, since you were already inside the chest cavity?"

The doctor repeated what he'd told me that night: it would have caused trauma to the body and delayed the healing process. And it wouldn't have altered the outcome. I spoke up. "Why didn't you remove the affected lung if the other one was clear?"

The doctor explained that, had he done so, the outcome would still not have been any different. There were certainly microscopic cells throughout José's body, he said. Furthermore, to take a lung is the most painful of operations, requiring a long recovery period.

José asked, "How much time are we looking at?"

The surgeon said, "You will die from this disease. But you're young, and so far, there is no spread to the bones, adrenals, brain, liver." The surgeon's eyebrows lifted. "—And, with good nutrition, and appropriate chemotherapy, you could live for two years, and should be vigorous for several more months."

He had honored my wish. He had softened the blow. The doctor said he was sorry, shook José's hand, and left. Fearful of breaking down, I hardly dared look at José's face, but a glance told me it was waxen.

In a minute, a nurse removed the staples running down José's back. After that, we walked to the nurses' station to make an appointment with the oncology doctor. José stood patiently at the desk. While he waited, I walked nonchalantly down the hall and back, pretending an interest in the framed prints decorating the walls. But my scalp bristled and my eyes burned with popping tears.

After the scheduling, we left the James. We kissed and parted, but I stood still, observing José, walking with stoic dignity across Neil Avenue to his temporary job in West European Studies. His posture was erect and graceful. I saw that his hair had come back after the chemo. He needed a haircut. A few silver brown curls touched the back of his collar.

Saturday, October 9th was one of the last decent days, warm Indian summer. We pretended that everything was normal. José had an appetite that morning, and after breakfast, he went to the thrift store on High Street. He liked to do that on the weekends. Ethan needed stability, and we made the effort for him. He cracked us up that afternoon. Describing the mandatory square dancing in his 6th grade gym class, he commented, "Amanda is the worst one to dance with. She's definitely an ectomorph." He delivered this information with utmost seriousness.

By mid-October, José was moving more slowly, and his appetite was almost gone. I didn't like how he looked. His color was bad. He was very thin. Yet he didn't say that he was sad, worried, frightened, or in pain. He was pleasant, even a smart ass from time to time. When I told him my church group was praying for him, he made the hand horn and said, "Pray *harder*, dudes." Despite his attempt at joviality, I knew he was suffering. The oncologist put him on Zoloft for his mood. But he never let me comfort him, and would never discuss his emotions.

His chest was still numb from the nerves that were cut during surgery. It would have been a good time, a logical time, to rest and take care of himself. But his presence was critical at work. For the past several months, he'd been working on a grant application that had to be mailed before midnight on October 18th. The purpose of the application was to gain "center" status for the Western European Studies program at Ohio State. José was juggling a morass of faculty vitae, timelines, budgets, and meetings with the Research Foundation people. In light of José's illness, his boss helped write the abstract and the narrative.

From Monday through Sunday, October 17th, José worked 12-hour days. He hardly ate or slept, and now felt a burning pain in his back and shoulder--at several points during the work day, he lay on the carpet, his strength sapped. Everyone in International Studies knew that José had just had major surgery, and that he had inoperable lung cancer. His colleagues were both moved by his dedication and appalled by his struggle. Once, the Director of Middle East Studies happened by José's office and saw him through the half opened door, lying on the floor.

"Oh! *Where* is your director?" he cried out. When José told me, I thought, good, so someone else understands the injustice, the barbarism. Someone of importance has denounced it.

On the evening of the mailing deadline, José drove the grant application to the post office downtown, and washed his hands of the project. But the workload in West European Studies didn't let up. A big mailing was the next task, which went on for days.

One evening late in October, José pulled into the garage. Instead of walking into the kitchen, he lingered in the laundry room, gasping. I rushed to him and asked if the pain was worse. "I'm losing lung power," he rasped between shallow breaths. Again I urged him to insist on an answer to his thankless, temporary position. After all he'd done for West European Studies, surely they owed him a permanent job. He'd gotten short shrift forever. Tears stinging, I thought again of his dissertation, moldering somewhere in Thorndyke's house, unread.

The pain in José's shoulder and back was getting worse. He stifled a groan as he lay down. The tight set of his lips told of his suffering. I called the oncologist. The doctor said he thought it was the tumor, and recommended that José get a second opinion, and to come back in for more chemo.

A malevolent thought hit: the surgeon performed surgery only on Tuesdays and Wednesdays. José's operation had been the last one on a Wednesday night, and it began late, after 10:00. It was to have been a three-hour procedure. What if the guy just crapped out? What if he made up his findings about "inoperability" to spare himself a lengthy surgery? He would have been paid, either way. Yes, the residents were there, too, providing oversight as well as learning their applications. But the thought churned through my brain.

It was then that my mind disgorged a recollection from early childhood. I was six. Mommy and I had been to a matinee downtown, *The Yearling,* with Gregory Peck. A big boy called Jody killed his pet deer. The boy's sweet crippled friend, Fodderwing, was also dead. The yearling deer and Fodderwing didn't fit into the mean scheme of things, so they had to be sacrificed. From their deaths, came Jody's manhood. But I didn't understand any of that. I was only shocked at the betrayal, the double loss.

With a sorry jumble of thoughts in my head, Mommy and I emerged from the theater into the sharp brilliance of a summer afternoon. We walked along. We didn't say anything. I looked down at my polished cotton dress, yellow-gold with purple pansies embroidered on the pockets. Near my shoes, a cellophane wrapper scudded along the sidewalk; cigarette butts littered the gutters. It must have been a weekend, because there wasn't much traffic. Sharp, vertical buildings, mysterious and sterile, loomed above and around us.

Suddenly, I saw a fat man sitting pretzel-legged on the sidewalk, his back against a wall. His legs looked rubbery. Something was wrong with his eyes: where the colored part should have been, blank opalescence. He had a dreamy, gentle smile. He held a tin cup filled with yellow pencils, cleanly sharpened.

Mommy dropped some coins into a bucket near the man. He thanked her and gave her a pencil. I was struck by the strange event. What did it mean? Why was the man like that? I looked at the pencil in Mommy's hand. It had a perfectly clean pink eraser.

"He should really keep his pencils," she commented as we walked on. "It probably costs him money to get them."

As I weighed this startling new information, she said, "It probably has a lot of germs, too." She tossed the brand new pencil into a trash can.

After a four-decade slumber in my subconscious, why had the pencil man reconstituted himself? As I lay sleepless, I mulled it over. The pencil man hadn't asked for his lot in life, and the fact that he seemed not to struggle against it didn't make it any prettier. I sighed and flipped the squashed pillow to the cool side. I wanted to imagine a life in which pain, ugliness, and struggle had no function. Yet I knew it's the spectrum of conditions that drives us to survive and even create. And survive we must, sometimes on the ashes of others, selfishly rising above the dirty sidewalks and the sharpened pencils that have never written and never erased.

As the sleepless nights continued, I thought about seeing a counselor, but reconsidered. I wasn't really clinically depressed. I wouldn't have been a good candidate for therapy, anyway, reacting to others with an eye to how they're reacting—a useful skill for an interviewer, but counter-productive when you're on the other side of an interview.

At the end of October, José dutifully flew to Texas for his 97-year old grandmother's funeral. For months, I'd struggled with the thought that José's family needed to be told. Now, I still didn't know if he'd come clean with them, but surely they'd figure it out when they saw him. At Nanaw's visitation, they'd talk among themselves. "Joe looks terrible, so thin!" they'd say behind their hands. It was plain as day. The cancer was a secret he couldn't keep. So before he left for Texas, I asked him to give his mother a sealed envelope.

After the funeral, José handed the letter to his mother. And that's how his family found out.

October 21, 1999

Dear Rachael,

You must feel the loss of Nanaw very keenly. I am so sorry. Please know that you and Nanaw are in my thoughts, every day.

I've been wanting to share with you the news about José's illness all summer. And what a heartbreaking summer and fall it has been. My shock and grief over this have been bottomless. No words can describe the desolation, or the deepening comprehension of how much I love and treasure this unique, brilliant man. I've been convinced that you should have been told when we found out, in late May. But José wanted to shield you, and I went along with his wishes. It is his illness, and you are his mother. Now, I'm relieved it will finally become clear.

And yet the timing makes me wonder how you'll cope with this news alongside the loss of Nanaw. All I can hope is that, with your family surrounding you, you will be able to support each other now.

Love, Sharyn

As we drove home from the airport, José brought up my end run. Shouldn't it have been his responsibility? "Wasn't it a little disingenuous, dear?" he asked with raised eyebrows. I wasn't sure of anything, least of all my disingenuousness. What could probity be to me, consumed with daily obligations I hadn't asked for and couldn't deal with?

On Tuesday, October 26th, a few days after the Texas funeral, we belatedly celebrated our 13th wedding anniversary at a Grandview restaurant. José ate half his dinner. We drove home in silence and readied ourselves for bed. José took off his shirt. The incision was still red but not so angry. He pulled off his socks. I slipped on a nightgown.

We lay down. I kissed his forehead and mouth. We embraced and felt one another's bruised tenderness. Slowly we followed the arc of the dark bridge that links past and present, fielding the benediction of saints, the impression of dim, small lights behind our closed eyes, the sense of being born away on a deathless, impervious wave. We were gliding above a terraced dreamscape, wet with my tears. I knew it would be the last time. A guttural sob escaped my throat. It echoed in the dark bedroom.

The rest of that month, we simply went through the motions. People in our position can't escape the sorrow. We ate it, slept it, breathed it. Teetering between denial and despair, we struggled to find the precise angle where we could rest despite the hurtling uncertainties. In a blinding clinical setting, we felt bayoneted. Later, the pain morphed to a nagging ache punctuated by daily spikes: my throat swelled at the greyish face, the dry coughs, the furrowed stare before he could lighten his expression at my approach.

Through November, we didn't say much as we drove down High Street. What was there to say? Before the cancer, he'd been impatient in traffic--to people who forgot to use their signals, he'd mutter, "Knucklehead!" When he came up behind a driver who dilly-dallied, he'd remark in musical exasperation, "The World Is My Oyster." Now José drove like an old man, flat and resigned. He didn't joke anymore. It was as if we were already living a posthumous life.

In the late afternoon, I took the bus home, but José had to stay late, planning receptions, processing honoraria, filling out travel reimbursements and parking receipts, creating award letters, and developing the West European Studies website. That he was wasting his strength on such drudgery cut me to the quick.

Ethan was aware that his dad was sick, but he didn't grasp the gravity, and we still tried to shield him. As a sixth-grader, he had his own troubles. Two bullies, Scott and Trey, tormented the other kids. Scott was the verbal abuser. On the playground, Scott called Ethan and his buddies "dorks." "You're *gay!*" Scott yelled.

One afternoon during recess, Ethan and his friend Charlie contradicted Scott on some point. Scott sputtered, "Oh, you guys are just *homosapiens!*"

Trey, physically violent, repeatedly hit a boy named Kyle. After Ethan made a good play against him during football practice, Trey jammed the ball into Ethan's face. Wanting to get to the bottom of it, the principal called the sixth-graders to his office, including Trey himself. On the way, the children snickered, "Uh-Oh! *Busted!*" Being in sixth grade wasn't fun. And it was going to get worse for Ethan, so I told his teacher that his father was dying, alerting her to escalating stresses on her student.

José still insisted on dragging himself to work, stubbornly refusing to let me help him, including the hauling of crates of wine bottles into the building where that week's event was being held. On the first Tuesday of November, José and I walked slowly to the shelter house to cast our ballots. Later, we drew up our wills and trusts.

The next day, José emailed his boss about office issues. At the end of the email, he asked when he would be moved up to permanent status. His boss responded with breathtaking brevity.

José,

Thanks. I reviewed all files and have made the formal decision to appoint you as a permanent employee. Check with Frank.

Something seemed to be giving way. In a few days, it was all sewn up: the job was now a permanent position on the university's books. It was José's job. I'd suspected the worst, but they came through for us. Ohio State had acted magnanimously. It took a while to get used to the idea. José had finally gained a fulltime position at the university, just what we had both wished, from the beginning. For years, he shouldered temp jobs at Ohio State, Otterbein, Columbus State, the prison at Marion, The Josephinum, Ohio Wesleyan, without benefits or a retirement plan. Now, finally, finally, a permanent position at the university, a professional job. And death was staring him down.

A week later, José was exhausted and shaking. By the middle of November, he wasn't able to get to work until 11:00, working only half days and crashing when he got home. He ate a few tablespoons of food every day, but by the last of the month, in each 24-hour period, he was able to ingest only one Carnation Instant Breakfast. Somehow, he continued to work. He dragged a bar stool into the bathroom to sit on while he shaved. When I hung his clean shirts in the closet, he asked me to stop my practice of buttoning the collar button, not having the strength to undo it. But he was still working. He didn't complain.

On the weekends, he couldn't leave the bed except to use the bathroom. Movement hurt more than lying still. Yet I had to move. With the extra combination of chores associated with José's illness, I had to play catch up every day with cooking, cleaning, laundry. There was outside work, too. On the last Saturday in November, in nice fall weather, I decided to clean out the rain gutters, a job José performed. As I scooped dry leaves from the gutter above the deck, the ladder slipped. I crashed from the eaves to the deck, landing on my right cheekbone, with one leg under the ladder and one leg outside it. Ethan ran screaming, "Mom!"

Shaking uncontrollably, I picked myself up, put an ice pack on my face, and broke down. My eye turned black and my face swelled, and bruises the size of small American flags blossomed all over--black and purple with streaks of yellow. Things couldn't be any grimmer, so I decided to level with Mom about José. She hadn't been over for three weeks, and came the day after the ladder incident. I knew that she'd recognize José's deterioration, the sepulchral pall. "Oh, *my*," she breathed mournfully. Her mouth hung open with shock. She couldn't accept that Saint Joseph was mortal.

On Wednesday, José's mother and sister came for Thanksgiving. Their presence both added to the trauma and diluted the sorrow. I picked them up at the airport and the next day, cooked Thanksgiving dinner. Mom joined the crowd, but she was so upset by José's appearance that she couldn't eat. Nor did José. He spent most of the day lying on the bed.

Mom brought a poinsettia which I set on his bedside table. She'd penned a message in a blank note card:

Saint Joseph,

Please prove Louis Pasteur's last words correct: "The pathogen is nothing; the terrain is everything." You are loved!

Betty

Lung cancer wasn't caused by a pathogen. But Mom's heartfelt words touched us both.

By the end of November, it took hours for José to shower and dress; he had to stop again and again during the process to regain his strength and breath. It was impossible to make it to campus before  noon. By then, I'd taken over the driving, dropping José at Oxley Hall, where he made his way, slowly and unsteadily. Considering he hadn't eaten for a month, I wondered that he could walk at all.

On the 30th of November, he asked me to drive him around to the back of Dulles Hall. He wanted to check his History Department mailbox. He didn't say so, but I knew he was still hoping for a message from Professor Thorndyke about his dissertation chapters. As we pulled up to the loading dock, a co-worker stood smoking. Offering one another brief hellos, the co-worker inhaled and watched warily as we slowly climbed the stairs. She exhaled as I held the door for José. He made his way through the lobby and the department, and into the mailroom. His box was empty.

November was gone and December was with us. Although the handwriting was on the wall, we went to Grant Hospital for the big second opinion. After fifteen minutes of slow walking through an enormous hospital, we found the surgeon's office. The nurse weighed José. He wore several layers, an overcoat, and heavy shoes. He stepped on the scale. The nurse announced his weight so that everybody in the waiting room could plainly hear: 128 pounds.

"I wish I could give you some good news," said the tall, highly respected doctor.

We drove home in silence. José went to bed. Although it was a cold December day, I angrily cut the grass, jerking the mower and spitting, "What a freakin' *waste*." We'd gone through with the second opinion only to satisfy José's mother. Angling for us to fly to Houston, she'd insisted over the Thanksgiving weekend that, "the folks at M.D. Anderson would very likely achieve a remission in Joe."

Rolling his eyes, José responded, "I guess nobody ever dies in Texas."

By early December, the pain was increasing. José said it was in his chest, back, shoulders, and hips. He was always uncomfortable, and in agony when he sneezed or coughed. This was true even though he'd been wearing a Fentanyl patch for two weeks, supposedly delivering round-the-clock relief to cancer patients. So the doctor prescribed liquid morphine, Roxynol, which I administered several times a day. He also prescribed triple-strength Fentanyl patches, Prozac for depression, and some kind of tranquilizer. Despite the meds, José was in serious pain. He never complained, but he gritted his teeth as he moved.

I asked him how the cancer felt. His whole chest and back felt raw, he said, deep inside. I imagined the cancer, spreading through the right lung and into the shoulder joints. When he came out of the shower, ashen-faced and exhausted despite sitting on a plastic stool, he gasped for air. He'd bathed in my tub once or twice, while Rachael and Judi were visiting, but said it was a horror to confront his bony knees. So he'd gone back to the shower.

I started to notice a faint odor about him—sweet, ashy. The decay was winning, achieving empire, its colonies thriving. We were living through the dehumanization of a man of great dignity. He was still beautiful to me. His green-blue eyes were still brilliant, vulnerable, poetic. Even the tautness brought on by starvation couldn't corrupt his beauty: the same wide brow, badge of his intellect and wit; the high cheekbones; the square jawline with the slightly cleft chin. It was going to get worse. I didn't want to lose the essence of this unrepeatable man, but I knew that I was losing him. The cancer didn't care. There would be no negotiation, no mercy. We were participants in a fearful biology lesson.

During the first week of December, José continued to work, but half days. On the 2nd, I got him to work at noon. On the 3rd of December, he had to leave in the middle of a meeting. No showers on the weekends, still bedridden. On Monday, December 6th, after dropping José at Oxley, I returned the CAT scans and x-rays we'd borrowed from the James Cancer Hospital for the second opinion. I hunted down the oncologist to get a prescription for stronger meds. I hightailed it back to my office, stamped out a few crises, wrote a book abstract for *The Journal of Women's History*, and told the whole truth about José's illness to a co-worker, whose sympathy and collaboration I'd need in the coming weeks.

Then I ran back down to the 11th Avenue garage, got the car, pulled up to Oxley Hall, and drove José home. As usual, he crashed on the couch without removing his overcoat. I left for the pharmacy, where I waited in line to fill his prescriptions for stronger pain killers. By that time, it was 5:30. Home again, I fed the dogs, made dinner for Ethan, and prepared the usual milkshake for José. I did the laundry, the dishes, and made a batch of Christmas cookies. Martha Stewart with a gruesome twist.

Unbeknownst to us, December 7th would be José's last day in West European Studies. In the early afternoon, I drove him to Stone Ridge Clinic for a series of upper chest and bone scans. To prepare, he had to drink a quart of chalky liquid. As he lay on the examination table, wasted and nauseous, the nurse and technician gossiped and laughed. The scanning continued for twenty minutes. The nurses continued to gab. In the middle of it all, José rose, walked calmly to the sink, and vomited the chalky concoction. The chatterers finally realized that their victim was not where they'd left him.

The latest bone/brain/chest scan showed tumors proliferating in the lung, and also something on the lower spine and a spot on the skull. The doctors didn't see a metastasis in the brain itself yet. But the oncologist didn't give much guidance. I was bewildered and frightened.

In mid-December, I asked him if he'd like me to read him some poetry. Something delicate and earnest. "Maybe Wordsworth? Is he too romantic?"

"Wordsworth is so smarmy," he stated. "I'd like to hear some Swift."

December 10th: José hadn't been to work for three days. Secretly, I thought he'd never go back. We didn't discuss that topic, though. José needed the structure of work and the legitimacy that work conferred. Above all, he treasured his Ohio State job. It might have been delusion, or wishful thinking, but the unspoken idea was that he'd recover sufficiently and show up in Oxley in a day or two. But he wasn't able to walk from one end of the house to the other without reeling and gasping for breath.

Peggy and I talked about José's resolve to go back to work.

"It puzzles me," she said. "I've heard of other men doing that, and just can't understand. I know I wouldn't want to continue. But maybe it would be like ceasing to do home maintenance. When I straighten drawers or put away clean laundry, I feel like I've put my life in order. I don't always like doing it, but it would be hard to stop, even if I became very ill."

December 13th was Ethan's 12th birthday. We saw the oncologist for the last time that day: José weighed 125 pounds. As we waited for an hour to see the doctor, José sat in a wheelchair. From the corner of my eye, I saw him wince in pain.

The oncologist recommended more chemotherapy for palliative purposes, but José didn't commit. It was a quiet drive home. Breaking the silence, I asked rhetorically why anybody would want to be an oncologist. In response, José rubbed together his thumb and first two fingers.

On Dec 15th, José ate nothing but a mouthful of green Jell-O. He was lying on the couch, and I was stroking his hair. I murmured, "What do you want for Christmas, dearest?"

He said flatly, "My health."

On the 16th, he drank half a Carnation shake and ate a quarter cup of Campbell's tomato soup. Same thing the following day. He seemed to be getting sleepier, unable to rouse himself. There was no way José would be able to go with me to the Colonial Hills Christmas Play, "Treasure Island." Ethan had never enjoyed theatricality—in preschool, he plugged his ears while the other kids happily sang little ditties. Now, he was dreading "Treasure Island." But the sixth graders were forced into it. Meanwhile, I didn't want to leave José. Nobody was happy that night.

"I wish you could come, Dad," Ethan said in his pirate costume, a hollow ring to his voice.

"I wish I could, too, Sweetie," José said from the couch, bundled in sweats and his green robe.

The school cafeteria was arranged like a theater, teeming with parents of sixth graders, happy couples chatting and laughing before the curtain went up. I sat alone, smiling briefly to a few familiar faces but not speaking. The play began. The stage and backdrop suggested a pirate ship. Many students had speaking parts and others either danced or were featured in some sort of pratfall. Ethan was nowhere to be seen.

Meanwhile, the other parents laughed, snapped pictures, and filmed with their camcorders. I sat and watched and waited. The hour-long production was dragging, and I still hadn't spotted Ethan. Finally, there he was. Wearing an eye patch and a do-rag, he ambled to the front of the stage in a strange, side-to-side motion. He jerked a push broom, varoom, swipe, varoom, swipe. Ten seconds, and he retreated to the back of the treasure ship and disappeared.

Stunned, I gathered that he was supposed to be the deck swabber. He had no lines, didn't sing, didn't dance. He was just a janitor pirate. When the lights went up, a volcanic eruption of parental applause and appreciation. Everybody had the Christmas spirit. I hurried home.

During those weeks before Christmas, José's family members called every day. In one conversation, José's sister Judi asked me what he thought happens to us after death. I told her that, years before, he'd mentioned that he believes that the body simply disintegrates, and that there's no soul to speak of. Like Judi, I was curious to know what he was thinking as he lay dying. But given the implications, I decided not to ask.

We didn't know it but a condition called hypercalcemia was setting in. José lay motionless in bed, in a state of near unconsciousness, eyes half closed, unseeing. On Saturday, December 18th, he roused himself to drink nearly a whole chocolate ice cream shake, but ate nothing else that day. In the process of sitting up in bed, he gasped for air. After taking the nourishment, he immediately reverted to the horizontal state.

On the 19th, he spent the day in the den. In the afternoon, he ate half a cup of tomato soup. When he finished, he lay back on the couch, curling onto his side. After I washed the dishes, I bent over to kiss him. Tears ran over the bridge of his nose and onto the cushion, but his expression was impassive. "You are so brave," I whispered, blotting the tears from his face. The surgeon said he'd have several vigorous months before the illness took its final toll, but by the third week of December, José had lost 50 pounds. He'd never been heavy—his usual weight of 165 wasn't much for a six-footer.

On December 21st, he swallowed half a vanilla ice cream shake. Nothing else. On this day, I told Ethan that his dad was dying. He didn't cry but was very sober. He asked if we could get water from Lourdes, or go to a hypnotist. He also asked if I would get married again if Dad died.

On the night of the 21st, I dreamt that it was Ethan who had the cancer. I awoke, sobbing. In another dream, José and I walked down a street together. A co-worker in the History Department overtook us. Seeing José's face, she recoiled.

On December 22nd, José's brother John called, and although there was a phone in the bedroom, and even though he was so weak and short of breath that he panted when he simply sat up, José decided to walk into the den to talk to his brother. He tottered down the hall and crashed into the kitchen. He lay next to the refrigerator while I struggled to get him up, trying not to touch his back where his incision was still painful. Ethan took it in—white, saucer-eyed. He disappeared into the safety of his room.

José was lapsing in and out of coherence. On the 22nd, I got no response to my questions about what he wanted me to do for him—he just stared. On the 23rd, I asked him again what I could bring him for nourishment. He looked at me for a long time without speaking. Finally, he whispered, "They have a house."

"Who?"

He pondered for a second. "I *thought* they had a house." Then he slipped away again.

I asked him if he wanted to listen to the radio, and he said, "Four o'clock." After trying to remember the name of the drink, he finally remembered: 7-Up. He wanted another 7-Up. I held the glass and he drank a few sips before lying back again. I stole softly out of the room. The house seemed thick with some alien presence, lurking, malevolent. When I peered in at José, he was unmoving, lips parted, eyes half open and unblinking, fixed on the ceiling. He was in some sort of coma.

Later, he roused enough to drink a shake, and I administered three doses of morphine. That night, he didn't have the strength to hold a water glass, and after a swallow, lay wearily back. He occasionally drifted to some plane of consciousness to ask for more morphine. At night I helped him as he staggered into the bathroom. I pulled down his pants, helped him onto the toilet, and left. Minutes later, I went in. He sat with his head and arms sprawled forward. I helped him back to bed.

At 1:30 in the morning, Christmas Eve, I woke to the sound of the bedroom door knob grating noisily. Before I could jump up, I realized he was staggering down the hall. I ran after him—he'd decided to use the old bathroom. He went in. I helped him take down his pants and waited outside. When I went in again, he was on all fours, crawling toward the door. Then he collapsed. I put a pillow under his head and dragged him to the bedroom, pulling him backwards by the arms. At 3:00 and 4:00 a.m., the scenario repeated itself. It happened again at 7:00.

I called the oncology nurse and told her what was going on. She said if it were her husband, she'd call the squad. I hesitated. José detested hospitals. Maybe he should just be allowed to slip away at home, naturally. Or maybe that would be a terrible choice, a brutal death. José's brother Jim and his wife Cathie called. They said to call an ambulance. Still, I hesitated. At 10:00, I called Mom. She urged me to call the squad.

Three large, gentle young men came. They asked José's name. They put him on a stretcher and maneuvered him through the curve in the hallway. They covered his head with a blanket against the cold outside. After the stretcher was secured inside the squad, I jumped in. During the drive to Ohio State Medical Center, he lay without moving, but looked around with naïve wonderment, taking in the lights and the equipment and the gadgets. He didn't speak.

We got to the emergency room before noon. After José was admitted, the handsomest of the firemen came to our cubicle and shook my hand. He spoke in a soft voice. "I want you to know that you and your family will be in my prayers tonight." Tears stung.

During our wait, José lay quietly, covered with a light yellow blanket. I stroked his hand. Suddenly he said: "California."

"Do you like California?"

He whispered tersely, "No, let's get to the point. Atlanta won the World Series."

Lab work revealed that José's calcium level was off the charts. The cancer was in his bones, and calcium was leaching into the blood stream, a condition called hypercalcemia, which was causing the disorientation. So José was hooked to an I.V. for hydration and blood cleaning.

In the late afternoon, José was moved to the 9th floor of the James. When he was settled, I left. It was 5:15. All day, Ethan had been home alone. Christmas Eve.

On the morning of December 25th, Ethan and I hurried to the hospital. We didn't even think about Christmas. The hospital oncologist met us at the door to José's room. A middle-aged woman, reassuringly honest and strong, offered us some straight talk. She sympathetically said that, yes, he was dying. She said twice, "You need hospice."

I sent Ethan to visit with his dad. The doctor and I sat in her office across the hall. "Depending on his will to fight," she said, "I think he has less than a month." As I took this in, the doctor said she'd arrange hospice: the equipment would be delivered the next day, including a hospital bed and oxygen. As the doctor spoke, Ethan showed up on the verge of tears. José's confusion had frightened him away. The doctor put her hand on Ethan's back and gently told him that Americans view death from how it's depicted on TV and movies, which is wrong. "This is real," she said.

On the way home, Ethan cried in the car. He worried that his friends would make fun of him when they found out. That afternoon, I went back to the hospital with Mom. José was experiencing severe pain in his back. He groaned several times, saying that he needed more morphine. I told the nurse. He was also in distress from weeks of constipation.

Tibby and Norah came in the evening. Tibby was white-faced and quiet. Norah lingered over José and wept, touching his forehead.

On December 26th, José endured what he later called a "19th century surgical procedure," a nurse manually removing the calcified feces from his lower bowel. The process was torture. But by the end of that day, the physical pain was being managed. José even joked around, and was reading *The New York Times* again. The following day, he seemed more lucid and comfortable. But the lucidity wasn't complete. Insisting that the wastebasket was moving, he said, "There must be a poltergeist in here." I stroked his hair and held my cheek against his. He was hot and frail.

On the 28th, Will Roper and a woman named Mary Beth from José's job in West European Studies came by, but José wasn't well enough to see them. The director of all the International programs came, too. I said I'd give José his good wishes. Then I spoke with a hospice social worker, who was reassuring. Hospice had always meant despair, the end of hope. But now hospice sounded like relief. I wouldn't have to cope alone anymore. We would have people, equipment, pain management, and time off when I needed it. As the social worker and I talked, José slowly ate a few bites of grapefruit. He did not seem to be in terrible pain. He was very calm, looking around the hospital room with large, wondering eyes. The eyes of an infant.

Late that night, José was in a deep sleep. He woke with a start, conscious that someone was hovering over. A former Josephinum student was there to draw blood. The young man stood still, realizing he was looking at his history teacher.

José seemed better on the morning of December 28th, and correspondingly more critical of the hospital's bureaucracy. His pain was being managed through the IV. His bowel habits were

278

nearly back to normal, but he still wasn't eating. A snowstorm that day limited me to one visit in the morning. In the late afternoon, men came to the house, setting up the hospital bed and bringing oxygen tanks.

The following day, December 29th, José came home. Before being released, he ate part of a piece of cake. Home that evening, he had a small salad. After the hydration and blood cleansing, he was amazingly better, rational and joking. Still very weak, he was able to walk from room to room a few times a day.

The next day, he consumed half a grilled cheese sandwich with sliced tomato, and one bite of apple pie. He was able to go to the bathroom by himself, took a shower and washed his hair. He breathed hard after each exertion, but slept comfortably on the hospital bed in the den. The arrangements looked cozy: granny afghan, sunlight spilling over the bed. A snowy vista outside.

The hospital stay hadn't cured anything. José had been discharged with a poor prognosis. But at least he'd regained some comfort and dignity. And hospice was helpful—a competent, pleasant RN provided all the prescription drugs and monitored José's pain. We also had a social worker, whom José thought too chirpy, and a home health care worker who bathed José; she'd also be available if I had to go out. All the medical expenses would be covered by José's Ohio State employee insurance. Emergency room, hospital, hospice. I wouldn't have to worry about paying those bills.

Our friend Kathleen was in town for the holidays; on the 30th of December, she came to see José. Sitting next to his bed, she said with tears in her eyes, "This is so shitty."

José replied, "Somebody has to die."

On the last day of 1999, José ate a tiny bowl of Grape Nuts. That afternoon, we watched a movie called *The Doctor* with Mom, along with part of *Some Like it Hot*. Later, I was outside, picking up dog poop from the snow, when our neighbor Chick came over, bundled in coat, muffler, and cap with ear flaps. He'd noticed the squad in our driveway the week before, and wanted to know about José. I told him what was going on. Chick stared silently for a few seconds, his milky blue eyes blank and stunned. He said in his hoarse voice that he hated to hear that news about such a young person.

On the first day of January, José again ate a small bowl of Grape Nuts. He showered by himself at noon. He was still lucid. On the second day of the year, José ate a bite of toast, an egg, cheese, and some veggie bacon. He ate a little lunch and a small dinner. He took a long nap in the afternoon while I dismantled the Christmas tree. Afterwards, the three of us watched 1970s *Willy Wonka and the Chocolate Factory*. I was giving José liquid morphine three times a day. On the third, José ate a scrambled egg and half a piece of toast. While José rested, I took Ethan to the orthodontist and Molly to the vet. Home again, I gave José a snack: half a cup of chicken with rice soup. For dinner, he ate half a ham sandwich.

During these days, neither of us spoke about his job in West European Studies.

January 4th was the first day of the winter quarter. Vacation was over and work and classes were resuming. José showered, ate a mouthful of scrambled egg and toast, dressed, put on his overcoat, and made motions to leave. Despite my protestations, he said he was going to the office. He got as far as the garage, and surrendered, saying, "You'd better go on without me, dear. I have absolutely no stamina." He headed back to the hospital bed, still wearing his street clothes. I went to work for half a day.

January 5th was José's 49th birthday. That evening, Tibby came with a present. José wasn't uncomfortable, but his emaciation was extreme. He looked sad, but the Prozac and morphine must have been dulling his anguish. His diet that day consisted of two bites of Grape Nuts and half a turkey sandwich.

On January 6th, as she took his blood pressure, the hospice nurse asked briskly, "So, José, what was your specialty in history?" It was unintentional, but putting his life in the past tense couldn't have been right. I stood still, her words on instant replay in my head. But José only said that he studied Western Europe and modern France. He drank a third of an ice cream shake and ate half a piece of toast. He spoke little and moved less.

On January 8th, José was profoundly tired. He ate a few bites of toast, an egg, and a cup of tomato soup. The next day, Sunday, the ninth of January, José's brother Jim and his son Greg drove from New Hampshire for a day-long visit. I made brunch. José ate very little but later that morning, when Mom and her dogs came over, he was able to get up to let them in. Along with the big female Great Dane Jody, Mom had just acquired a second dog, a boxer-pit bull puppy she called Jill. Mom found Jill running loose in the grocery store parking lot and took her home. Now, in the sick room, Jill darted playfully under the hospital bed and all around the den, confounding Petey and Molly. All of us smiled at her puppy exuberance. After an hour, Mom left. Later that afternoon, Jim and

José spent time alone. As they embraced, Jim spoke in low tones to his dying younger brother.

Jim and Greg's visit made an impression on Ethan. He'd been courageous for months, but Uncle Jim's appearance made him see the gravity. The Talberts weren't a close family, and a visit in the dead of winter meant that something terribly bad was happening. The next morning as he was dressing for school, Ethan broke down. We sat on his bed and I tried to comfort him. Afterwards, he rode off to school on his Christmas bike with his helmet fastened, his face splotched red and white. As he rode away, he said so sadly, "I love you, Mom." The snow plows had just come and the streets were clear enough for a bike ride. But it was bitter.

After the hospital intervention, José had been on an even keel for ten days. But now he was becoming confused again. His responses were delayed. He hadn't been able to shower for a week. On the 11th, the hospice nurse looked at him closely, and said in quiet tones that he had less than two weeks.

Two weeks.

The nurse left, and the house was quiet again. José was deeply under, unmoving.Eyelids half open. I had to distract myself. I surveyed the house: everything clean and neat. The laundry, put away. The dogs, fed. Soup simmering on the stove. I remembered the broken-down Rabbit in the garage. José would never fix it now. It was just taking up space. I pushed aside my sentimentality and called the St. Vincent De Paul Society, which repairs old cars and donates them to needy families. I asked for someone to haul the Rabbit away.

In a couple of hours, a bearded man came. I'd raised the garage door, and was watching for him over the café curtains. Before he could knock, I opened the front door. Handing him the keys with a finger to my lips, I signaled the need for stealth. The man obeyed. He silently connected a heavy chain to the Rabbit, put the car in neutral, and pulled out of the driveway with only a little motor noise from his tow truck. I watched the yellow Rabbit disappear. I tiptoed to the den to make sure José hadn't heard. He was in the same position, respiration slow and shallow, eyes unseeing.

January 12th was the last day that José walked. At 11:00, he somehow made it from the den into the hallway, heading for the bathroom. I'd been emailing in Ethan's bedroom. When I heard his exertion, I got up and confronted him, startled to see him swaying haphazardly.

He cried, "Move!"

I waited fearfully outside the bathroom door and helped him walk out. He got as far as the love seat in the living room, unable to make it back to the den. As he slumped there, he asked with a distraught expression, "What time is it?"

"Eleven o'clock."

"In the day?" Sunlight shone through the windows.

After a few minutes, I helped him to the hospital bed, where he nearly collapsed. I tucked him in. When the hospice nurse came, I told her that he was much worse. She confirmed that he was indeed suffering again from hypercalcemia.

She told him in a low, urgent tone, "José, you can't walk to the bathroom anymore. It's much too dangerous. We're going to have to catheterize you." After she performed that unwanted task, she lifted the hospital bars around his bed and locked them into place. From then on, she said, someone would have to monitor José all the time. That someone would be me. I couldn't go to work, and would need to sleep on the couch beside him until the end. Wouldn't it be ironic, I thought, if a historian as meticulous as José slipped into death without anyone making note of the hour, the minute?

Later that day came a letter came from our friend Kathleen. I read it aloud to him:

Dear José,

I'm writing because I wasn't able to say what I felt the last week of December. Of course, there is nothing to say in such circumstances. The only thing I can offer is to tell you what I doubt you realize: how much pleasure and entertainment and comfort I've received from your gifts and your grace.

On the many days I'd walk into 168 Dulles Hall, with its skuzzy carpets and dreary atmosphere, I was never happy about facing the usual motley crew, not that I want to run down the general average of humanity. But if you were there, it always seemed that there was some sanity and dignity in the place. There is something about your mere presence that cuts through anything false.

And you helped me so many times, took any question I had seriously, and never said more or less than you knew. Your advice always meant the most. It wasn't until I knew you in your home with Sharyn and Ethan that I also learned what a good husband and father you are.

But it's all part of the person you are, someone of unusual integrity, honesty, and—what I think I liked best—great seriousness. I've got to put this in the mail before I write too much and the words cancel themselves out—you'll think them sentimental.

I cannot convey how fond I am of you, José. I can only give you these few words.

Love, Kathleen

The next morning, José tried to force down the bars on his bed, weakly shaking them, anger and pain on his face.He was too confused to verbalize his despair. The pain must have been terrible, but he couldn't tell us about that, either. I was still giving him Roxynol with the dropper, but swallowing was becoming harder by the day. So instead of the liquid morphine, the hospice people said I should crush a sedative and mix it with a few drops of water. I did that, but the white chalky paste was even less apt to go down—the grains gathered at the corners of his mouth. I wiped them away.

The rapid slide continued. While he'd been only confused the day before, he was once again in the coma-like sleep of late December. The hospice team looked at him. There would be no point in hospitalizing him again, they said. Once more, the nurse said she thought death would come in days.

The next morning was Saturday, January 15th. I woke up before dawn and found the hospital bed wet. In tears, I called hospice. "If he's losing bladder control," I said, "it's surely the end." A male nurse came at 9:45. "Wow," he said, standing over José. "He's so young." He got to work, washing José and changing his clothes and bedding. He guessed a week.

José was comatose all that day. In mid-afternoon, Norah came. She wept silently, holding his hand. From the kitchen I could see but a quarter of her face. A cascade of clear brown hair fell around her shoulders. She didn't speak and hardly moved.

My boss Dana arrived later, gazing at José and brushing away tears before playing computer games with Ethan for a couple of hours. I showed her the color photos of José I'd reproduced that morning. The pictures spanned his life, from babyhood through the previous summer. They were for the funeral home.

That night, José straightened from the fetal position. He'd been inert for days, and the abruptness of the motion startled me. I peered into his face. His eyes had been half-closed for days, but now they were wide open. It seemed he was trying to focus on something above. I glanced at the ceiling. Nothing unusual. Then he lifted his right arm and pointed straight up, arm and index finger rigid. Many seconds passed before he settled again. I wanted to ascribe it to something supernatural. He must have witnessed something we'll all see someday. Mom said it was the effects of the morphine.

The hospice nurse came by soon after and said that José could go within a few days. Although his heart was strong and he was still breathing on his own, she thought his kidneys were failing. By evening, my hands shook with exhaustion as I measured the morphine and squeezed the drops into his mouth. The other meds went under his tongue; I had to hold his jaw closed so the medications could dissolve. He wasn't responding to voices, words, or to his name, but seemed to feel comfort when we stroked his head and hands. We continued to talk to him and said how much we loved him.

On Sunday the 16th of January, José drifted deeper into the coma. But now there was a current of restlessness—sporadic groans and spasms. At 10:00, the hospice nurse came and together we changed the sodden bedclothes. The nurse washed him carefully. I cut one of his sweatshirts down the back for easier on-off. The nurse predicted in low tones that he could die within days or hours, but as she gave him a crushed dose of Lorazepam, she again remarked that his heart was strong.

Early in the afternoon, José began to battle something fierce and unspeakable, something he fought from the depths, like an undertow that wanted to drag him out, the sand rushing violently beneath him. His knees were no longer in the passive fetal posture but had angled themselves upwards. He began to strike his bent knees against the metal rails. The first bang passed without my notice. But the relentless rhythm quickly became frightening. With every collision came an exhalation of pain, a sunken, fathomless moan.

Again, again, and again—Bang! UUnnnhhh. Bang! UUU-hhnnnnh! Bang! Unnnhgh!

It went on all afternoon. I could not push his knees into a more comfortable posture. I couldn't soothe him. After hours of watching him, I slumped helplessly, laying my head on his left arm. "Don't leave me. Don't leave me." I rested my cheek against his. My tears fell onto the side of his face and into his ear. I told him how much I loved him, how wonderful he had made my life.

At around five o'clock, Tibby came. I was in the laundry room, trying to distract myself by folding clothes. I was still crying. José was still banging and groaning.

Tibby looked at the misery, and asked, "Oh Mom, how can you bear this?"

She sat and held José's hand. She stroked his arm. She put her face next to his, her rosy beauty contrasting with his partly opened lips and sunken, unseeing eyes. Amid the commotion, she talked to him soothingly and sang to him. She stroked his head and hair. The sun was setting as Tibby said, in a soft cadence, "You are the perfect stepfather. You never told on me." Gradually, José began to relax, and after dark fell, the moaning ceased. That night he lay quietly.

The next morning, Monday the 17th, a deacon from St. Michael's came and blessed him. Lucid, José would have scoffed at that ritual. He'd have been insulted by some sanctimonious stranger mouthing Catholic mumbo jumbo over his emaciated, insensible state. But I'd take any kind of support--physical, emotional, or spiritual. José didn't react to the deacon's presence. He was peaceful, responding neither to touch or sound, his eyes, unseeing. I thought they were fixed on some other landscape, a more pleasant place.

When I held his cheeks, though, forcing the crushed, moistened sedative into his mouth, he grimaced painfully, baring his teeth. My ministrations seemed to jolt some remnant of his consciousness. At the very least, turning his head surely hurt his neck and spine. I thought the cancer must surely have spread to those places. As I loosened my hold on José's face, his expression returned to its passionless cast, preoccupied with what was to come.

On the morning of Tuesday, January 18th, my first thought, as usual, was of José. I scrambled up, lowering my face and listening. The breathing was still sporadic and shallow. I touched his hand and face. Unresponsive. As I drank my tea, the den looked sunny and inviting. A deep layer of snow sparkled outside the long windows. José was covered in quilts and comforters, topped with the brown and tan duck blanket. He breathed short, quiet breaths.

Late morning, the hospice nurse came and bathed him. He was impossibly wasted, his mid-section shrunken almost to the level of the mattress. On either side, the fearful hip bones, vertical, cliff-like protrusions. I tried not to look.

After changing his sweats, the nurse tucked him back in. Worn out, I sat dumbly. As always, classical music was playing. The nurse urged me to take a break. "It'll do you good," she said. After considering, I decided that maybe I did need a change of scene. I'd gas up the car. I'd be right back.

After filling the tank, I decided to stop at the mall. I was out anyway. It wouldn't take long. I wanted a new pair of earrings. I didn't need earrings, but wanted to buy a pair anyway. Mountains of snow had been bulldozed to the edges of the parking lot. It's good to get away, even for a few minutes, I told myself, breathing deeply as I hurried, the frigid air clearing my lungs and brain. The accessory counter was close. I spun the earring racks. Studs with all sorts of fake gems. No. Drop earrings, no, too gaudy. Hoops—no, I wasn't a hoop type. I decided on a pair of ear wires with a little golden cube and black bead. Simple, nicely designed. I made my purchase and headed for home.

I pulled into the garage and shut off the ignition. The car clock said 1:00. I'd been gone for 45 minutes. I opened the laundry room door and stepped inside. The hospice nurse blocked me. She was waiting. Her eyes were large. I looked at her.

"What?"

"He's gone," she said.

I pulled in air. No. No. I hadn't been at his side. He couldn't have left me while I was at the mall. He could not have done that.

It was true, and nothing could fix it. I couldn't get back that last sliver of time. Now he was gone, forever. I couldn't change my mind and stay with him, just a little longer.

I would find out that it's common for terminal patients to take their last breath when their family has left them after a constant vigil. Somehow, the exit conveys that it's time. Whether it's the result of being abandoned or whether it comes from a sudden release of obligation, the medical experts couldn't tell me.

Either way, th4 information didn't help. And nothing could have helped at the moment of truth. I stood rooted, unbreathing and unseeing. I felt my features melt and twist. The nurse's voice came from some direction. José died at 12:47, she said. As he took his last breath, she said, the final track on the CD was finishing up. Later, I looked--Liszt's "Consolation."

The first two or three seconds stretched themselves, like I was on one of those airport people movers, a smooth, confining sensation. Suddenly, I was ditched onto solid ground. I lurched forward. I sank onto the hospital bed. There he was.

I kissed his face and forehead. "Oh, this poor man."

I pulled the beautiful hand from under the covers and held it against my cheek. It was still warm.

8

THE UNKNOWN COUNTRY

And who or what shall fill his place? -Thomas Hardy

E than had to be told, but I lingered for a while. I slowly caressed the hollow plane of his cheek. I took off his heavy gold wedding ring and slid it onto my middle finger. I smoothed his hair and felt the contours of his skull. It was so familiar, that head and that hair, thin and straight on top, curling a little at the nape of the neck. I'd cut his hair so many times. Now, as the hospice workers called the funeral home, I cut a lock from the back of his head.

For a time I sat on the bed. The duck blanket concealed the wasted body, straightened again to full length. The lips were slightly parted, showing an edge of teeth. The eyes were closed. The expression, utterly noncommittal. I could see no sign of where he was or what he might be feeling. And his erudition, so deeply carved, now entombed in a lifeless machine. I touched the magisterial forehead. Right now, I thought, his brain cells are dying. Like bubbles in a dishpan, iridescent and quivering, giving way one by one to flat grey water. In life, his dignity was responsive to what was outside of him, tinged with playfulness, elegance. But now the outside world had become irrelevant, the body taking its orders from the ruin inside.

After a while, I left for Colonial Hills School. I parked the car without mishap and headed robot-like up the steps and into the school office. I prodded myself, thinking, it's best to get this over. Slightly conscious of my blotchy face, I approached one of the secretaries.

"Ethan Talbert's father just died." My voice sounded unfamiliar, unyielding. "Please call him out of class so I can take him home."

The woman blanched and rushed down the hall. In a minute, the twelve-year old came at the side of the shepherding secretary, anxious strain on his young face. I said, Dad died. We burst into tears and huddled together, weeping as we walked, indifferent to the stares. When we got home, Ethan would not look at his father's body but retreated, sobbing, to his bedroom where he stayed the rest of that day and night. Later Mr. Novak the mortician came with his adult daughter. They removed José's body without a sound and drove away in a small utility van. I sat with Ethan while that business was taking place. When I emerged a little later, I found a long-stemmed rose on the pillow of the empty hospital bed.

Next morning, a cold Wednesday, I picked one of José's suits, and a shirt and tie. Ethan and I took these to the funeral home, along with a laminated photo that I'd ask the funeral director to slip into the breast pocket of the dark jacket. It was the picture of Ethan gazing toward the Pacific Ocean, the picture that José had been so taken with. A week earlier, my friend Ronda from Social Work had offered to help me--she'd said, "I'll do anything, Sharyn. Anything." I thought about the photo and asked Ronda to have it laminated. Now I held the stiffened, shiny image. José would lie with it forever, just above his heart.

Mr. Novak, the funeral director, welcomed us gently and guided us to the coffin room. Ethan and I moved around in bewildered silence. Dozens of coffins. Not to mention the variety of satin pillows. We also found out about vault liners, which I'd never heard of. Mr. Novak said firmly, "Oh, a vault liner is a must. It protects the coffin and its contents from the water table." I stared at him. In almost a whisper, he stated, "--you don't want water leaking in." I acquiesced, and he made a note in his executive ledger. Back to the coffins. We kept looking. Mr. Novak reverently suggested a mahogany number. I squinted at the price tag. Deciding not to obsess, I picked poplar, a warm and shining wood. Metal didn't seem right for José.

Later, Norah and I drove north on High Street to the Catholic cemetery. She wept as we surveyed snow-covered grave sites, our mittened hands in our pockets. "I don't like any of these spots too well, Mom," she said. I agreed. We finally found a sheltered place at the southern edge of the cemetery near a curve in the narrow driveway, in a section called "The Annunciation." Copper sculptures livened the vista—a kneeling Virgin and the Angel Gabriel with upstretched arms. The elongated figures, engaged in the process of revelation, were meant to soften the earthbound realities below.

Norah stood in thought, turning this way and that, looking at the site from José's point of view. Serious in the responsibility of the choice, she lifted some of the strain. We decided that the Annunciation plot was as good as any. I paid at the cemetery office.

The next day was Thursday, January 20th, 2000. I'd written José's obituary a few weeks earlier. Now it appeared in *The Columbus Dispatch.*

TALBERT

Joseph A. Talbert, age 49, truly beloved husband, father, son, and brother. Tuesday, January 18, 2000, at home. Born January 5, 1951, in Houston. Assistant Director, West European Studies Program, Ohio State University, he also taught history at Ohio State and the Pontifical College Josephinum from 1991-1998. Attended Ohio Wesleyan and Ohio State Universities, where he was an honors graduate. Member of Phi Beta Kappa and recipient of numerous academic distinctions, he pursued master's and doctoral programs in modern European history. Joseph's generosity of spirit, scope of intellect, humility, grace, and wit will live on in the hearts of all who loved him.

That evening, José's family came from New Hampshire and Texas, taking rooms in a nearby motel. The funeral home was ready—photos of José were arranged on black felt boards. Five-years old in a cowboy hat, wide smile with baby teeth. Twenty, with hippie hair and bare chest, cigarette between two fingers. Thirty-five, a bridegroom, refracting the ambient light. Forty-two, a dad in cut-offs and sneakers, hand in hand with Ethan at the zoo.

On Friday, we got to the funeral home before the visitation. The coffin was open. The mortician wanted us to see his efforts at recreating the blush of life. He wanted us to know that he'd earned his fee. But the shape lying there in José's dark grey suit was unfamiliar, and with a hint of peach-colored lipstick. He would have been repelled. So I asked them to close the lid just as the wailing broke its bonds. Ethan wasn't prepared for the sight of his father wrapped in death's mantle. If only there could have been a rewinding of the brutal encounter.

Visitors began to arrive. More than fifty of my co-workers from Social Work and History came. Many of José's T.A. colleagues came, including the exuberant young guys who had drawn the "Baby Boaz" flyer twelve years before. José's professors came, even Bamberger.

José's dissertation advisor, Professor Thorndyke, didn't come, nor did he send a note of condolence.

My friend Kathleen flew in and my friend Peggy drove up from South Carolina. Old friends and new came, including entire Catholic families from St. Michael's. Students and seminarians from the Josephinum came. Ethan's third, fourth, and fifth grade teachers came. My cousins and my aunt came. And Mom sat in the middle of everything.

"Those *doctors*! Never trust them!" Her arthritic hands drooped helplessly. She seemed caught in a net, smothering. She stared past the cousins and shook her head. "All the *suffering* they put poor Saint Joseph through. It's an outrage!"

Ethan had slowly regained his control. Dressed in a black suit with white shirt and navy tie, he wore black boots he'd soon outgrow. His face was pale. As he responded to people, his eyes didn't sparkle at all. The full set of braces looked torturous. But he tried to be brave and gracious as he sat on a sofa, a murmur of respectful activity all around. White-haired, even-featured Professor Richard Hamilton was standing over him, expressing his regrets. Ethan glanced my way for guidance, and I motioned with my fingertips for him to stand. He rose and took in the professor's words.

The evening visitation was more sparsely attended. Graduate students read aloud their recollections of José. One of the priests prayed. My cousin Valerie sat next to me. During the service, she broke into tears. "Oh, Sharyn!" A feeling of satisfaction jolted me. "Yes, cry!" I thought. "Your tears help me, Valerie. Cry, scream, holler! Fling yourself on the floor! Show everyone just how cruel this is. Because I can't do it. Not yet. Attempts at purging will have to be done later, in solitude."

At the end of the night, the funeral director opened the casket so that family members could look one last time. I couldn't do it. I hoped that the image of the embalmed José wouldn't usurp my memories of the living José. But his sister Judi wanted to look again, and so did Tibby. She was the last one to stroke his hair and cheek, to kiss him.

Saturday, January 22nd, 2000: José's burial. Private in life, his burial would be private, too—only immediate family and a few friends. Seven cars drove north on High Street. We were just south of Delaware, Ohio. Resurrection Cemetery. Resurrection. If only it were true. For one last kiss. One last declaration of love.

A thick snowfall buried the roads and gravestones. Slowly we followed the hearse to the site. The funeral director and the pallbearers, who included Ethan, Tibby, and Norah, hoisted the coffin and set it slowly down next to the opening. It moved me inexpressibly that the girls wanted to carry the coffin of their stepfather.

The morning was silent. An endless crust of glittering white surrounded us. The winter sun gave no heat. It was so frigid that the inside of my nose shriveled. Ethan, Rachael, and I sat. The others stood behind us, pressing together closely. Kathleen tucked the wool scarf more tightly around my neck. I was touched but didn't care about physical discomfort. As the priest recited the words, I felt etherized, dead myself save a slow spinning of the head.

Suddenly the *Our Father* was over. As I placed a rose on the poplar box, a lopsided sob burst halfway out. When I turned, I saw the red-rimmed eyes of José's brother, Jim. Our gazes locked for a second. We reached out gloved hands in a clumsy attempt at comfort.

We moved like mute, woolly creatures from prehistoric times, drifting past one another. I got into the Dodge Colt and lowered myself behind the driver's wheel. I'd decided to drive, to save money. Tibby and Norah sobbed softly in the back seat. An aroma of fleece and microfiber mixed with steely air. We waited for Ethan.

My old friend Peggy was walking with him, her arm around his shoulder. They were the last to pass the priests. Peggy could tell that the shorter, darker priest was looking for the right moment to approach Ethan, so she brought the priest's presence to his attention.

"As usual, Ethan reacted with poise and politeness," Peggy said. "But before he could fully turn in the priest's direction, the priest put his arms around Ethan's chest and shoulders, in a tender embrace, and he nearly buried his nose into Ethan's neck. I heard him say, 'Ethan, your father is here. He is living in you!'"

"He said it with such urgency," Peggy said. "It was delivered with so much compassion and affection. I wanted to share that with you. It was one of those moments that your mind takes a snapshot of and permanently stores."

We went back to the house and ate and chatted. I felt a little better, warm again and temporarily occupied. Co-workers had brought homemade bread, salads, and a big pot of chicken soup, setting things up while we were at the cemetery and leaving everything fragrant and ready. I felt chastened, regretting all the nasty thoughts I'd had about the Social Work people. They were generous and kind and sorry for my suffering. A few of them had cried at the funeral home.

There was plenty of food. Patty, my lifelong friend, came with a pan of bubbling lasagna. His duties over, Mr. Novak stood expansively in the kitchen and sampled everything with a hearty appetite. As people ate and talked, I heard the bump and slam of the mailbox. I fished out a sheaf of condolence messages. Curling into the loveseat in the quiet living room, I saw that many of the notes were from History Department faculty. Nobody offered clichés. The words expressed a bracing blend of sorrow and praise.

José's former advisor, Professor Riegert, said how shocked and sorry she was. She hadn't even known he was sick. Professor Fulton, a historian of the Middle East, wrote how sad it was "to lose a valued member of the university community at such a young age." Professor Lisa Rhys: "What a terrible tragedy this is—he was so young and talented." Professor James Kittelson, writing from Minnesota, spoke of his desire to console me; he wished he were back in Columbus. Professor Stanley from Social Work assured me that the experience of a loving relationship with such a remarkable man would always be a part of me.

Will Roper, José's co-worker in International Studies, talked about José's unflagging sense of humor, his professional example, and his toughness: "I never once heard him complain, seek pity, or in any way call attention to his plight. Instead he consistently came to work and did his job despite physical pain and undoubtedly great mental anguish. I don't expect to see that standard of courage and dignity repeated in my lifetime."

A fellow T.A. from History wrote that José and I had been his surrogate older brother and sister, steering him through his first several years of grad school. Another former History grad student called José a fine man whom he both liked and esteemed. Another viewed José as "patient, kind, understanding, passionate about his scholarship and life calling, and positively erudite. I will never forget his wonderful, wry sense of humor, and neither will anyone who had the fortune of knowing him." A friend whose field was Tudor-Stuart history remembered José walking into 168 Dulles with his old black briefcase, "quiet, but never shying away from an argument about Bamberger's view of fractals in history."

My neighbor couldn't imagine losing such a treasure in the realm of men.

For a long time I sat reading the messages. Suddenly, I realized I was being inattentive and returned to the relatives and friends talking quietly the den. Once more, I embraced José's eighty-year old mother.

"Rachael, this is so hard for you. To lose your son."

"Honey, we have to take comfort in the fact that Joe is in heaven," Rachael stated firmly, patting my hand. Her eyes protruded, blood-shot and ravaged. "The Bible says that if you accept Jesus Christ as your Lord and Savior, you will be saved. So I know that Joe is with Jesus now."

I hugged Rachael's shoulder and turned to Judi, who was seriously shaken. She felt cheated that she hadn't been told about her brother's cancer until it was almost over. Kathleen tearfully embraced me before leaving with one of her sick headaches. Tibby and Norah cried and hugged me tightly before departing.

The Talberts eventually dispersed for the airport. Later that day, Peggy and I went to the grocery store—we were out of dog chow. Finally, even Peggy left.

Now it was just Ethan, me, and the dogs. A new status-quo, amputated, wobbly. Ethan played a computer game and I moved slowly around the kitchen. The winter light was waning. In semi-darkness, I dried the dishes and put them away. I wiped the counters and the refrigerator handle. I filled the teakettle and set it on the stove. The clinks and clatters hung inside my ear canal, a sensation both shapeless and pointed.

I walked into the laundry room and stepped into a lake. For seconds, it didn't compute. Then I understood. The water heater had failed on the day of my husband's burial, on a Saturday evening in sub-zero weather with two feet of snow on the ground. I ran to the phone and grabbed the yellow book. With shaking hands, I found "Plumbers." I called several, but none would come. So I called cousin Valerie, whose husband Phil worked as a contractor. She didn't answer. I left a panicky message.

I turned off the water at the source and mopped the floor, soaking every bath towel and dish rag. Unaware of my plight, Ethan continued to play. I silently heaved the sopping towels into the washing machine, silently wiped the remnants of the water, silently, silently, alone. Sullen resentment crept in. For a little while, it offset the grief.

The next morning, a scritch-scratch, scrape-scrape-scraping broke the silence, waking me from an uneasy sleep. I peered into the dawn. It had snowed again. There was Phil, bent at the waist, rapidly shoveling the front sidewalk. Making a stab at fixing my hair, self-conscious about my swollen eyes, I went out to meet him. Phil had bought a water heater. He installed it that morning, free of charge. He also brought hot coffee and donuts. His kindness that day lifted me from abandonment.

Five days after José's burial, I drove to campus, parked in the 12th Avenue garage, and walked to José's office in West European Studies. I had to empty out his belongings. It would be painful. Keep going, keep going, I encouraged myself, one foot in front of the other. I was a soldier, no turning back. My boots chewed and squeaked the hard-packed snow. As I stepped, I kept time with sayings I'd lived by.

"A stitch in time saves nine." (Saves none?)

"Enough is as good as a feast." (Enough is never enough.)

"There's no great loss without some small gain." (Maybe, but what is it?)

"Whistling girls and crowing hens always come to some bad ends." (Do tell.)

"Kill one fly in May and keep thousands away." (Yep.)

"No good deed goes unpunished." (That is correct.)

"My mother told me to pick the very best one, and y-o-u spells you, and I do mean *you*."

In José's office, I sifted through dozens of his neatly written notes to co-workers, and copies of typed memos to students seeking foreign language scholarships. The messages were succinct and respectful. Reading through, I felt shame. José would never have answered a deserving student as I had at times in Social Work, abruptly, snidely, as if I my agenda was more important than theirs. Some of the notes had nothing to do with work. One little post-it reminded him to get his glasses fixed. Another said "blue books."

After cleaning out the desk, I looked around. The lamp with a handsome brass base he'd found at the thrift store—I could use that at home. The historical prints he'd framed himself, cutting thin pieces of trim into angles, staining them, and gluing them together to fit his maps of France and Europe, a poster of Queen Elizabeth I, and enlarged photos of Chartres Cathedral he'd taken thirty years earlier. I stood back and looked at the framed images, picturing José in his office, deciding just where to hang them. I thought about his satisfaction and relief at having the new job, a steady income, smart colleagues, a place in the world. Now I carefully removed the pictures. They'd hang in our home office.

My eyes fell on the phone. Soon, his co-workers would delete his recording, eradicating his words. But I couldn't bear to hear his sober, measured tone, which echoed in my head:

"You have reached (slight pause) the West European Studies Program (slight pause) at The Ohio State University. Please leave your name, phone number, and a brief message (slight pause), and we will return your call as soon as we are able. (Lower tone, now) Thank you."

Among his computer disks were several labeled "dissertation." These I handled with special care. At home, I slid them into the computer. Chapters one through five popped up. They were intact. Then, a file called "Conclusion." I was unaware that he'd started a conclusion. I opened the document and scrolled through. It seemed to be a collection of random thoughts about how to summarize his study.

At the very end, three sentences jumped off the screen.

The landscape we seek is a figment of our imagination. The life we must seek is located in the valley. From the peaks, we see only other peaks, but these are largely barren and serve to delimit the valleys.

I blinked. The words pulsed. The three sentences had nothing to do with pandemic influenza. "The life we *must* seek," he'd written, not the life we wanted, not the life we hungered for. It was José, admonishing me to be brave, to be satisfied, to find beauty in the valley.

A few weeks after the funeral, I stood on the back step, hugging myself in the cold. The roar of a train pocked the stillness, the rhythmic beat of wheels flying over the ties, a metallic clang. The noise climaxed and dwindled, drifting farther away, finally overtaken by a giant, lonesome sigh. Gazing upward at the silver maple, I stared at the heavy horizontal limbs criss-crossing the greyness. Moving along the trunk, my eyes rested on a hole where the limbs branched off.

"Where are you?" I asked aloud. "Where *are* you?"

At that second, a black bird poked its head out of the hole. It looked at me, motionless. It was a sign. José was there. He had heard me. I felt the flesh shrinking on my face and the tears brimming. But was that all? A black bird was no substitute.

In those dark days, I became fixated on the number 13. I recalled that thirteen people had attended the burial. I started to figure: there are thirteen letters in his name. His son was born on the thirteenth of December. We were married thirteen months after we met. Our marriage lasted until death parted us: thirteen years, three months, thirteen days. He died on the thirteenth day after his 49th birthday, and four plus nine equals thirteen. He died at 12:47, which is thirteen minutes before 1:00. And one o'clock is the thirteenth hour.

I knew it had to be a coincidence. A million other things about José's life and mine would never add up to 13. It was just silly. Thirteen couldn't be that bad—the United States started with 13 colonies. Or maybe I was the unlucky one. Faced with the ultimate mystery, I searched for the right questions. But like José, the answers were beyond reach.

A few days after José's death, the galloping, deregulated stock market of the 1990s scored a paralyzing correction that would repeat itself for a decade and beyond. José would never find out about the collapse of Enron or World Com or Arthur Andersen or the dot-com bubble, or later, the housing bubble, credit default swaps, derivatives, government bailouts, "too big to fail." He also died without knowing that Ethan and I would be okay, financially.

José survived ten days past the minimum point at which he would be eligible for all the benefits of a full-time permanent employee of Ohio State University. These extended to his survivors, so Ethan and I got what was called, in ghastly bureaucratese, a "lump sum death benefit"--two and a half times his yearly salary at Ohio

State. The insurance I'd purchased at the last minute the previous summer also came through, paying $40,000. And there was his final paycheck with accumulated vacation and sick leave.

More reassuring news: until Ethan graduated from college in 2010, I'd receive several hundred dollars every month from the state. We could also count on a monthly benefit from Social Security, which would persist for six years until Ethan's 18th birthday. And as survivors of a state employee, Ethan and I would have medical and dental coverage, so no money had to be taken out of my Ohio State paycheck for those things.

Thank goodness for safety nets.

Nor did José know what his colleagues in International Studies would do on his behalf. After his death, Will Roper spearheaded a drive for Ethan's college expenses, and after hundreds of letters and emails to our friends and co-workers at Ohio State, more than $10,000 was in the 529 account. Several years later, I used the money to send Ethan to Russia and to Oxford.

The sorrow remained, but the necessities were working themselves out. I paid off the balance of the house, and the second mortgage. I bought a new car, paying for it outright. No more installment plans. I bought a Roth IRA. I purchased rain gutters, more insulation in the attic, a glass block window in the garage, a concrete driveway.Prosperity had come to our family. It had cost José's life to get us there.

***

After the finances were settled came the small matter of José's dissertation. In the spring I made an appointment to see

Professor Lisa Rhys, now the chair of History. It felt both strange and reassuring to be back. Lisa led the way into her office and gestured toward a couch. She regarded me expectantly with calm blue eyes. Her eyelashes were naturally black—no mascara or any other makeup. She had not aged. Her distinctive hairstyle was just the same, a short geometric cut with a poufy top. One section of hair at the back was longer, and as always, Lisa braided the lock and fastened it with a silver cylinder. She wore a loose orchid-colored blouse.

She expressed her sadness, saying that José had been so young, that he'd had so much promise. She was forthright and kind. I thanked Lisa, and told her I wanted to discuss José's dissertation. She didn't know the background, so I brought her up to speed.

"His argument is that the movement of French troops during the First World War lessened the virulence of influenza in France. Five chapters are complete," I said, "but the work lacks a conclusion." I explained that José had planned to go back to France that fall to finish the research. He'd already written three hundred pages of rigorously argued history. "The work is carefully documented," I said. "--some of the single-spaced footnotes are a page long."

Lisa Rhys was confused. "But if the work is in good shape, why didn't José and his advisor wrap it up before he got too sick?"

I told her the whole story. José had been researching the dissertation for ten years, since his general examination in 1989. But the dissertation writing had been on-again, off-again because, to make ends meet, José took temporary teaching jobs every quarter, sometimes three or four at a time. That meant three or four preparations, three or four different course schedules and grading schedules, and a lot of driving. I told her about José's research trip to France in 1992. And for the past three years, he'd worked on the dissertation feverishly. But he hadn't received any guidance or encouragement from Professor Thorndyke.

Yes, I admitted, maybe José was partly to blame for the delay. He should have insisted on communication and direction, and, last resort, he should have complained to the chair. "But what about Charles Thorndyke's culpability?" my voice held an angry edge. "He was the doctoral advisor. He is the French historian of some repute. He's the one who's paid to work with doctoral students." I swallowed. "He's been sitting on José's chapters for years."

José hadn't gotten one single word of feedback, I said, despite his many notes to Thorndyke, full of details and perceptions and questions, including his thoughts for the conclusion. None of the messages had been answered.

Lisa's expression was stiffly solemn. I felt the lump rising again and took a breath as I looked at her. "I'm a little emotional about this," I said. "But I've been . . . I'm determined to see that something comes of José's work. For it to go unrecognized is too awful to think about."

She nodded. "What do you propose, Sharyn?" she asked.

"I can format the document and add some sort of conclusion, using his chapters as a guide to suggest how future research should proceed."

Lisa considered. "Well, I can tell you that the History Department would very much like to give José credit for his work."

She said that three faculty members would have to approve the dissertation before it could be filed in the Graduate School. She asked me to keep in close touch. I left her office with renewed hope, but the jagged points of betrayal burned hot.

Next day, with shaking hands, I inserted José's disks into my Social Work computer. When a chapter opened, I copied it to the hard drive. The thought of losing the documents terrified me. For the next two months, I worked on the project whenever I found a few minutes between work tasks. I adjusted the margins, the pagination, the footnotes. I wrote an abstract, prepared a table of contents, and a curriculum vitae. I corrected the bibliography, adding entries as needed. I put together a conclusion that suggested further questions into pandemic influenza during the Great War.

In late June, I handed the finished document to History's Graduate Chair, Jim Balthasar. He assured me that he'd have an answer soon. In less than a week, I was notified that the dissertation had been approved by the committee—Professor Rhys, the department chair; Professor Balthasar, the expert on the history of medicine; and Professor Thorndyke. No revisions or corrections would be required. Professors Rhys and Balthasar expressed their astonishment over the density and sophistication of the scholarship and the eloquence of the writing. Professor Thorndyke remained silent. As advisor of record, his sole contribution was to sign his name.

The Unknown Country

Everything's ready, the secretary said on the phone. I flew to the History Department and took up José's dissertation and the approval forms. I felt the weight of the scholarship, hefting it for a few seconds. I went out into the sun.

As usual, the sidewalks were teeming with students and professors, but my purpose was all that mattered. I cradled the dissertation, a perfect newborn, finally delivered after an endless, tortured pregnancy. Feeling like the 50-foot woman in an old science fiction movie, I strode across to the Graduate School. I heard the solid rhythm of my steps: whump, whump, whump. Teeth clenched in victory, I pulled open the heavy door of University Hall and bounded up two flights of stairs, making my way toward the office where José's dissertation would be scrutinized one last time.

A brown-haired woman wet her finger and paged through, checking things off: table of contents, curriculum vitae, page numbers, chapter headings, bibliography. With a little ruler, she measured the margin widths. When the woman was finished, she looked up and said, I'll take it from here. --It's okay, she went on. We have everything we need. So with one last touch, I left the dissertation in her hands and headed back to my office.

Stillness fell upon my heart. All the loose ends were tied up. In September of 2000, seven months after his death, Joseph Talbert was awarded a Ph.D.

About a year later, on a bright late summer day just before the 9/11 attacks, I was at the Worthington library when I ran into a History Department professor. I would have known Ava Cohen anywhere—the same short curls and lively brown eyes, the same open-toed sandals. When I worked in the department ten years earlier, Ava and I joked about her addiction to chocolate. We talked about sex in history--Ava was frank and forthcoming about subjects that others avoided. She even admitted her fondness for romance novels. But I was impressed with her scholarship on medieval Russia, her ability to wade through primary documents written in Old Church Slavonic.

I was surprised to find that, after twenty years at Ohio State, Ava was leaving. She said she'd taken a teaching job elsewhere and was about to go. Abruptly, she changed the tone of the conversation. Her eyes fixed on mine. She said she'd always remember José and what happened to him.

I thought she meant the cancer. Then I got it. She was talking about Thorndyke's negligence. It seemed that José's unread dissertation had become a topic of discussion among the History Department faculty.

"--do History faculty know?"

"Oh, yes," Ava said with a serious knit in her dark brows. She was free to talk about it only because she was leaving the department.

I tried to imagine how the news had circulated. José hadn't mentioned it to anyone but me—not to other grad students, not to any faculty member or administrator, not even to Thorndyke himself. I'd mentioned the neglect only to Lisa Rhys. But she would have had to explain the situation to Jim Balthasar, the second reader of the dissertation. Now that the cat was out of the bag, maybe Lisa Rhys decided that the subject should be brought up in a faculty meeting. I hoped she had said, Let's all of us get on the same page here and make sure we're accountable to our graduate students. This kind of thing can't ever happen again.

Or maybe Lisa Rhys wanted to warn the department about negative publicity. Maybe she feared a lawsuit. Ava Cohen didn't say how the news got around, or in what context, and I didn't ask the specifics. I was too stunned by her candor. She continued, shaking her head as she talked.

"It's shameful, just shameful, what happened to José. It's terrible. And when I'm at my new place, you can bet I'll try to make sure nothing like that happens there."

When José died, almost everybody in the History Department expressed sympathy. But no one had brought up the grievous injustice. Nobody had said how sorry they were that José's efforts of ten years had been in vain, that he had died without a shred of recognition for his scholarship. That was because no one except the guilty party had any idea. Now at least some of the faculty knew. Maybe a lot of them knew. Maybe by now most of them had forgotten all about it, Ava Cohen being the exception. Or maybe they were still silently thinking, Holy Christ, what a sorry set of circumstances.

Some years later, when Ethan was in Russia on a study abroad, I emailed Ava Cohen to let her know that Ethan shared her interest in Russian culture and language. She emailed back, in Moscow herself at the time. At the end of her message, she said that she was now Graduate Studies Chair in the History Department of her new university. With José in mind, she had implemented two policy changes. First, graduate advisors were required to provide bi-annual reports about their students' progress. And advisors had a maximum of one month to respond in writing to grad students about their thesis or dissertation chapters.

The absence was searing. For months, grief grinned behind my eyes and pressed its clubbed fingers against my diaphragm. A liquid fire encased my brain and heart. How to escape it? I held the lock of his hair at my nostrils, trying to inhale his scent or a left-behind molecule. I tried to reconstruct him in my mind's eye, but didn't recognize the image. One-dimensional, no comic or intellectual sharpness at all. Where was the real human being, brave but vulnerable, cynical but honest, manly but not macho?

And where was the routine? I'd timed my own schedule by his morning ablutions. I could always predict when he would finish showering and shaving: 5, 4, 3, 2, 1—the bathroom door is about to open. Now he's wheeling into the kitchen in his green robe. I adjust my expression to meet his, and feel the damp, just-shaven smoothness against my own cheek.

I slept fitfully, with disorienting dreams.
1) We were standing together, bodies touching. He emanated warmth. We kissed,
   sharing a film of perspiration. Without friction, the bones of our faces articulated, cheek to cheek, jawbone to jawbone, a rolling sensation like kissing oneself in a mirror. We were bathed in a golden light . Then I heard

the steady respiration of the dogs curled next to me. My eyes opened. It was daybreak. José wasn't there. I uttered, "Oh, no. He's gone."

2) I was in a Catholic gift shop and came upon a table laden with religious medals. I touched the raised images of the saints. In the center of the table, I spotted the largest, thickest medal, a silver oval. It bore the image of St. Joseph, the gentle foster father of Jesus. I brought the heavy medal to my lips and wept.

3) I saw José walking on campus in his tan trench coat. It was definitely José--his hair, his build, his gait. He didn't see me. He didn't know I was trying to catch him. He was making for High Street, heading for the bus stop. I struggled to keep sight of him, trotting and running. The COTA bus pulled up. José got on. My lungs were bursting. As I reached the door, the bus roared away.

4) Ethan and I were in Paris. It was twilight. The weathered stone battlements were slimy and moss-covered. Ethan and I fell into the river. As we were carried downstream, we struggled to grab hold of an iron railing. I boosted Ethan over the embankment and grasped at a slick slab with a gargoyle on top. As I pulled myself up, the slab opened. Ethan's toys and costumes spilled out into the moving water.

One morning, as the end of such a dream filtered through my consciousness like sediment in a wine bottle, I realized that I'd been resentful of hanging his clean clothes. Now, no more trousers and shirts and boxer shorts to hang or fold. No more smoothing that warm impression on the bed where he sat to pull on his socks. I knew that widowed people sometimes guard the physical remnants of their former life. But turning our bedroom into a mausoleum? I thought of Miss Havisham covered in mold and cobwebs. I didn't want to end up like that. So a week after José was buried, I bundled his clothes and shoes and took them to Volunteers of America. Somebody might be able to use them. José would have thought the same.

Home again, I looked at the half-empty bedroom closet. Some would find heartbreak in that. I saw advantage, filling José's half with my summer things. Now my clothes could breathe, arranged according to season, and in appealing spectrum sequence. I felt organized and proud. After that, I forced myself to tackle chores I disliked, washing windows and curtains, scrubbing blinds, purging garage and attic, and reorganizing the contents of the cedar chest and kitchen cupboards. I hurt, but I was alive, productive.

Along with not being sentimental about José's clothes, I was unconcerned about going to the cemetery. Five months after his death, I stopped by. It was June. It was hot then, the snow long gone. Grass grew thickly on the site. I stood by the marker, thinking a little, talking a little. I told him that Ethan was at "Adventure

Camp." "We're going on a road trip this summer," I said. "We're okay. But we miss you, so much, dearest. So . . . much."

I was eating a ripe peach. A juicy bit fell from my lips and plunked onto the gravestone, landing in one of the letters of his name. "Oh, sorry, dear!" I said as I bent and scooped out the soft piece of fruit. The only other time I visited the grave was a year after his death. I put a red rose on the stone. Only a sprinkle of snow had fallen. After that, I kept away. He wasn't there.

Six months into widowhood, friends began asking if they could fix me up. "Carl is *such* a nice man—really bright, and what a sense of humor!" I was surprised and touched that people thought of me in that way, that they'd recommend me as someone who might fill a precious role. But always I demurred. True, when sharp loneliness kicked in, I sometimes wondered, isn't it possible that another José is out there, waiting and hoping? It happened once. Couldn't it happen again? But I knew the truth. José was a one-time deal. He was the only man for whom I was willing to pay the price. After José, I became like a fertilized ovum, barricaded from further invasion.

Other questions played out, over and again. If I hadn't pursued José, would he have lived a dismal, loveless reality? Did my insistence on "Progress" propel him toward an early grave? Why did José have to die while so many hateful, ignorant, menacing people live to old age? I tried to imagine José's responses to historical events. What would he have said about George Bush? Barack Obama? Or, the one who came after? How would he have reacted to 9/11?

One year into widowhood, I gave up religion. I wish he could know that. As a student of English literature, suspension of disbelief had taken me a long way. But after José vanished, I concluded that religious mythology is too thickly entwined with bureaucratic hypocrisy, internal contradictions, patriarchal prejudices. Deep down, I'd always doubted the existence of the supernatural. In José's absence, and especially after 9/11, I settled things for myself: the world is tragic and wondrous enough without religion. So I abandoned the idea of gods and put my belief in the best of people. Of course, in releasing myself from the religious enterprise, I also released myself from the hope that José will ever re-materialize, in the shape of a black bird or in any other form. I won't see him again, even when I'm dead myself. José is gone. Isn't the finality the reason we mourn?

José was spared Mr. Petey's demise five months after his own. As he lay dying in the car in the vet's parking lot, Petey raised a paw, the final symbol of his loyalty and love. In June of 2002, Molly died of heart failure. She took her last breath on the floor of the laundry room. It was good that José missed all that, but I'm sorry he didn't get to know our future dogs: Arthur the fawn greyhound, Ella, whose own life was cut short—she was the gentlest treat taker ever--, and Gabe and Dolly, the soulful, comic Treeing Walker coonhounds.

Through the years, José missed fielding Ethan's questions, so many questions, about history and politics and a million other things. I tried my best to answer, but often came up short. It was, as widowed people always say, bittersweet watching our son graduate with honors from Ohio State in 2010, a double major in International Studies and English, and minors in Legal Foundations and Russian. José would have loved to hear Ethan talk about his study abroads in Siberia and Oxford, and his subsequent law studies, at Ohio State, of course. Class of 2015. Ethan broke our family's habit of goofing up in the third decade of life.

José's death denied both of us long years of love and companionship. Death let him bypass my occasional callousness, my vanity, and my intractable envy, and in dying at age 49, he also escaped my urge to pin him down, to bring his limitations to the forefront. But he would have preferred life with those challenges any day of the week.

Was José happy? In an everyday sense, he was not unhappy. He was prone to inwardness, even depression, but his routine, his family, and his cerebral drive were the antidotes. His contemplative power was the muscular sort. He took joy in his quicksilver insights, which he shared too rarely with the rest of us. You could see it on his face: a slight smile and a dart of the eye were the signs of private editorializing. Whenever I noticed that, I'd ask in a hopeful tone, "What?" But he usually kept his fancies to himself, dismissing them with a gentle, "Oh, nothing, dear." Along with the life of the mind, José was devoted to the simple joys. Any small kindness filled him with surprise and gratitude.

Still, an underlying tragedy belonged to him, the greatest part being that his gifts and his struggle went unacknowledged. He made a pact with scholarship too late to fit the base economies of higher education, and a negligent advisor wreaked untold damage. On all of us. It didn't help that José was reticent, but that trait should never have been put to the test.

***

In 2002, two years after his death, I took an advising job in Ohio State's English Department. A year later, I experienced the ripple effect of José's goodness. Religious people talk about the ripple effect of sin--how a mean, selfish action spreads out from its source, invariably harming the innocent. True enough, but the incident in my office was just the opposite. I was as usual filling out a form for a student who was ready to graduate. On his transcript, I noticed that he'd taken History 111 early in his undergraduate program. I looked up and asked if he recalled who had taught the course.

"Oh, yes, I do remember," the student said. "Professor Talbert taught History 111 at the Mansfield campus. Without that man's encouragement, I wouldn't have stayed in college."

The student didn't know that the so-called Professor Talbert had been my husband.

"Really?" I asked. "What happened?"

"Well," he said, "when I started college seven years ago, I was struggling. I was miserable, really struggling emotionally. I failed some courses, math and the first English composition. When I took History 111, I got an incomplete because I didn't finish the final paper in time. But the professor talked to me. He helped me to think it through, and allowed me to turn in my paper late so I could make up the incomplete."

"Professor Talbert?"

"Yeah. He talked to me on the phone. He told me I was intellectually competent. Those were his words: intellectually competent. I guess something in my writing told him I wasn't a total loss. I mean, that was the turning point. It was . . . I don't know, it was what I needed. Just somebody to recognize me and say something." Now the student was on the dean's list, graduating with a 3.7 GPA. He would be starting his graduate program in the fall.

After he finished his story, I said that José had been my husband, and that he had died three years before. The student took in the information. He solemnly shook my hand. "Oh, wow," he breathed.He left without saying anything more.

Alone in my office again, the silence reverberated. José had never mentioned it.

Soon after the encounter with the student, I was found a bulky envelope in our battered old *Joy of Cooking*. In his neat handwriting, José had labeled the envelope, "Les Fleurs." I peered inside and found a bunch of plastic tabs used to identify commercially grown flowers. José must have saved the tabs whenever he planted something in our yard. I shuffled the tabs, dozens and dozens of them. As I thumbed through, I thought about José's work in the garden, about his love of plants and flowers.

Les Fleurs. How magical they are. Once I peered into the petals of African violets. The pale lavender blooms seemed coated with the finest dusting of sugar, a field of tiny, winking diamonds. The petals of the magenta violet showed ruby flecks, denser than the blood red panes in a stained-glass window. That which seems ordinary might hold the most resplendent treasures. It takes only a little attention.

Just consider the common names of flowers, so vital and life affirming. Lady's Mantle. Bleeding Hearts. The blue Forget Me Not.

At the thrift store, I bought a bunch of scratched dinner plates, white with cobalt borders. Home again, I hurled the dishes one by one onto the brick walk in the back yard. It was freeing to do that.

I picked up the pieces.

Next, I found a stout wooden plank, 18 by 30 inches. I covered it with joint compound, smoothing it evenly, like icing on a cake. Around the edges of the plank, I arranged the shards, creating a mosaic. The jagged pieces didn't fit like a jigsaw puzzle, but close enough. They sparkled, geometric white and blue.

Rummaging around in the back of the garage, I found some 3 x 3 inch terra cotta tiles, left over from the fireplace surround. I counted them—I'd need eleven. On each, I painted a large black letter. Once dry, I pushed the rosy tiles in careful order into the wet center of the plank. I stood back and read aloud the three words framed by the blue and white border.

FORGET

ME

NOT

No, José, I will not forget. I search for you still. When I'm lost in a crowd, I look for you. When I behold an endless city or a single spear of grass thrusting toward the sun, I feel you. In the shifting tides of my memory, I follow your every move. I will never stop missing you, my husband, my teacher, my beloved scholar.

ACKNOWLEDGEMENTS

Thank you, my lifelong friend Peggy, for your stalwart, joyful presence, for your humor and keen eye, and for reading with such tender honesty and sharp insights. I love you.

Ronda, my deepest thanks for saving me and for lifting my sorrow. You are so special.

Sebastian Knowles, I was bereft and bewildered when I quit the university in 2001. Thank you for hiring me back for the final ten-year stretch. You, too, saved my life, a fact that becomes clearer all the time.

To Patrick Mullen: your expert guidance stays with me. You are the gold standard of doctoral advisors.

My undying appreciation to the many people, on campus and off, who supported José and me. You came up with so many thoughtful, creative, and often work-intensive projects to show your devotion. I remain humbled and in your debt.

Thank you, my family members in all your permutations, for your love of José throughout our marriage. Because of you, he knew how deeply he was loved and respected.

I thank our dogs who delighted us and loved us and helped knit our family so firmly: dear Lady, Molly, and Mr. Petey.

Ohio State, you bestowed sustenance, structure, and joy. You filled us up and shaped our personal history. You injected life and hope. At the very end, you came through. That an errant player within your walls wreaked heartache does not cancel the abundance. As my late friend Elsbeth said, "They're a good bunch, smart people, really gifted people. A few bad eppels. . . .but you'll do well here."

And to my dear son, thank you for your love, devotion, and loyalty, for your discipline and courage, and for turning out exactly as your father would have dreamed. I will love you until the end of time.

Made in United States
Troutdale, OR
08/14/2024

22022623R00186